On Children Who Privilege the Body

On Children Who Privilege the Body: Reflections of an Independent Psychotherapist brings together selected papers from the career of Ann Horne, and draws upon her considerable experience in the field of child and adolescent mental health.

Many of the papers collected in this volume reflect Ann Horne's important work with 'troubled' children and young people, and the technique and theory on which it is based. Across her writing, she demonstrates that the roots of their deviant behaviour are to be found in their earliest experiences, which not only fail to offer them an opportunity to thrive but also actively contribute to their dysfunctional behaviour.

On Children Who Privilege the Body will be of considerable interest and use to child psychotherapists, social workers and all other mental health professionals working with children and adolescents in a range of settings.

Ann Horne was head of the Independent child psychotherapy training and post-graduate development at the BAP (now IPCAPA). She is co-editor of *The Handbook of Child and Adolescent Psychotherapy* and of the four earlier books in this series. Now retired, she gives talks and writes, retaining a special interest in children who act with the body rather than reflect.

Independent Psychoanalytic Approaches with Children and Adolescents series
Series Editors: Ann Horne and Monica Lanyado

On Children Who Privilege the Body

Reflections of an Independent Psychotherapist

Ann Horne

Routledge
Taylor & Francis Group

LONDON AND NEW YORK

First published 2019
by Routledge
2 Park Square, Milton Park, Abingdon, Oxon OX14 4RN

and by Routledge
711 Third Avenue, New York, NY 10017

Routledge is an imprint of the Taylor & Francis Group, an informa business

British Library Cataloguing in Publication Data
A catalogue record for this book is available from the British Library

Library of Congress Cataloging in Publication Data
Names: Horne, Ann, 1944– author.
Title: On children who privilege the body : reflections of an independent
    psychotherapist / Ann Horne.
Description: New York, NY : Routledge, 2018. | Includes bibliographical
    references and index.
Identifiers: LCCN 2018014839| ISBN 9780815399773 (hbk) | ISBN
    9780815399827 (pbk.) | ISBN 9781351171281 (ebk) | ISBN
    9781351171274 (web) | ISBN 9781351171267 (epub) | ISBN
    9781351171250 (mobipocket)
Subjects: | MESH: Child Behavior Disorders—therapy | Psychotherapy |
    Acting Out | Psychology, Child | Adolescent Psychiatry | Collected
    Works
Classification: LCC RJ506.B44 | NLM WS 7 | DDC 618.92/89—dc23
LC record available at https://lccn.loc.gov/2018014839

ISBN: 978-0-8153-9977-3 (hbk)
ISBN: 978-0-8153-9982-7 (pbk)
ISBN: 978-1-351-17128-1 (ebk)

Typeset in Times New Roman
by Swales & Willis Ltd, Exeter, Devon, UK

For Chris

Contents

Contributors

Ann Horne is a Fellow of the BPF, the British Psychotherapy Foundation, and an Honorary Member of ČSPAP, the Czech Society for Psychoanalytic Psychotherapy. Trained as a child and adolescent psychoanalytic psychotherapist at the BAP (British Association of Psychotherapists, now IPCAPA at the bpf) in the Independent tradition, she was later head of training and then of post-graduate development. She has taught and supervised on several training courses in the UK and abroad. A former joint editor of the *Journal of Child Psychotherapy*, she co-edited with Monica Lanyado *The Handbook of Child and Adolescent Psychotherapy: Psychoanalytic Approaches* (1st edition 1999; 2nd edition 2009) and conceived and developed the Independent Psychoanalytic Approaches with Children and Adolescents book series for Routledge. Retired from NHS work, lastly as a Consultant Child Psychotherapist at the Portman Clinic in London, she writes, teaches, consults and still retains a particular interest in children who use the body and activity rather than being able to access thought and reflection.

Lydia Tischler is a Fellow of the BPF, an Honoured Member of the ACP and an Honorary Member of ČSPAP. Trained as a child analyst at the Hampstead Child Therapy Clinic (now the Anna Freud Centre) with Anna Freud, she was Head of the Child Psychotherapy Department at the Cassel Hospital, London, for 23 years. She has been Chair of the Training Council of the Association of Child Psychotherapists, Chair of the Child and Adolescent Psychotherapy Training at the BAP (now IPCAPA at the bpf) and Chair of the BAP itself. Co-founder of the European Federation for Psychoanalytic Psychotherapy in the Public Sector and its first Honorary Secretary, she later became Convenor of the subcommittee for Central and Eastern European Networks for the EFPP. A co-founder of the Child Psychotherapy training programme in the Czech Republic, she contributed as well to trainings in Estonia and St Petersburg. In addition, she taught on the Child and Adolescent Psychoanalysis training programme at the Han Groen-Prakken Psychoanalytic Institute for Eastern Europe.

Acknowledgements

Immediate responsibility for this book lies with Lydia Tischler whose quiet insistence over the past few years that it would be useful to collect papers on – especially – body-based defensive manoeuvres in children finally resulted in action. Her writing the Foreword was both a kindness on her part and a penance for her insistence . . . I remain indebted to this great friend who has taken me to talk across central Europe many times in the last 20 years, been so generous with her advice and company, and who remains special, even in the list of very good friends.

I have been fortunate to have experienced several workplaces where I have been encouraged to think, to encounter the new and have my knowledge (and comfort zone) expanded and challenged. The most influential of these have been the Social Policy teaching team at the School of Community Studies, Moray House College, Edinburgh (1974–79); Camberwell Child Guidance Unit in South London (now CAMHS at the Lister Health Centre and where I worked as a PSW for 10 years from 1981); and the Portman Clinic in North London (1995–2004). To colleagues and friends from all these settings I remain extremely grateful.

When I applied in 1982 to train as a child psychotherapist with the British Association of Psychotherapists (now the Independent Psychoanalytic Child and Adolescent Psychotherapy Association at the British Psychotherapy Foundation), I had no idea other than the most general about the traditions and disputes of the world of psychoanalysis; I simply knew that, since leaving secondary school teaching in 1969, I had been seeking training in how to work with children and young people in a way that enabled conversation, reflection, understanding and change. At the BAP I found it – and blessedly without any sense of rivalrous fundamentalism in its approach to psychoanalytic theory. I have been indebted ever since. Indeed, developing this book series has offered me one way of thanking my BAP grandmothers and grandfathers for an excellent training.

My especial thanks to Monica Lanyado, who accepted the invitation to join in editing an Independent book series and who remains enthusiastic and creative, even as it grows.

And to Chris – without whom life would have contained far less music and far fewer colours . . .

My thanks to the following for permission to publish papers and chapters:

Taylor & Francis Ltd (www.tandfonline.com) and the editors of the *Journal of Child Psychotherapy* for 'Brief communications from the edge' *JCP* 27(1) 2001; '"Gonnae no' dae that!" The internal and external worlds of the delinquent adolescent' *JCP* 30(3) 2004; and 'Oedipal aspirations and phallic fears: on fetishism in childhood and young adulthood' *JCP* 29(1) 2003 – all copyright Association of Child Psychotherapists;

Taylor & Francis Ltd (www.tandfonline.com) and the editors for 'The Independent position in psychoanalytic psychotherapy with children and adolescents: roots and implications' and 'Interesting things to say – and why', both from M Lanyado & A Horne (eds.) *A Question of Technique* London & New York: Routledge 2006; 'From intimacy to acting out' from A Horne & M Lanyado (eds.) *Through Assessment to Consultation* London & New York: Routledge 2009; and 'Entertaining the body in mind: thoughts on incest, the body, sexuality and the self' in P Williams, J Keane & S Dermen (eds.) *Independent Psychoanalysis Today* London: Karnac 2012;

Wiley and the editor of the *British Journal of Psychotherapy* for 'Rhythm, blues, affirmation and enactment: it's tough soloing without a rhythm section' from the *British Journal of Psychotherapy* 26(1) 2010.

The chapter entitled 'Thinking about gender in theory and practice with children and adolescents' was originally commissioned by the editor of the *Journal of the British Association of Psychotherapists* for an anniversary edition of that journal and published in 1999 – volume 37. The *JBAP* no longer exists, nor does the BAP, and I have been unable to seek permissions for this.

Finally – and certainly not least – my heartfelt thanks to the children and young people who educated me and whose courage permitted our joint journeying into what had been and who they might become.

AH
February 2018

Foreword

Lydia Tischler

I feel honoured to have been asked to provide a foreword to this volume of clinical papers. Readers of this book will learn why the children and young people who find their way to specialist services like the Portman Clinic displayed the kind of behaviours they did. They are troubled individuals and a trouble to society. What Horne so clearly – and with empathy but not sentimentality – shows is that the roots of their deviant behaviour are to be found in their earliest experiences where their environment not only did not offer them a soil in which to thrive but actively contributed to their distorted development and functioning. As Horne states: 'If as psychoanalytic practitioners we lose our capacity to see and engage with the individual in our therapy rooms, responding instead to a symptom or a condition – "the delinquent", "the fetishist", "the violent child" – we diminish our patients as they have already been diminished by an uncaring or abusive environment.' How much more does this apply to society's propensity to generalise and demonise those whose behaviour makes us feel uncomfortable.

Horne, with her unique combination of profound theoretical knowledge and technical skill, larded with a sense of humour, manages sensitively and carefully to unpick the defensive armour of those individuals who were lucky enough to become her patients and, with patience, to get through to the vulnerable individual. To understand why the individual was driven to make the choices he/she did is not to condone but, through understanding, to help the individual to make different, more constructive and creative choices.

Horne is too modest to claim the concept of 'body-based defences' as her own, a concept which she formulated based on her extensive clinical experience. Given the nature of the disturbances for which most children and adolescents are now referred to CAHMs teams, this concept forms an indispensable tool at the therapist's disposal and has taken a rightful place in the curriculum of the IPCAPA training.

The bulk of the book deals with clinical material illustrating the diversity of conditions she has encountered. Horne's style of writing enables the reader to join her in the consulting room and follow the interaction between therapist and patient, the painstaking and often very slow process of change, the successes and, at times, the failures. Horne eschews therapeutic zeal and is honest in recognising her limitations. This is clearly demonstrated in Chapter 5 when she was asked to consult to an organisation about a youngster whose dangerous behaviour put lives at risk. She is very honest about reaching her own limits when she states that when her levels of anxiety prevent her from being able to think, she cannot function and be of use to the patient. This no doubt applies to most of us.

Technique is derived from theory and the first and last two chapters discuss these subjects to show how her theoretical orientation informs her technique. She considers the countertransference as developed by Heimann, in which both the patient's projections and the therapist's own feelings play a part, as the most important part of the therapy. Indeed, she cautions that the therapist must pay attention to her countertransference if the therapy is to have meaning.

The BAP (British Association of Psychotherapists), as it was when she trained, was based on the Independent tradition of Psychoanalysis and as she makes clear she found the theories of Winnicott and Anna Freud most relevant in her work. Although, as she points out, Winnicott was averse to becoming a leader of a school, I think Ann would consider herself to be a Winnicottian. Finally, every graduate must take responsibility for the kind of therapist they have become. I think she has become an outstanding one and our profession can be proud to count Ann Horne among its members.

This book will make edifying reading for all clinicians, even the most seasoned ones, but should be compulsory reading for all those professionals, be it in the law, social services, special education, who meet those disturbed and disturbing young people.

I cannot recommend this book highly enough.

Part I
Setting the scene

1 On children who privilege the body
Introductory reflections

It is pleasing to see that there has been a recent revival of interest in the body and how/whether the psyche is able to relate to it and sustain an integration. It is, after all, almost 100 years since Freud pointed out that 'the ego is first and foremost a bodily ego' (Freud 1923: 26). Christine Anzieu-Premmereur describes the current resurgence of curiosity as a

> renewal of interest in the unconscious forces behind the contemporary burgeoning of identity pathology; work with disturbances in identity, autistic features, eating disorders, addiction and gender issues has reinforced the unassailable association between a loss of the connection with the body and archaic anxieties. When the capacity for adequate mental and emotional development finds itself at risk, sensation and action intervene to decrease anxieties linked with primitive non-mentalized experiences.
>
> (Anzieu-Premmereur 2018: 187)

While I do agree with this statement – especially concerning action directed towards containing anxiety arising from what has never been able to be named or processed – we may view this 'capacity for adequate mental and emotional development' slightly differently when we engage with the child's desperate search for a position, in relation to the body, that might allow the ego simply to survive. It is for many children a matter of life and death, the relationship that develops between psyche and soma; and often less a 'loss of connection' than a connection that dare not be made.

The book

This collection of papers bids to tell the stories of several young people whose internal worlds became enacted. For some the enactment is directed towards their own bodies; for others the activity aims to project intolerable internal states onto the world outside and make an impact upon the environment.

Encounters with children and young people form the central section – 'Children, activity and the body: case explorations'. The themes which led to their referrals include delinquency, sexual abuse and abusing, violence, fetishism, transsexualism and gender dysphoria, but mainly the chapters speak to the exceptional nature of each child's experience. As Alessandra Lemma stressed when she wrote of the uniqueness of her transsexual patients' experiences (Lemma 2015: 99), these are not examples of 'a unitary "condition" afflicting a homogeneous group of individuals' but they are distinctively personal responses to perceived and actual trauma that give rise to uniquely subjective psychological positions as the only developmental solution each child can find.

I cannot emphasise this enough. If as psychoanalytic practitioners we lose our capacity to see and engage with the individual in our therapy rooms, responding instead to a symptom or a condition ('the delinquent', 'the fetishist', 'the violent child'), we diminish our patients – as they have already been diminished by an uncaring or abusive environment. It is a counter-transference response that denies the singularity, individuality, of the child and attempts to create an 'other', separate and not-me, in response to the potency of counter-transference feelings. Where the body is concerned, the counter-transference can be challenging – and it is challenging to allow oneself to feel how unbearable are the unprocessed emotions that have to be projected. This work, then, needs us to be held ourselves – good supervision, good and available colleagues who (as in Chapter 6) know when to proffer a cup of coffee and a listening ear, and a capacity to explore one's own responses in depth.

This is perhaps most important when we find our patients arriving in our therapy rooms conflicted by issues of gender. In the 20 years since Chapter 9 was written, a more open, robust discussion of the social construction of gender and sexuality has developed across and between academic disciplines, informing and contesting, questioning theoretical stances. The wish to be a girl, in an 8-year-old boy, is not a typical position for a child to find in relation to his body. Such atypical positions seemingly adopted by children in relation to gender are becoming a matter of public debate and political intervention in the UK. The current focus tends to be on gender as a personal choice, an adaptable and flexible self that one may find when social responses permit, a self-conceived construct rather than a presumed biological 'given' – a stance that appears to recognise the acute disjunction experienced by some between felt body/gender experience and the 'reality' of endocrinological assessment (which itself experiences scientific challenge as we learn more about fluid biological states). This comes at the same time as society addresses an urgent need to take account of the experience and situation of – especially – transgendered adults who have found a voice in the political arena and seek social recognition and protection. The engagement of politics in giving validity to transsexuality has been important. It is vital, however, that we *also* remain able to keep ambivalence in mind – that where a child is gender-conflicted, there is room to reflect on that internal conflict and that we do not as a society insist on a dash to gender reassignment, immediately allocating the child to Lemma's unitary and homogeneous groupings: we have to temper our rush to action in order to create for the child a space to reflect. Activity is the main defence of the children in this book; we should seek to understand this but not ally ourselves with it: 'it is the imperative to "do", to adopt the child's defence and be active, as being passive, reflective, receptive feels intolerable' (Chapter 7).

There is considerable reflection on theory in these chapters and on process and technique – perhaps the latter is more evident as it permeates the sessional material rather than in any didactic imperatives, although there is included a chapter on the development of Independent thinking (Chapter 2) and a later one on thoughts on the process of work (Chapter 10), locating this approach to children who use the body clearly within the Independent tradition in British psychoanalysis. Theory, of course, must be examined and, as Winnicott noted 50 years ago, 'If observations do not fit in with theory, then theory must alter' (Winnicott 1967: 110). A further theme, therefore, is that the institutionalisation of theoretical stances is not helpful – indeed, it results less in the growth of enquiring minds in our training establishments than in the production of clones. That may be comfortable at times, but it does leave us with a remarkably restricted arsenal of thought on which to draw.

Key issues

There is an assumption, in these papers, that good-enough child development depends on the provision of good-enough relationships and environment. We can turn to Winnicott for an assessment of what is sufficient to enable the infant to find a creative developmental track.

'Communication between infant and mother, and mother and infant, compared and contrasted' provides an affecting description of precisely what is involved in lively, non-verbal communication between mother and infant (Winnicott 1968) and must make us pause when we think of our patients' experiences of the body. Initially there is 'communication . . . in terms of mutuality in physical experience' – i.e. the mother's movement, breathing, smell, rocking, the sound of her heartbeat; there is playing and common ground ('the no-man's land that is each man's land'), transitional space; the uses of gaze; and the mother's provision of an anticipatory adaptation that allows to the baby an experience of omnipotence and omnipotent ownership of the object. Winnicott writes:

> As development proceeds, . . . the environmental reliability becomes a belief, an introject based on the *experience of reliability* [human, not mechanically perfect] . . . The baby does not hear or register the communication, only the effects of the reliability.
>
> (Winnicott 1968: 97)

This is not a perfect mother – the baby experiences the failures of ordinary day to day care, mended and amended by the mother who is, in his experience, reliable-enough. Small failures and recoveries in mothering build up a rhythm, internalised by the baby and serving a protective function for him. But where 'gross failures' of care, reliability and adaptation are all that is available for the infant:

These gross failures of holding produce in the baby *unthinkable anxiety* – the content of such anxiety is:

Going to pieces

Falling for ever

Complete isolation because of there being no means of communication

Disunion of psyche and soma.

These are the fruits of *privation*, environmental failure essentially unmended.

(Winnicott 1968: 98–99)

Recent child development and neurobiological research would support Winnicott's 'fruits of privation' observation:

One of the effects of trauma on the brain is that neuronal pathways are intensively created in parts of the brain that stimulate hypervigilance . . . A hardwired 'superhighway' develops, through which new experience is filtered.

(Sutton 2017)

Sarah Sutton goes on to describe how this is useful in times of danger; but means that 'the parts of the brain that process ordinary positive experience wither' (ibid.: 9) and thus are not available to the child who is coping with the sequelae of early trauma and neglect. She also, incidentally, reminds us that research has already established the fact that relationships are 'the medium through which minds are made'. For the children whose stories form the major part of this book, good-enough parenting did not feature, nor the early Winnicottian physical intimacy, whether by result of neglect, depression, ambivalence, hatred, abandonment or physical, emotional and sexual abuse.

Several themes in work with children who act and who use what I have termed 'body-based defensive manoeuvres' reappear, in action, in the chapters that follow. Indeed, Chapters 2 and particularly 10 focus on factors such as pace, intimacy, timing, affect recognition, moving between developmental and new object, working in the displacement and a range of ways of simply being with children. Those key issues that now follow are merely those that I feel we too often lose sight of.

Aggression/ agency/ potency/ violence

Chapter 11 puts it fairly clearly:

It is essential that today's trainees can understand the origins of aggression and distinguish what is developmentally an achievement and the advent of potency, what is a primitive defence and that which is affect that overwhelms, where words cannot be found to make sense of it and bind it.

It matters that we are able to see aggression as a necessary developmental achievement in childhood (Winnicott 1950–1955), and that we can separate this from violence. Chapter 2 explains the Independent understanding of this and in Chapter 5 Parsons and Dermen

> suggest . . . that violence be understood as an attempted solution to a trauma the individual has not been able to process, and we define this trauma as helplessness in the absence of a protective object. . . . The youngster is both a perpetrator (in the external world and in his ideal image of himself) and also a victim (having been failed at a point of maximum helplessness and lacking an internalised protective membrane). He enacts this disjunction, causing harm to others and inviting punishment unconsciously from the law.
>
> (Parsons & Dermen 1999: 345)

The implications for how we work, then, become clearer: 'the unhooking of 'violence' and 'aggression' allows us to think of what might be helpful in therapy. When we think 'defence' and 'anxiety' we tend to find very different phrasing from when we think 'aggression' and 'attack'.' Indeed, with Martin – the child struggling with violent responses in Chapter 5 (where this quote can be found) – the *in*ability of staff to recognise that his verbal abusing of others (often with very sexually disparaging language) was essentially a sign of anxiety, led to his having to act.

Taking a developmental line is also vital when we encounter young people like Stanley (Chapter 8) where there was gross inhibition of the development of a sense of muscularity and agency and of a body self. The role of illness, scoliosis and lengthy hospitalisation, compounded by the loss of his father and ambivalent parenting, led to a subsequent dependency on fetishism to inhibit any aggressive affect. This impinged in turn on the growth of positive aggressive affect which would become an achievement in the therapy: '. . . the analyst must expect to find acting-out in the transference, and must understand the significance of this acting-out, and be able to give it positive value' (Winnicott 1963: 210).

In the therapy room, when a child is compelled to attack aggressively, his/her reliance at that moment will be on the oldest, reptilian part of the brain, used in fight/flight. We cannot talk to this. Complex interpretations of anxiety will simply be felt as further intrusion, needing to be obliterated. Using the briefest of phrases (I have found 'Oops!' and 'Ouch!' to be particularly valuable . . .), creating a safe space and distance, and waiting for calm are far more useful – and for this we need to be able to see the child as vulnerable and intruded upon, using attack as a defence, rather than attack as a perverse pleasure. As Winnicott writes (above) the recognition that this was the only response available to the child lets us construe the acting out differently and see its necessity.

History taking

'The essential thing is I do base my work on diagnosis,' said Winnicott to the British Psycho-analytic Society (Winnicott 1962: 169).

There is a place for State of Mind assessments with children. These should not, however, be the only psychoanalytic assessments undertaken before a child who uses activity and the body is taken into therapy. Activity has a reason, a source; when it appears, we need to have a very clear knowledge (or as clear as we can assemble) of that child's history in order to be alert to the re-enactments that inevitably inform the symptomatology. We cannot be lazy about this but must insist to referring colleagues that the child's story is pieced together, and that information is requested.

There is a further reason for pulling together a child's history: for every child, a sense of 'going on being' matters. Children who come to us from looked-after settings or from perversely abusive families may well lack this. There is *always* more information in the system than comes with the referral – as is made plain in Chapter 5 where the Unit had a clear record of just how Martin was decompensating but no-one read it. We owe it to the children to help unravel the narrative and to be a person who can keep it in mind when the child dares not access memory.

Ideal states and the role of shame

A brief note on the role of the ideal ego and the ego ideal – concepts which I find helpful in work with children who act. In developing the thinking which resulted in his theory of the superego, Freud first posited an ideal ego and an ego ideal – seemingly conflated later but to my mind still valuable to the clinician as separate concepts (Freud 1914). The 'ideal ego' one can see as the one which sustains us in daydreaming and fantasy, an omnipotent state of an illusory kind, the first compromise between the loss of infantile omnipotence and the advent of the reality principle. In time, the child can tolerate not being omnipotent and develops an ego ideal – 'the self's conception of how he wishes to be' (as Rycroft defined it in 1995) with the addition, for me, of how he would wish the world to see him – 'potent but not omnipotent' (Rycroft 1968: 39). 'Being seen' is such an important part of this. The ego ideal in health shows the child in a state of aspiration and knowing his capabilities, a self with possibilities. Where the child's development has gone well enough, this becomes a resilient ego ideal. When we fall short of our ego ideal, we feel shame and try to take ourselves away from the gaze of those who observe this failure. When the children we work with can come to conceive of an ego syntonic ideal self, the work has progressed considerably; where there is still reliance on the brittle omnipotence of an ideal ego, it is probably indicative of a history of being relentlessly shamed in the eyes of others and of ourselves and thus being compelled to have recourse to an ideal, powerful fantasy state. This latter is often found with violent youth, easily alert to humiliation and 'being dissed' (Chapter 4).

When thinking of Martin's increasing threats to staff in Chapter 5, we conclude that the only position available to him at this lowest point appeared to be identification with the objects of violence, pictures of which he masturbated over. He had become such an object with an internal ideal image, ideal ego, as perpetrator. Orlando, too, sought a mechanistic solution – 'I'm a machine' (Chapter 9).

I wonder if a mechanistic ideal-self, for young people who have experienced hatred in the acts and the gaze of the other, is the only possible psychological construct available to them, not only because it is a minimalist identification without fear of human attachments and therefore humiliation, but also because it gives an illusion of control. It may be the only position to be found by the child for whom an experience of omnipotence has never occurred and could never be envisioned. We recall the child, described by Fairbairn (1946), who perceives himself as bad in order to sustain the idea of a parent who might love him – it is his fault, not the parent's, that he is hated.

Triangulation: 'Isn't it interesting what your body gets up to!'

Issues of intimacy and distance are of especial importance when we encounter children who act. Anna Freud was clear that working in the displacement was an effective intervention for children who need to approach their anxiety carefully (Sandler, J, Kennedy, H & Tyson, R 1980: 165). With children who act, I have found we can also triangulate the situation, as with displacement, and address the body as a separate entity that cannot think but that does operate as a source of memories and at times acts on these. 'Isn't it interesting what your body gets up to!' can surprise a child – you are not, then, going to engage in telling them off – and seeks to ally with the thinking part of the child in observing the acting part. The space gained for thought is so important – see Chapter 3 for comment on this in the case of Matthew.

The final chapter

The last chapter was given as a talk at the 60th anniversary of the founding of the BAP with the specified focus of reflecting back and observing change. It is interwoven with vignettes from my first training patient (well, we don't forget patients, especially first ones) and the careful reader will recognise extracts from Chapters 6, 8 and 10. It fits in this collection as the third of the chapters that take as their theme an Independent training. The style is at times celebratory and the chapter notes the achievements of a unique training school. I make no apologies for this – I am most grateful to the BAP and IPCAPA at the bpf.

Conclusion

When we think of the body and our child and adolescent patients who are driven to act, to depend on soma rather than psyche-in-soma, we think of a spectrum of bodily responses or positions that are all the child can see to adopt in the circumstances in which he finds himself. These may – as with George in Chapter 9 – be what the child assumes the parent wishes and lead to the structuring of an ideal self that depends heavily on introjected parental objects: the parental trauma is then articulated through the body of the child. With Martin (Chapter 5), where there was no expectation or early experience of an alert – never mind an attuned – adult, his primitive actions were responses to previously relentless trauma, the memory of humiliation, and a desperate need to act to survive, and led to reliance on an ideal self as perpetrator. With the body, it is psychologically a matter of life and death.

I hope this collection of papers adds something to debate, understanding and practice in work with children who act.

References

Anzieu-Premmereur, C (2018) Concluding remarks. In V Tsolas & C Anzieu-Premmereur (eds.) *A Psychoanalytic Exploration of the Body in Today's World – On the Body* London & New York: Routledge

Fairbairn, WRD (1946) Object relations and dynamic structure *International Journal of Psychoanalysis* 27: 30–37

Freud, S (1914) On narcissism: an introduction *SE* 14: 67–104 London: Hogarth Press

Freud, S (1923) The Ego and the Id *SE* 19 London: Hogarth Press

Lemma, A (2015) *Minding the Body – The Body in Psychoanalysis and Beyond* Hove & New York: Routledge

Parsons, M & Dermen, S (1999) The violent child and adolescent. In M Lanyado & A Horne (eds.) *The Handbook of Child & Adolescent Psychotherapy: Psychoanalytic Approaches* London: Routledge

Rycroft, C (1968) *Imagination and Reality* New York: International Universities Press

Rycroft, C (1995) *A Critical Dictionary of Psychoanalysis* 2nd edition London: Penguin Books

Sandler, J, Kennedy, H & Tyson, R (1980) *The Technique of Child Psychoanalysis: Discussions with Anna Freud* London: Hogarth Press

Sutton, S (2017) Who do we think we are? The myth of the individual. Unpublished paper given at the annual conference of the ACP, June 2017

Winnicott, DW (1950–1955) Aggression in relation to emotional development. In *Collected Papers: Through Paediatrics to Psychoanalysis* London: Tavistock

Winnicott, DW (1962) The aims of psychoanalytical treatment. In DW Winnicott *The Maturational Processes and the Facilitating Environment* London: Hogarth Press 1965

Winnicott, DW (1963) 'Psychotherapy of character disorders'. In *The Maturational Processes and the Facilitating Environment* London: Hogarth Press 1965

Winnicott, DW (1967) A tribute on the occasion of Willi Hoffer's seventieth birthday. In L Caldwell & H Taylor Robinson *The Collected Works of DW Winnicott* Vol 8 Part 1 p 110

Winnicott, DW (1968) Communication between infant and mother, and mother and infant, compared and contrasted. In DW Winnicott *Babies and Their Mothers* eds. C Winnicott, R Shepherd & M Davis London: Free Association Books 1988

2 The Independent position in psychoanalytic psychotherapy with children and adolescents

Roots and implications[1]

The split in 1944 within the British Psychoanalytic Society (BP-AS), highlighted by the 'controversial discussions' (King & Steiner 1991), did not simply result in the formation of the 'A' Group (Kleinians) and the 'B' Group (identified with Vienna and Anna Freud) within the Society; the majority of members adopted a very British position and became the 'Middle Group', later (from 1973) the Independents. I call it a very British position as it is a feature of many British institutions that, in the face of dispute, a compromise is reached – we do not seem to be creatures of extremes. It must be the climate. British social policy, for example, has frequently been described as 'muddling through' – not dogmatic or extreme in political stance, but reaching, on a good day, the best available compromise. The Independents are thus part (and the majority part) of 'the British School' in psychoanalysis – importantly to be differentiated from the term 'English School' which was applied early on by colleagues in Europe and the USA to the followers of Mrs Klein after her arrival in the United Kingdom in 1926.

It is more than simply a compromise, however – to rest with this proposition would be a great over-simplification. The thrust of the early Independents was a determination to preserve precisely that, independence of mind. As Rayner puts it, 'The key to an understanding of the Independents is their avowed openness to learning from any psychoanalytical theories' (Rayner 1991: 4). Rayner, following Gillespie, locates this British tradition within the political and philosophical liberalism of the 17th and 18th centuries, a profound influence on British intellectual life:

> Here is empiricism, and pragmatism, in practice. Love of it brings a natural leaning towards experiment and trial and error. When using this mode of learning, the experience of error is often as valuable as correctness. We will find this philosophy in the Independents' approach to psychoanalysis as a therapy as well as a theory.
>
> (Rayner 1991: 8)

> Such an approach, in contrast to the European tradition of deductive rationalism, leads empiricists to 'place greater emphasis on the senses . . . and experiment to frame ideas'.
>
> (Jones 2004, paraphrasing Grayling 1995)

Most commentators would see this style of empiricism and curiosity as evident in the British Psychoanalytic Society prior to the controversial discussions. At a physical distance from Europe, it was perhaps easier to think freely, away from the immediacy of the transference to Freud and Vienna. Thus, Mrs Klein was invited by the BP-AS to give six lectures to the Society in 1925 and, a year after the death of Abraham, feeling less supported in Berlin, she returned permanently to London. The arrival of the Freud family from Vienna in 1938 heightened the tensions that had already caused rumblings on the continent.

Although ardently a non-political grouping without a leader, the Independents have often been associated with Winnicott whose ideas have been very influential. While frequently assumed to be leader of the Middle Group, in fact he always declined to be seen as such and worked unavailingly for reconciliation between the A and B groups.

Becoming an Independent

Statements about empiricism and curiosity can be open to misconstruction and may be treated as if one is somehow arguing for an eclecticism that omits rigour or rigorous theoretical underpinning. The taunt of 'eclecticism' tends to be used by those who would cling to narrower identifications and supposed orthodoxies. Yet such 'orthodoxy' brings its own dilemmas.

The greatest issue facing psychoanalysis in Britain today, paradoxically, is not the assumed threats from other psychological approaches or even the slowness in establishing an evidence-base. It lies for many of us in the incapacity of the profession to analyse its own tendency to idealisation. That most independent of Independents, Charles Rycroft, in an early paper explored ideas of 'pathological idealisation' and 'normal idealisation' (Rycroft 1955) linking these to Winnicott's concepts of illusion and disillusion in the development of the infant (Winnicott 1945) and here describing the process in the 'healthy child':

> Though this illusion will require an eventual disillusion, the disillusionment will be confined to its belief in its omnipotent control of reality, not to reality itself. The healthy child's hero-worship of its parents and its belief in their omnipotence is to be seen as a process of idealisation which tides it over this period of disillusion until such time as it can rely on its own powers and discovers itself as an individual, potent but not omnipotent.
>
> (Rycroft 1968: 39)

It is, perhaps, with a wry smile that we read Rycroft's own account of the reception accorded this paper when read at the BP-AS in 1954:

> I entered the analytical movement without appreciating the passionate intensity, the absolute certainty, with which many analysts held their views. Too many did not have opinions that were open to discussion and possible modification but, instead, had unalterable convictions – including the conviction

that anyone who disagreed with them had not had a sufficiently deep analysis. As a result, the so-called scientific meetings were all too often not discussions but collisions. I once read a paper to the Society about a woman who had dreamed that the moon fell out of the sky into a dustbin (Rycroft 1955). During the discussion Melanie Klein expressed her regret that I had not had a sufficiently deep analysis; at the time I took this as an insult to Dr Payne [Dr Sylvia Payne, Rycroft's analyst]. I heard later that some of the audience had construed my paper as a conscious, deliberate allegory about Klein; it wasn't, but it's a pleasing idea.

(Rycroft 1993 reprinted in Pearson 2004: 244)

Idealisation tends, all too speedily, to be followed by institutionalisation – perhaps a variation on Rycroft's 'pathological idealisation', which has no reference point in an external reality that knows to foster disillusionment but depends upon ideal internal objects. Such a process often brings an accompanying reluctance to question the ideas and tenets of one's theoretical forebears and carries with it an assumption that what one is taught are 'set' and 'right' techniques and principles. The danger of this process possibly lies more with those whom Winnicott called 'the proselytizers' (Casement 2002: xxiv) rather than the original figures themselves, as the story of Winnicott's tolerable relationship with Mrs Klein, until close to her death, demonstrates. Understandable as such rigidity might have been in the years close to Freud's death, and it must be considered a major factor in the 'controversial discussions', it is disappointing that, 60 years on, we may sustain the polarised theoretical positions of the 1940s. Kohon reminds us that, in the world of British psychoanalysis:

Although there has been peaceful co-existence between the three groups, they have remained separate . . . . it is in theoretical work that the separations are – for some analysts – tightly maintained: they would never be found quoting from colleagues of any of the rival groups.

(Kohon 1986: 45)

Whereas Rayner points to a growing sense that this 'necessary expedient' of the three groups is no longer useful, he too comments that 'there is frequent acrimony about group-ideological matters' (Rayner 1991: 21).

Anne Hayman (2001) tenaciously pursues a similar theme when she comments, for example, that Bion's 'eschewing memory and desire' (Bion 1970) is predated by Freud's 'evenly suspended attention', as Freud develops it in 1912, and that Annie Reich, in 1951, describes 'confusing incomprehensible disconnected presentations [which] suddenly make sense and become a *Gestalt* [whole]' anticipating Bion's (1967) 'selected fact'. Neither, however, is credited. Roazen raises a related point, that 'history-writing is inherently a subversive activity: students of history necessarily undermine generally received wisdom. . . . A typical lack of respect for historical sequences has, I think, bedevilled the writing about psychoanalysis to an exceptional extent' (Roazen 2004: 43). As theories develop and ideas are encountered and shared in this process, it may be difficult to tease out just who first thought of what. We cannot in that respect omit what Adam Phillips has called Winnicott's 'infamous statement' (Phillips 2000: 91):

> I shall not first give an historical survey and show the development of my ideas from the theories of others, because my mind doesn't work that way. What happens is that I gather this and that, here and there, settle down to clinical experience, form my own theories, and then, last of all, interest myself to see where I stole what. Perhaps this is as good a method as any.
>
> (Winnicott 1945: 145)

Today, however, in the service of clarity and theoretical rigour, and perhaps as an aide to integration and mutual respect, one would hope for generosity in the trans-ideological acknowledgement of sources.

I am reminded of the Association of Child Psychotherapy (ACP) conference in 2001 when, asked what has most aided the 'crossing of borders' between training schools of different theoretical orientations, a senior Kleinian psychoanalyst proposed in all seriousness that it was the acceptance by all groups of the Kleinian concept of projective identification. There was a sharp intake of breath . . . One might – from an Independent point of view, of course – offer that the saving of psychoanalysis in 1944 in Britain was the refusal of the majority of the members of the British Psychoanalytic Society to follow any charismatic leader or omnipotent theory, and so sanity lay in the formation of the Middle, later Independent, Group. But I would say that – wouldn't I?

A new child and adolescent psychotherapy training

The arrival of an Independent training in child and adolescent psychotherapy grew from a situation that was not unlike the controversial discussions – a situation of increasing polarity and lack of communication, perhaps the controversial discussions without the discussion.

Although established in the aftermath of the disputes within the BP-AS in the 1940s, the early atmosphere of the Kleinian Child Psychotherapy training at the Tavistock was one wherein Bick in the 1950s could readily invite Winnicott to teach the Child Psychotherapy trainees. Juliet Hopkins also describes the possibility of some leeway within prevailing convention:

> [In 1961] I was fortunate to have Winnicott as the supervisor of one of my training cases. As far as I know, no other student child psychotherapist ever shared this good fortune, since doctrinal differences dictated that students should be supervised only by the orthodox. However, the Tavistock Clinic training, though Kleinian in orientation, allowed some latitude to its few 'middle group' students like myself to select our own supervisors.
>
> (Hopkins 1996: 20)

This 'latitude' – tenuous enough in 1961 – appears to have encountered a period of sudden frost by the late 1960s. Khar comments:

> The Kleinian bitterness towards Winnicott and his burgeoning independence reached such proportions that during the late 1960s certain tutors on the Child Psychotherapy course at the Tavistock Clinic . . . expressly forbade their students to attend Winnicott's public lectures, even though Melanie Klein had died some years previously. Mrs Frances Tustin (personal communication, 22 February 1994), a renowned child psychotherapist, . . . confessed that 'I in my training was brought up not to read Winnicott'. Another of those trainees, now a seasoned professional, laughed as she recalled how she visited Winnicott in secret, as though he epitomised some dreadful subversive underground movement.
>
> (Khar 1996: 77)

By the late 1970s there were three Training Schools in the UK. The Lowenfeld Institute of Child Psychology had closed in 1978:

> Although economic reasons finally led to the closure of the ICP as a clinic, the search for comparability across trainings was felt to have been an influence as the ACP and its Training Council consolidated around a more purely psychoanalytic approach than the holistic Lowenfeld one was felt to be. It is somewhat ironic today that many admired senior members of the profession are ICP graduates and some of the most stimulating and creative writing on children and psychoanalysis comes from that stable.
>
> (Lanyado & Horne 1999: 8–9)

Within this brief account there lies a sense that the ICP had failed, somehow, to be 'orthodox'. Of the three remaining schools, one was Jungian (the SAP where training began in 1974); the others – the Hampstead Clinic (to be renamed the Anna Freud Centre after Miss Freud's death) and the Tavistock Clinic – centred on the thinking and teaching of each of the two women around whom the controversial discussions had stormed.

There was little communication between these two major centres. Rather, it was felt that further entrenchment had occurred. At the Hampstead Clinic there was additionally grave concern about funding and the future of the institution: dependent on American financial goodwill and applicants from outside Britain presenting for training, the staff felt that both sources seemed to be drying up. The solution to finding a transitional (independent) position 'between Anna and Melanie' and perhaps keeping alive the teaching and theory of Miss Freud was the brainchild of Anne Hurry, a Hampstead staff member who had also trained in Adult Psychotherapy at the British Association of Psychotherapists (BAP) where the new training was to be located. She carefully chose her planning committee to comprise Hampstead trained and Tavistock trained child psychotherapists, all sympathetic to Independent thought, and the new BAP child training had its first intake of trainees in 1982. The flyer for the training announces:

A new training in Child Psychotherapy

The British Association of Psychotherapists has trained adult psychotherapists since 1951. This new venture has been planned in response to the national shortage of child psychotherapists, and the need to provide a training which represents the thinking of the classical and Independent groups in British psycho-analysis.

(BAP archive 1981)

The Training Committee demonstrated this range of experience, comprising Anne Hurry, Charlotte Balkanyi, Irmi Elkan, Wallace Hamilton, Juliet Hopkins, Rosalie Joffe, Dolly Lush, Eileen Orford, Pat Radford, Margaret Tonnesmann and Peter Wilson. As Dolly Lush (a Tavistock staff member until her retirement) described, 'Anne Hurry asked if I would lend my name to it, that's all that was needed.' This was said as she retired from the BAP Child Training Committee after 20 years of stalwart service. The training was 21 years old in September 2003 – it has come of age and with a strong identity.[2]

Trainees may be in analysis with analysts of all three sections of the Institute of Psychoanalysis and supervisors are equally Anna Freudian, Independent or Kleinian. Similarly, seminar leaders are from all three orientations: it seems particularly important to have a specialist Freudian teach Freud, Oedipus and latency, and to have a Kleinian specialist teach, for example, Klein and Bion.

A by-product of this training has been a greater integration across the profession as, in teaching and supervision, ideas have been shared across theoretical divides. Anne Alvarez, who had resigned her post at the Tavistock, was later to return there and find her work rightly valued. In the interim years, however, she was an engaging and stimulating teacher at the BAP. Lively discussions took place, especially around technique, and her paper 'Beyond the unpleasure principle' (Alvarez 1988), she has said, owed a small measure to her BAP trainees. Recent trainees in supervision with her report that she still says, 'But you Independents know this! This is easy for you!' – usually about technical issues.

Where does it leave us as child psychotherapists? One has fantasies – even in the Middle Group – of what happens in other trainings. One can speculate as to the containment offered by trainings that take one theoretical perspective – a consistency and nurturing that is at times enviable. Such trainees may be viewed as young plants that are growing in a greenhouse, protected from the winds of controversy and theoretical conflict. Being in the middle of an Independent training can occasionally feel like being planted out, where frosts might still come, and told, 'Grow, damn you! Grow!' To experience all weathers, however, is somehow also 'very British' – and it is essential in character formation!

Establishing an identity

With the seminal contributions of Kohon (1986) and Rayner (1991), we see a new consolidation of the Independent Group within the British Society, clarification of the principal theoretical positions and a group defining itself by what it is as well as by what it is not, gathering the commonalities of theoretical thought but not denying the breadth of theoretical positions possible. There had long been a flourishing of ideas (Brierley, Bowlby, Balint, Milner, Rycroft, Winnicott amongst the earlier independent minds; Bollas, Coltart, Casement, Klauber, King, Khan, Parsons, Rayner, Wright more recently – and those only a few) and much of more recent writing develops perceptions stimulated by 'the genius of British analysis', Winnicott (Rycroft, quoted in Roazen 2002: 23). It is not surprising, therefore, in this volume, to find Winnicott to be a common thread.

What, then, would we say are the major theoretical and technical issues for those of us who once lay 'between Freud and Klein' (Limentani 1989)? Rayner (1991) provides us with a great deal of information here and what follows is indebted to him for his erudition and clarity. He notes, initially, that the fundamentals remain the same: basic classical theory and technique – the unconscious, defence and resistance, interpretation and the transference, and metapsychology – are taken as given. To this, he notes, most Independents would add from Mrs Klein and her followers the concept of projective identification and the use of 'the mechanisms of denial, projection and introjection creating splits for defensive purposes in the personality' (Rayner 1991: 22). Equally, Anna Freud's contributions of the analysis of the ego and the defences, and her concept of developmental lines, have become part of the repertoire of Independents.

It is interesting that, in the detail of theory, the Independents appear to have taken time particularly to position themselves in relation to Kleinian theory – possibly from valuing Klein as the co-progenitor of object relations theory (Brierley's 1937 pivotal paper on affects placing her equally here). Yet Fairbairn holds a key role and, for the child psychotherapist, his emphasis on the importance of environment and real experience – taken up by Winnicott – has a necessary impact on how we understand and engage with our young patients. Most 'Independents do not widely subscribe to Klein's theory of neonatal development, either in her dating or in the means by which one position is said to succeed the other' (Rayner 1991: 23). For Fairbairn and Winnicott, when paranoid-schizoid features appear, these are a *reaction* to trauma and to interactions with or impingements by the environment and not a necessary developmental stage – although both value the concept greatly in thinking about pathology. Similar importance is accorded to the environment when contemplating the origins of psychopathology: Klein saw these as rooted in conflict, originally between the life and death instincts. Independents see the roots in the early experience of interaction with the environment – 'real external object-relations' out of which phantasy then arises: hence 'phantasy is an "inference" or "interpretation"'. 'Imagination or phantasy thus probably arises out of the interplay between infant and environment and has no meaning as an innate faculty' (Rayner 1991: 24). From such a perspective it becomes easier to see the progression to Khan's later concept of cumulative trauma and the further impact of the real environment (Khan 1963). Indeed, to the child psychotherapist working nowadays, infantile trauma, loss, perversion and distortion of reality, neglect and abuse are such a feature of the histories of the children whom we see that we could no longer – in any tradition – only perceive innate conflict.

Some Independents do subscribe to the death instinct theory very much in the form that Klein took it from Freud. But Gillespie's contrasting view [1971], both about the idea of the instinct itself and with regard to its consequence that aggressiveness must then be seen as an original sin of a sort, would probably be subscribed to by the majority (Rayner 1991: 109).

This is an essential difference – for Mrs Klein destructiveness is innate and so intra-psychic. Darwinian to the last, most Independents, and certainly Independent child psychotherapists, view aggression as necessary for survival, part of the self-protective function of the organism. Aggressiveness thus has a central position in Independent thought, with the emphasis on its role in normal development. In this we are, perhaps, closer to Anna Freud. Both Winnicott and Fairbairn perceive pathological aggression as *reactive*: this may be to the actual, assumed or phantasised impingement of the environment. Winnicott adds the point that muscular aggression (which the mother has to survive) is the beginning of motility and a sense of assertiveness and potency – essential for healthy development (Winnicott 1950–1955: 204). In her revision of her initial conceptualisation of the life and death instincts, based on clinical experience that she found challenged her earlier position, Heimann explored the possibility of two types of aggression – that (as Winnicott) in the service of survival and agency, and another expressed in sadism and cruelty. This latter, interestingly, she saw as derived from failures in the care offered by the environment (Heimann 1964). A similar view was expressed by Suttie (whose influence on the object relations tradition was profound, if at times rather unacknowledged) who based it on his very early formulation of attachment theory (Suttie 1935).

The fundamental axis of the Independent position may well be that originally articulated by Suttie and Fairbairn, that the human being is object seeking rather than, as in drive theory, pleasure seeking (Suttie 1935; Fairbairn 1941, 1946): 'the orientation of the infant to others is there from the very beginning because the infant has adaptive genic roots for his biological survival' (Sutherland 1989). This differs from Klein in that the object is not simply a means towards pleasure: 'pleasure is not the end goal of the impulse, but a means to its real end – relations with another' (Greenberg & Mitchell 1983: 154).

Finally, the place of creativity and ideas around transitional space, transitional objects and transformational space in Independent thought more than merit attention. The third area of the mind – between internal and external, between me and not-me, where play and thought and psychoanalysis can happen – is after all one of the most readily recognised contributions of Winnicott and one developed and enhanced by several later theorists, principally Bollas (e.g. Bollas 1987). The influence of work in these two areas has relevance for the therapist in establishing the setting of the room, the nature of the interaction, and indeed in understanding the purpose of the analytic encounter.

Brief implications of Independent theory for technique in work with children

Perceiving the child as 'object seeking' – rather than seeking relations in the service of undoing displeasure – takes us immediately into the arena of the external as well as the internal world. With Fairbairn, Ferenczi and Winnicott, we find the importance of the role of real but flawed object relations, objects who have failed to meet the creativity of the child – or who have imposed their own perversion on the child-treated-as-object. How these 'mis-steps in the dance' become replayed in the child's pathology and in the transference relationship becomes the focus of work. However, in order *not* to replicate the mis-shapen dance that the child expects and replays in his object relationships, one has to keep in mind Winnicott's injunction that psychoanalysis offers a further intimacy, like the early infant-mother relationship, in which the curiosity of the child – and the 'true self' – may be called forth. One is therefore always seeking space in which the child's defences and affect are held in mind, yet curiosity becomes possible. To be careful about 'shame' and 'humiliation' (and the vulnerability of the ego ideal) need not mean avoiding anxiety or avoiding interpretation; it does mean actively taking great care about timing. In this, the Independent motif matters – that the interpretation that is most useful to the patient is the one the patient finds, in the therapeutic process, for himself.

Aggression

To perceive aggression as fundamental for development, healthy narcissism and a sense of agency does have serious implications for treatment. The Kleinian concept of innate destructiveness and hate, based on developments away from Freud's theory of the death instinct, leads to the need to analyse these impulses and their impact on the internal world. Following Winnicott, the Independent working with the child who is prone to attack would see the need to indicate the importance and necessity of the defence and articulate this – it is, after all, life or death – and the immaturity of the ego that can only resort to such early, primitive manoeuvres must be borne in mind. Often the therapist therefore begins by understanding and according meaning to the aggressive defence as necessary (not condoning or encouraging it, simply recognising and articulating its essential function); the subsequent lessening of anxiety may then afford a space for thought (rather than action) and enable mutual curiosity to be engaged. A similar stance is helpful when faced with the child whose main defensive preoccupation is activity.

The working alliance and the setting

It would seem axiomatic that the therapist encounters a measure of 'ego' in the patient for engagement in therapy, and that one would seek to connect with this in a treatment alliance. It is not, however, uncommon to encounter censure in relation to the concept of the working alliance, as if to foster it is indicative somehow of indulgence or gratification of the patient. It seems, at times, as if it gets confused with the idea of the positive transference and can be taken to imply an over-cultivation of this. The two are separate, if overlapping:

> In practice, the state of the transference always has repercussions on the treatment alliance, and the alliance is not completely autonomous and independent of the transference, even though a conceptual distinction is made between treatment alliance and transference.
>
> (Sandler, Kennedy & Tyson 1980: 48)

For many Independent therapists, simple matters like the therapy room being quietly but overtly a place that is welcoming to children would be of importance and would be seen as part of the process of establishing a treatment/working alliance. Although each child has a protected box of toys and play materials, it is unusual for an Independent only to have the box in an otherwise fairly bare room. Perhaps this is not unconnected to the conviction that paranoid-schizoid manifestation is reactive to external impingement and not an innate, initial 'given', hence not a state that a child might be *expected* to regress to. The model of early mother-infant interaction that Winnicott would have us keep in mind as the model for therapeutic work means that we present an environment not overwhelming in its possibilities but definitely offering a curious and engaged 'other'.

The process

With the pronouncement that 'there is no such thing as a baby' (Winnicott 1947a) the important recognition that the process of therapy is an interplay of two minds, of the patient's transference and the therapist's counter-transference, has led to interesting developments in how the counter-transference is monitored (Casement 1985) and used (Winnicott 1947b). The constant reminder that this is a process which occurs in the transitional space between two people, not a procedure applied by one to the other, requires a continuous capacity to monitor oneself as therapist and to seek room in the therapeutic session for observing this interaction. This is particularly important with active children and technical inventions like 'thinking time' (see Chapter 10) arise from this realisation.

One would also include the general tendency not to go immediately for the manifest content (anxiety) below the defences but rather to wait for the individual psychological structure to emerge before going for deep interpretation. Again, this varies according to the needs of patient and therapeutic situation, but it would seem therefore that pace and timing are fundamental principles, as outlined in the following chapter. Moving, too, from a developmental to an analytic stance and being able to go between the two would take us closer to Anna Freud's teaching in terms of technique, as would keeping the developmental position and tasks in mind. There is a certain freedom generated by the recognition that, with children, one seeks to do sufficient work to enable them to regain the natural developmental thrust – and developmental track – that then takes them forward once more. No ideal personality structure is in mind, simply a spectrum of pos-sibilities on which the child hopefully takes up a more appropriately defended and more optimistic position.

'Play' and 'playfulness' equally merit serious consideration, not simply because they are such Winnicottian concepts but because they take us into the arena of *how* the therapist is with the patient. This is also not unadjacent to Paula Heimann's concept of the 'naturalness' of the analyst and the question of 'neutral-ity', sterility, emotional responsiveness and alert attention all feature strongly in Independent writing over many years, from Balint to Bollas. Perhaps Balint can sum it up, as long ago as 1939:

> The objective task demands that a patient analysed in any of the many indi-vidual ways shall learn to know his own unconscious mind and not that of his analyst. The subjective task demands that analysing shall not be too heavy an emotional burden, that the individual variety of technique shall procure suf-ficient emotional outlet for the analyst. A sound and adequate technique must therefore be doubly individual.
>
> (Balint 1939: 206–207)

Counter-transference

There will be a great deal in common amongst the different theoretical schools when counter-transference is considered. However, there is a perception that counter-transference has often seemed to centre, for Kleinian analysts, on the patients' projective identifications. This is undoubtedly part of the process but not its entirety. Both Winnicott and Anna Freud would argue forcefully that a certain amount of ego development is necessary before projection and projective identification is possible (remember Anna Freud's rueful comment, 'First you have to build the house before you can throw anybody out of it!'). This would take us to the concept of developmental therapy (Hurry 1998). Additionally, the Independent would be more inclined to Heimann's revision of her major work 'On Counter-transference' (1950), a revision published in 1960, and developed in 1965. There we find not only the position that the counter-transference is more than the projections of the patient, being created by *both* analyst and patient, but also the understanding that projective identification is in fact the analyst's counter-transference at work, but a little late. The balance of perception is important: active intrusion by the patient or a failure of discernment as to the nature of the transference by the analyst. Each will call forth a different technical response.

Assumptions about parent-infant observation

Esther Bick made a major contribution to the training of psychoanalysts and psy-chotherapists when she developed her method of observing infants (Bick 1964). Despite the commonality of observational skills and the commonality of paying acute attention to infant development, however, there is a subtle yet important distinction in these titles – Bick's 'Notes on infant observation . . .' and the heading 'Parent-infant observation' perhaps demonstrate where the Independent would add an important emphasis. This is the infant in his/her environment. 'There is no such thing as a baby' after all (Winnicott 1947a). In observing, therefore, one is perhaps hesitant about leaping to assumptions as to the internal phantasy world of the infant, reluctant to impose a prism of theoretical knowledge, but rather always considering what is happening in the space between parent or carer and infant. The following vignettes show something of the process:

> Lisa, age 6 months, lay close to her mother's breast and gazed into her eyes as the nipple of the bottle played with her mouth. Enjoying this, she smiled at her mother and accepted the bottle. As she sucked, her right hand came up to the bottle and began to explore the feel of her mother's fingers on it. She stroked these, rather dreamily, seemingly enjoying the touch. Her mother stroked her fingers with one of her own. Lisa stopped sucking and held her mother's gaze. 'She's enjoying her feed,' said her mother. 'Isn't she?' – to Lisa. Lisa gurgled contentedly and resumed sucking. There was no urgency, simply seeming contentment.

This feeding sequence occurred once Lisa had learned to crawl. Before this her mother fed her from the bottle, the baby perched distantly at the end of her knee. Lisa had to become evidently separate – crawling and mobile – before such an intimate feeding as in this observation could take place. Lisa responds at once with sensual enjoyment, very attuned to her mother's stroking finger. It is 'parent-infant' observation. One may fantasise about the internal possibilities for Lisa – omnipotence, gratitude – but one could certainly see an infant alert and responsive to her environment and ready to be receptive to change – i.e. object seeking. This was also evident in a less comfortable situation:

> Lisa at the age of 3 months was being bottle-fed by her young 17-year-old aunt who was simultaneously conversing with another relative. Lisa's mother was elsewhere. The bottle was being held at an angle that did not allow Lisa to suck the milk. She gazed for quite a time at her aunt's face, as if trying to engage her with her gaze. A few noises of protest followed. The bottle moved about, sometimes allowing her to feed, sometimes not. Finally, Lisa stretched her legs right out, bent up her knees, arched her back, straightened her left leg, twisted her right leg beneath her left and stretched out her arms, as if trying to find a balance that allowed her to control the flow of the liquid. She gobbled it down, not her usual feeding pattern.

In this observation one can see the role of normal development and the impact of an unavailable environment. When faced with mild 'unpleasure' – or lack of attunement – or care that is not 'good enough' – the baby tries gaze, then vocalisation, to alert the object's attention. These failing, she reverts to dependency on the body ego – a regression to body-based mechanisms for containing anxiety. Without a developmental construct, one cannot understand the process. And without a knowledge base that has the infant as an object-seeking entity from the beginning, we could not make sense of Lisa's regression to the body – there is no such thing as a baby, and if there is we can see how pathology might follow.

Conclusions

There is an established tradition for the psychotherapist training in an Independent school – although the words 'Independent' and 'school' when conjoined might well be perceived as an oxymoron. While valuing Freud, Klein and Anna Freud, the trainee child psychotherapist can take pride in a subsequent body of critical and creative theoretical and technical writing. The role of object relatedness, the importance of the environment and of trauma, the relevance of development and the real-life experience, the essential capacity to observe scientifically and to be able to alter theory when it does not fit observation, and the concepts of transitional and transformational space give rise to originality in technique and in one's response to the child patient: it is less the pursuit of a theory than an engagement with a person. 'Why is this child communicating in this way with me now?' is a constant thought in the therapy room where the work happening in the space between patient and therapist is a co-construct, not something a therapist does to a child. Beyond this lies the other great Winnicottian question, as valid for therapist as for developing child, 'Now, what can I do with this object?'

Notes

1 This chapter appeared originally as chapter 2 in Lanyado, M & Horne, A (eds.) (2006) *A Question of Technique* London & New York: Routledge
2 Now 35 years old, the Training is still going strong.

References

Alvarez, A (1988) Beyond the unpleasure principle: some preconditions for thinking through play *Journal of Child Psychotherapy* 14(2): 1–13

Balint, M & A (1939) On transference and counter-transference. In M Balint (1965) *Primary Love and Psycho-Analytic Technique* London: Tavistock

Bick, E (1964) Notes on infant observation in psychoanalytic training *International Journal of Psychoanalysis* 45: 558–566.

Bion, WR (1967) *Second Thoughts* London: Karnac

Bion, WR (1970) *Attention and Interpretation* London: Karnac

Bollas, C (1987) The Shadow of the Object: Psychoanalysis of the Unthought Known London: Free Association Books

Brierley, M (1937) Affects in theory and practice *International Journal of Psychoanalysis* 18: 256–263

Casement, P (1985) *On Learning from the Patient* London: Tavistock

Casement, P (2002) Foreword. In B Kahr (ed.) The Legacy of Winnicott: Essays on Infant and Child Mental Health London: Karnac

Fairbairn, WRD (1941) A revised psychopathology of the psychoses and psycho-neuroses *International Journal of Psychoanalysis* 22: 250–279

Fairbairn, WRD (1946) Object relations and dynamic structure *International Journal of Psychoanalysis* 27: 30–37

Freud, S (1912) Recommendations to physicians practising psychoanalysis *SE* 12: 109–120

Gillespie, WH (1971) Aggression and instinct theory *International Journal of Psychoanalysis* 52: 155–160. Reprinted in M Sinason (ed.) *Life, Sex and Death: Selected Writings of William H Gillespie* London: Routledge 1995

Grayling, AC (1995) The empiricists. In *Philosophy: A Guide Through the Subject* Oxford: Oxford University Press

Greenberg, JR & Mitchell, SA (1983) *Object Relations in Psychoanalytic Theory* Cambridge, MA & London: Harvard University Press

Hayman, A (2001) What do our terms mean? In R Steiner & J Johns (eds.) *Within Time and Beyond Time – A Festschrift for Pearl King* London: Karnac

Heimann, P (1950) On counter-transference *International Journal of Psychoanalysis* 31: 1–2

Heimann, P (1964) Evolutionary leaps and the origin of cruelty. In *About Children and Children-No-Longer: Collected Papers 1942–80* edited by Margret Tonnesmann London: Tavistock/Routledge 1989

Hopkins, J (1996) From baby games to let's pretend *Journal of the British Association of Psychotherapists* 31 (1 Part 2): 20–27

Hurry, A (ed.) (1998) Psychoanalysis and Developmental Therapy London: Karnac

Jones, E (2004) Charles Rycroft and the historical perspective. In J Pearson (ed.) *Analyst of the Imagination: The Life and Work of Charles Rycroft* London: Karnac

Khan, MMR (1963) The concept of cumulative trauma. In The Privacy of the Self: Papers on Psychoanalytic Theory and Technique London: Hogarth Press 1974

Khar, B (1996) D W Winnicott – A Biographical Portrait London: Karnac

King, P & Steiner, R (eds.) (1991) *The Freud-Klein Controversies, 1941–45* London: Routledge

Kohon, G (ed.) (1986) The British School of Psychoanalysis – The Independent Tradition London: Free Association Books

Lanyado. M & Horne, A (1999) The Handbook of Child and Adolescent Psychotherapy: Psychoanalytic Approaches London & New York: Routledge

Limentani, A (1989) Between Freud and Klein: The Psychoanalytic Quest for Knowledge and Truth London: Free Association Books

Pearson, J (ed.) (2004) Analyst of the Imagination – The Life and Work of Charles Rycroft London: Karnac

Phillips, A (1988) *Winnicott* London: Fontana Press

Phillips, A (2000) Winnicott's Hamlet. In *Promises, Promises: Essays on Literature and Psychoanalysis* London: Faber & Faber

Rayner, E (1991) *The Independent Mind in British Psychoanalysis* London: Free Association Books

Reich, A (1951) On counter-transference *International Journal of Psycho-analysis* 32: 25–31

Roazen, P (2002) A meeting with Donald Winnicott in 1965. In B Kahr (ed.) *The Legacy of Winnicott: Essays on Infant and Child Mental Health* London: Karnac

Roazen, P (2004) Charles Rycroft and ablation. In J Pearson (ed.) *Analyst of the Imagination – The Life and Work of Charles Rycroft* London: Karnac

Rycroft, C (1955) On idealisation, illusion and catastrophic disillusion *International Journal of Psychoanalysis* 36

Rycroft, C (1968) *Imagination and Reality* New York: International Universities Press

Rycroft, C (1993) Reminiscences of a survivor: psychoanalysis 1937–1993. Graduation Address given at Regent's College, London published as Chapter 15 The Last Word in J Pearson (ed.) *Analyst of the Imagination – The Life and Work of Charles Rycroft* London: Karnac

Sandler, J, Kennedy, H & Tyson, RL (1980) The Technique of Child Psychoanalysis: Discussions with Anna Freud London: Hogarth Press

Sutherland, JD (1989) *Fairbairn's Journey into the Interior* London: Free Association Books. Extract published as 'Fairbairn's achievement' in JS Grotstein & DB Rinsley (eds.) *Fairbairn and the Origins of Object Relations* London: Free Association Books 1994

Suttie, ID (1935) *The Origins of Love and Hate* London: Free Association Books 1988

Winnicott, DW (1945) Primitive emotional development. In *Collected Papers: Through Paediatrics to Psychoanalysis* London: Tavistock 1958

Winnicott, DW (1947a) Further thoughts on babies as persons. In *The Child, the Family and the Outside World* Harmondsworth: Penguin 1964

Winnicott, DW (1947b) Hate in the counter-transference. In *Collected Papers: Through Paediatrics to Psycho-Analysis* London: Tavistock 1958

Winnicott, DW (1950–55) Aggression in relation to emotional development. In *Collected Papers: Through Paediatrics to Psychoanalysis* London: Tavistock

Part II

Children, activity and the body

Case explorations

3 Brief communications from the edge

Psychotherapy with challenging adolescents[1]

Prologue

The Winnicottian child, allowed an experience of 'good-enough' in-tune mothering, is in a position to meet the world with confident curiosity. As a profession with different theoretical emphases in our trainings, we would hope equally as child psychotherapists to be able to greet each other with a similar curiosity – grounded in our own experience but engaging with the 'other' with interest. In this area of work – with the adolescent who is on the cusp of a perverse or delinquent solution that may harden into character disorder – we need to be able to share ideas, think flexibly about what makes sense theoretically and what works clinically, and find an arena for sharing the burden of managing especially difficult counter-transferences (Winnicott 1947; Lloyd-Owen 1997; Wilson 1999). Parsons and Dermen (1999), writing about the violent child and adolescent, describe this burden well:

> From the therapist's point of view, she has to deal with the impact of the child's very primitive anxieties which will inevitably trigger her own. In practice, the twin dangers are that she may either defend against her own anxieties by denying that she is with a patient who could well attack her, or be so afraid of this possibility that she cannot be receptive to the patient's needs. . . . The patient will find it intolerable to be at the receiving end of the very defences he relies upon. . . . Additionally, the therapist will have to contend with the arousal of her sadism when attacked. She may respond to this by wishing to control or get rid of the patient. Since the work proceeds slowly and acting out is inevitable, she will also have to deal with feeling useless, helpless and guilty.
>
> (Parsons & Dermen 1999: 344)

We may argue as to whether to interpret anxiety at once or not. When we do not do so, it is for the very good reason that interpreting such primitive anxiety too early in the analytic process may be counter-productive and simply strengthen maladaptive and perverse defences – a technical issue often elaborated by Anna Freud in her writings (Freud 1936: 36–37; 1968: 143). Indeed, in sustaining traditional and often fundamentalist theoretical positions, rather than engaging with

curiosity with each other, we can attack each other with theoretical and technical difference, not recognising in *our* rigidity and *our* activity that we mirror the
defences of the challenging adolescent.

The challenging adolescent, who if an adult would attract a forensic label, has
not found a position of confident curiosity in relation to his world. Where early
trauma, overwhelming to the immature ego and not able to be processed, has been
a feature (as it frequently has), the young person has often been left with early
body-centred defences as a way of blocking out the primitive anxieties of annihilation, abandonment, disintegration, falling endlessly and merging. In the therapy
room we encounter in the patient and ourselves the capacity to act in and out, and
experience anxiety about acting-out outside – when society may well intervene.
As Winnicott (1963a) notes, '. . . the analyst must expect to find acting-out in the
transference, and must understand the significance of this acting-out, and be able
to give it positive value' (210).

In the counter-transference we find ourselves in touch with fundamental primitive fears, cruel and punishing superegos, immature atoll-like egos, and defences
designed to deny intimacy, attachment, affect and pain. We need to cope with
not-knowing – often for long spells – and to think both developmentally and
psychoanalytically (Alvarez 1996; Fonagy & Target 1996), recognising when the
opportunity of becoming a 'new object' glimmers, yet in touch with the dangers
inherent in this for the patient (Loewald 1960).

Introducing Matthew

Matthew was 14 years old when he abused the 6-year-old sister of a friend. The
court requested, through the Youth Justice social worker, an assessment as to the
suitability of psychotherapy for Matthew in relation to his offence. I saw him three
times around his 15th birthday, a colleague meeting his paternal grandmother and
stepmother and then his father and stepmother. Once weekly therapy began two
months later.

Matthew's parents married when his mother was 17 and his father 18, his
mother being 6 months pregnant with Matthew. Matthew's mother had been
brought up in an abusive home and was sexually and physically abused by her
stepfather as well as suffering severe emotional neglect. Her mother died when
she was 13. Mr P (Matthew's father) had suffered serious depression from his
early teens, attempting suicide twice and having a spell of adolescent in-patient
psychiatric treatment. He had, according to his own mother, suffered most in the
family when his parents separated when he was 4 years old. When Matthew was
3 years old his father's depression worsened and Matthew's mother ended their
relationship. Mr P moved in with his mother, Matthew's grandmother, who came
to the clinic. His wife moved a boyfriend, Sean, into the home with Matthew
and her. There were violent episodes between the parents, occurring over Mr P's
requests for access to Matthew, and an injunction was granted by the court banning Mr P from approaching the home. He spent a few weeks in prison, having
destroyed their kitchen, and did not see his son for over a year.

Sean disliked Matthew. It was only following the referral that Sean's gross physical abuse of Matthew emerged as the family began to be able to talk of it. Matthew knows that this relationship was abusive but has blocked out his memory of it. He does, however, recall his parents arguing and fighting.

When Matthew was 5, his mother was killed in a road traffic accident – she was knocked down by a car on a zebra crossing. Matthew was left in the 'care' of his abuser as his mother had stated that this was her wish in her Last Will and Testament. There ensued a long custody battle, Matthew being made a Ward of Court, and at one point when he had been sent to stay with his abusive maternal stepgrandfather he was kidnapped by his father and grandmother, so anxious were they about his care. Matthew's father finally won custody. When Matthew was 6½, he and his father moved in with Mr P's girlfriend, Sammie, and her daughter, Emma, who is a year younger than Matthew. They now have a son, Alex, who is 11 years younger than Matthew.

Matthew's past and present functioning

Mr P and Sammie approached their local Child and Family Consultation Service when Matthew was 7 years old, for help with his aggression, but it was felt that time to adjust to the new family was all that was needed. By the age of 9, Matthew had been expelled from six schools, sometimes for violence, sometimes for not being there. He described escaping out of school windows and commented, 'I thought that was mad – being expelled for not even being there!' There was no sense of a comprehending or a pursuing adult. Finally, he ended up in a day school for children with emotional and behavioural difficulties, a school that creditably managed to hold on to him.

In school he was said to be 'bright' – brighter than most of his peers, 'capable of clear thinking but stubborn'. He could attack other children with words, and be rude, unpleasant and undermining to others. This verbal aggression remained worrying to the school and it tipped over into physical fights at perceived slights.

Peer relations were said by school and family to be poor, although it emerged in therapy that Matthew belonged to a group of delinquent lads with whom he spent much of his spare time. His descriptions of their meetings contained much excitement and activity, and were empty of thought or reflection. Matthew had an ambivalent relationship with his father whom he tried to like but who shouted at him, hit him and only rarely listened. He could have been allied to his step-mother, Sammie, as both are intelligent, but he felt excluded by the birth of his half-brother, Alex. His paternal grandmother remained a 'good object' for him.

His offence occurred when he was at a friend's watching TV where England were being beaten by Argentina in the World Cup. This friend often had sexual intercourse with his girlfriend in the presence of a group of friends, which Matthew found exciting and disturbing. When he went to the toilet, his friend's 6-year-old little sister pounced on him from her bedroom to play, punching him and jumping on his back, and he threw her onto her bed. There he began to tickle her and what began as a game moved to his touching her genitals. When he found that he was trying to remove her pants, he stopped himself, wondered what he was doing, and went home. The others in the family, however, had a sense of something more sinister and asked the little girl what had happened later in the evening. Matthew was arrested at 2a.m. and taken to the police station. He told me his father followed but, in fact, it was Sammie who came to see him. Initially insistently denying everything, when faced finally with the video interview with the child he agreed that her version was right. He received a 3-year Supervision Order, with a strong injunction from the judge that, should he appear in court on any count in future, he would be given a custodial sentence. When I saw him, he was embarrassed to talk of it and ashamed of what he had done – hopeful signs. Like many violated young people, however, he was furious that the police had kept his clothes for analysis – as if he were trying to focus on the external to avoid thinking of the body, its actions and the internal.

Thinking about work with adolescents

The key tasks of adolescence, as we all know, involve separation, individuation and becoming responsible for the self. In classical theory where psychosexual development is the main thrust, this means taking ownership of the body and sexuality at a time of great change. Where there has been early trauma and the immature ego has been overwhelmed, we have to think with care about technique. Defences are often pre-verbal, pre-representational, centring on the body-self, its traumatisation and its survival. What the young person does *with* the body, therefore, is significant

1)   in the offence of sexually abusing others (the victim's report is extremely helpful in letting us know just what is so intolerable that it has to be decanted outside the self);
2)   in delinquency and putting the body at risk;
3)   in violence or aggression where we often encounter either violent provocation designed to repeat an earlier experience of being violated, or self-preservative violence in Glasser's (1998) terms, designed to protect the fragile ego from perceived threat;
4)   in the unconscious use of the body in ensuring one's exploitation. The prime example of this is the rent boy whose repetition-compulsion in relation to his own abuse is masked by a veneer of being in control of those whom he chooses to think he seduces and who are made to 'pay'.

Thus, issues around the body, bodily conflicts and its use need to be addressed. Yet the adolescent task is to take over this body at a time when infantile fantasy and curiosity is revived. One solution for the therapist is to separate mind and body – 'Isn't it interesting what your body gets up to – being chased, being hit, being where it shouldn't be?' Addressing the functioning part to explore together the infantile part can help 'save face' and avoid humiliation. Sometimes, though, this is not enough. Edgcumbe (1988) approached such issues when thinking about the technical problems of interpreting (or not) in the transference with adolescents, and 'whether to take up defence, content or affect, and at what depth or level to deal with content of conflicts' in the light of 'the adolescent's heightened fear and shame about regression . . .' (Edgcumbe 1988: 1). Following case illustrations, she concludes:

> I have stressed the importance of taking up material from the angle of the higher-level conflicts which have engendered regression, rather than the infantile instinctual wishes and modes of relating which are expressed in the regression. . . .
>
> Shame and anxiety are likely to be best relieved by making sense of the situation which led to the regression. In this way the analyst can remain aligned with the part of the patient's self which is striving for growth, without denying the regression.
>
> (*ibid.* p 12)

It is just this kind of carefully thought-out, conscious choice of what to take up that often seems to have been totally misunderstood in the past in disputes between theoretical traditions. It led Winnicott in 1962 to an interim, transitional position that he called 'working as a psychoanalyst' when the 'anti-social tendency' (amongst other clinical issues) was present. Today, one hopes, we are clearer that this *is* psychotherapy and that it is, moreover, a question of conscious, sophisticated analytic choice.

In parallel with issues about the body comes the danger of relationships and especially of intimacy. Of particular importance in work with young people in search of a perverse solution (a survival technique) is Glasser's (1979; 1996) concept of the core complex. Here, one sees the search for intimacy as the start of what becomes a vicious circle. Gaining intimacy, the adolescent is overwhelmed by anxieties of a primitive nature – anxiety about merging with the object, of suffocation and loss of individuation. This arouses a violent response – violence in the service of protecting the immature ego – in order to escape anxiety; and a consequent sense of abandonment (again, a primitive anxiety) ensues with the necessity once more to pursue intimacy. And 'la ronde' continues. Glasser finds this to underlie all perverse psychopathology.

Psychotherapy requires a relationship of considerable intimacy, yet the adolescent process, too, is contrary to this. Apart from the danger in hoping that this relationship might be different from earlier ones, the adolescent can experience being understood both as a relief and as an enormous threat, bringing back just such primitive fears of merging with the object, of not being separate. One has to *pace* this experience of being understood, and be aware of what is too intimate, and know that the young person may be driven to disparage it when it is desired, arousing as it does memories of vulnerability. Even pauses and silence need judgment: silence may become a threatening absence of the object, especially if this mirrors the young person's early life. At times, one has to be an 'enlivening object' (Alvarez 1992); otherwise one is perceived as abandoning and annihilating. It is 'either – or': there is little middle ground here – indeed, the process of therapy seeks to develop this. The 'all or nothing' quality Winnicott encapsulates in 'There is not yet a capacity to identify with parent figures without loss of personal identity' (Winnicott 1963b: 244) is exacerbated in the adolescent who has still to achieve a capacity for symbolisation, for whom emotional states *are* bodily experiences (Parsons & Dermen 1999: 341). The risk involved in 'hope', too, may be one reason why, with adolescents, one often gets 'brief communications' followed by escape.

We are all used to adolescents as escapologists. In a sense, this is a healthy adolescent process, distancing oneself. It contains elements of the toddler who has learned how to make the adults pursue him – except that with adolescents we are made to feel great uncertainty as to how much we should pursue. This capacity to put the grown-up into a 'double bind' seems to arrive with the hormones at puberty. Again, this requires delicacy: the conflict belongs in the adolescent, not in the therapist or network, and should be gently returned there. A very simple example would be the adolescent who invariably arrives 15 minutes late for his session. One can say how important taking control is, and how essential; it is a pity, however, that in taking this necessary step he costs himself 15 minutes of *his* time. That's an interesting dilemma he has there – and the conflict is quietly returned to its owner but not in the tone of his own dismissive and shaming superego. The other side of escapology is the defence of activity – a return to the body-self of toddler years. Activity often occurs as a way of blocking out thought, which itself involves unbearable recollection and memory. It is, in this context, unfortunate that the UK Government has instructed the Probation Service in England & Wales to breach offenders (i.e. to bring them back before the court) if they miss two appointments. One could point to a recourse to action and an absence of thought in Government for this anti-adolescent decision. Thinking, too, in adolescence is a further aspect of intimacy – intimacy of mind – and:

> The fear of thinking may derive both from conflicts over curiosity and from reluctance to let the analyst/mother intrude on painful private matters. Here, again, transference interpretation may have to be used sparingly, to free the patient's thinking.
>
> (Edgcumbe 1988: 13)

Creating a space for thought is not easy when the drive is to activity and not thinking. Making space for curiosity about the self helps, and one can often capture adolescents by picking up the paradoxes in their lives or offering the unexpected in comment, especially when the unexpected is in contrast to their dismissive, abandoning or punitive superego:

> Matthew described being on the back of a friend's motorbike (legitimately) in the park and the police cruising past. By their actions, the group made the police pursue them, but eluded them. I said that was interesting. Matthew had expected something more negative. 'How?' I said that he had really made the police pay attention. Perhaps he had wished people had done so when he was little.

Matthew went on to say how his father often thought he was 'up to something' when he was not, then told of his favourite teacher, a female Art teacher, who had taken his side in a dispute that he had actually caused, leading to another youth being punished. He grinned. I said that perhaps I needed to hear the warning – all is not necessarily as it seems? He grinned more widely. I said that this was another area for me to be curious about – he can change reality.

It is worth thinking here about the concept of 'therapist as developmental object', so well described by Hurry (1998) and a part of the work of the Hampstead Clinic for many years. The young person engages with a curious ego and supportive superego in the 'developmental object therapist' who *deliberately* takes up a position of *not* being used as a projection of the child's cruel, shaming and undermining superego. When one thinks of early trauma and the 'breaching of the shame shield' described by Campbell (1994) in the young abusers whom he has treated over 30 years, one sees a further reason for creating possibilities for alternative identifications and routes to a different ego ideal. Wilson (1999), writing about delinquents, put it rather well:

> The key therapeutic task is to resist the young person's implicit invitation to repeat the past . . . The . . . ability to find ways of responding that are different from what young people expect and which do not meet the dictates of the transference is essential. Ultimately, it is through the child psychotherapists' behaviour that they convey their understanding of the meaning of the young person's delinquency and provide the safety and boundary that the delinquent needs. Such behaviour, sustained by the child psychotherapists' own insights, constitutes interpretation and serves as a stimulus and basis for further verbal forms of communication and understanding.
>
> (Wilson 1999: 318)

It is also important, with the drive to acting-out in adolescence and the risk of self-harm, that there is a functioning network that enables the therapy to continue, a subject addressed later.

Issues of sexuality appear throughout the treatment, often beginning in the form of remarkably crude jokes that show very early childish fantasies of destruction, inadequacy and incorporation in intercourse. The fantasies of adolescence, after all, overlay for such young people a very often traumatically abusive childhood reality. Work in this area tends, I find, to be consolidated nearer the end of treatment although it appears throughout – it is only after much work that the young person can, with confidence, face exploring the kind of adult sexual being that s/he would wish to be, and the fears and fantasies around that. Issues of a procreative body are acute for abusing and violated boys and girls. The necessary fusion of aggression, agency and sexuality for adult functioning is terrifying in its potential for destruction and much work on the positive role of aggression is necessary first.

Young people, defending against the memory of helplessness in the absence of a protective object, find aggression paradoxically difficult. It emerges in an uncontrollable fashion in their lives, overwhelming others and themselves. They need practice in appropriately assertive aggression and righteous anger, and a capacity to recognise and name emotions and affects, in order not to be swamped by them. Identifying with the adolescent's victim role can mean the therapist missing aggression: it is important to have in mind as a constant undercurrent, and to connote aggression and agency as necessary and, where it is problematic, to perceive the roots in an early defence against intolerable feelings. 'Anger management' strategies work well where there is a more integrated, functioning 'self'; where this is not so, the construction of an emotional vocabulary and 'anger practice' – the capacity to recognise agency and aggression, to note when they are appropriate and to begin to exercise them – are essential. Attention to such ego developments as affect recognition and affect tolerance is vital in psychoanalytic work with young people where the ego is immature and patchwork.

There are implications within all of this for assessment – the information one needs, the environment necessary for an assessment to be relevant and if therapy is to be considered, and the assessment encounter itself. These are beyond the remit of this paper but must be flagged up: 'The essential thing is I do base my work on diagnosis,' said Winnicott to the British Psycho-analytic Society (Winnicott 1962: 169).

Thinking about Matthew

Matthew presents as not typical of young abusers but rather demonstrating the mixed symptomatology of mid-adolescents who arouse concern. Most abusing adolescents appear either to be rather isolated individuals with one clear *known* abusive incident, or to be multiple abusers with a real polymorphous feel. Matthew's history shows difficulties in equal peer relations (his mates are all less bright than he is), long-standing outbursts of aggression and seeking violent situations, delinquency and sexual abusing. His capacity for putting himself at risk is also becoming clearer.

With Matthew we can see the clear pattern of early violence where there is no protective figure, outlined in the Great Ormond Street Hospital research on young abusers: the two main factors correlating with abusing others are

a) an experience of unpredictable and unprocessable violence and trauma, when the ego is too immature to make sense of it (Lanyado et al 1995). Matthew witnessed early marital warfare, was beaten from the age of 3 and traumatically abandoned to his abuser at age 5.
b) having a mother who has herself been abused and unconsciously projects onto her male child the expectation that he, too, will abuse.

The memory of such victimisation (especially the humiliation and vulnerability) can be dealt with by developing a fantasy of abusing someone weaker and smaller, becoming powerful in the process and making someone else into the victim – identification with the aggressor. Part of the treatment thus involves exploring the patient's own 'victim' experience before one can reach the victimising.

There is also 'the ambivalence of the object' – a mother who consciously and deliberately leaves him with an abuser – and who turns a blind eye to his abuse when she is there. We should not be surprised that he 'tricks' the grown-ups in return and should expect this in the therapy. Thinking inter-generationally, Matthew's mother was abused and abandoned on her mother's death to her abuser and the scenario was repeated with Matthew. Matthew's father lost his father at age 4; his mother lost her natural father at a very young age; Matthew lost his for a considerable spell at age 3. Welldon (1988) has alerted us to the necessity of thinking across at least three generations where abuse is concerned.

We can also note the use of activity as a defence, beginning with his early escaping from school – but no-one pursues, instead he unconsciously makes the process of his being abandoned happen repeatedly – and continuing in his delin-quency. Indeed, one might find his delinquent activities to be a seduction of me, as therapist, away from the abusing that formed his offence, as well as a prac-tised way of using excitement to mask depression. There is also the compulsion to repeat sensations of fear, as we will see in the clinical material: in some of his delinquent activities, Matthew scares himself. More profoundly, one might think about identification with the dead mother: it is unusual for a 22-year-old to have made a will and colleagues have suggested that her accident may have been suicide. Being alert as to Matthew's unconscious suicidal behaviour, therefore, becomes a factor, and the meaning of an abandoning, not protective, even malevo-lent maternal object important.

Finally, it is worth commenting on aggression, an issue of long-standing for Matthew, noted first at the age of 7. This use of self-preservative violence has begun to turn into an enjoyment of others getting into trouble – the early begin-nings of a sadistic quality – and it is essential for his development that work is done with Matthew on this.

An encounter with Matthew

This session occurred in early December, almost nine months into therapy. Matthew at this point is living with his grandmother.

Matthew arrived early for his session, wearing a new, padded, warm jacket. (He had come the previous week in a sweatshirt and with an awful cold.) Although his cold was still bad, he said that he was OK, that he had taken lots of soup. This comment came with a smile – in our last session he had told me that his grandmother was very good at making soup. [Paternal grandmother has transference implications.] He hadn't been allowed to take a day off school, however. I wondered if he could have been able to bear that – not being active and just sitting with his thoughts. He agreed he could not, he would rather be in school. I reflected on this unusually intimate start and wondered when reaction would set in. [When Matthew attends, he always takes time to re-discover his object: he seems, indeed, to expect a corrupt object.]

There was a sustained pause. He looked very sad. I wondered if he were thoughtful now or just fed up? Fed up. His father had said that the moped was too much for his Christmas and he probably wouldn't get it. He expanded on how it would have cost £200. His father was giving his brother Alex a computer worth £200; Matthew would get a new mobile phone worth £100 and his sister, Emma, a present worth £75. There was a pause, half sad, half angry. I wondered rather weakly if that seemed unfair? *Yes* – Alex gets everything. [Alex, indulged at age 5, contrasts with Matthew, abused and abandoned.]

After a further pause Matthew wondered if his father would give him the money and he could put it towards a bike himself. Then he deflated, recalling that his father preferred to pay things up week by week. I said that it seemed impossible for the adults to get things right for him. We reflected in silence.

'Do you know a Pa . . . Po . . . something like that – it's a bike.' It emerged as a Piaggio. 'They're *very* nice! I really like them. I was out last night on one!' I felt anxiety begin to rise and wondered inside about this need to make the adult anxious, and why. There followed a story of Matthew and five or six friends. Dave had brought the bike and all had tried it out in the local park. Steve did a 'wheelie' and drove into a tree. Matthew also tried it – 'It was really good!' He described sharp turns, sudden acceleration, mud flying, excitement. As he was in full flow, his mobile phone rang. He looked apologetic, muttered, 'Sorry,' said the answering service would pick it up, and could not resist checking the screen. It was Dave leaving a message: 'He already phoned twice when I was on the train coming here! It's about meeting tonight.' The phone was switched off and put away. He continued with the bike tale – taking it out on the road out of town, a vivid description of Dave nearly coming off the back of the bike as Matthew accelerated, 'It can do 45 miles an hour!' and finally return to town.

I thought about the sense of life and energy in the midst of this extremely dangerous behaviour. 'You know, you really like being "on the edge", don't you?' Matthew looked questioning. I said that on the bike he liked being in control himself (he didn't like it on the back) but it could tip over – Steve had managed to hit a tree. I suggested he was also 'on the edge' with the police, were he found, and with the court as the judge had told him that his return to court on *any* count would mean a custodial sentence. And he had told me before (in an earlier session) that being on a bike could be scary and he didn't like that. 'Yes, that's why I won't let Steve drive.'

There was a pause. I interpreted then that it was interesting that this 'on the edge' excitement had actually followed a very painful description of him and Emma feeling 'on the edge' in the family. He gave me a very direct look.

I offered that one way he had learned of being in control of these very difficult, sad feelings was through the excited 'on the edge' feelings, but they were risky. I wondered, too, about the excitement keeping *me* 'on the edge', not sure of his safety, and wondered if he was good at making the adults and me feel this. He smiled gently.

There was quite a long pause. Matthew launched into a story of his friend, Joseph, a very small 14-year-old. Joseph's passion was cars – with a particular emphasis on taking and driving them away. I noted to myself the connection between my interpretation of the pain in the family and his further recourse to excitement and danger, moving from bikes to cars, but did not interrupt. Matthew gave great detail of how Joseph would break into the black boxes behind the steering wheel panel, where to locate these in a Rover Metro, and diverted into a variety of ways to break into a car. Joseph had been doing this since he was 7 years old. The police knew him well – had been to see him the other day as he is the first port of call when cars go missing. 'He has been cautioned and the police know him. Pathetic!' 'Pathetic – who?' I asked. 'Joe. He knows they'll come to see him first. When he takes a car, he drives with the headlights on full beam so that he can't be seen himself. He just gets very excited by cars. Once when I was with him he saw a Jaguar. I said, "NO!" but Joe kept talking about what it would be like to drive it when we were walking away.' I wondered if Joe had the same sense of excitement in relation to cars that Matthew had talked of with bikes. He looked surprised: 'No, he's pathetic.' I commented that sometimes things are both pathetic and exciting, reminding him of the large screen television set he said his father had bought that in one way seemed pathetic to him but in another seemed full of excitement and potential. This had been in an earlier session. He grinned – 'That's true!' I continued, 'So you know some things that are both pathetic-daft-dangerous and pathetic-exciting-"on the edge"?' He nodded thoughtfully.

The story of Joe continued. He had 'torched' a car. This felt suddenly very unsafe, as if the juxtaposition of 'pathetic' and 'excitement' had to be avoided. He had tried to break into a car in Tesco's car park (the known area where local youth find and dump cars and bikes) but couldn't get at the black box. Realising that he had left his fingerprints all over the vehicle, he had found a cloth and jerrycan of petrol in the boot and poured it over the front seats, leaving the can in the car before striking a match. He had singed his hair. 'He's totally pathetic! He could have burned himself badly. He had the rag from the boot – he could have wiped off his fingerprints. He ran off and it went "Whump!" exploding. The Fire Brigade was called. He could have hurt people!' Matthew sounded very upset. I said gently that I thought he had witnessed this, been there with Joe. He nodded. I added that it was frightening that the excitement and 'on the edge' bits could tip right over into danger and wondered if he scared himself. He nodded, saying, 'He could have been harmed!' Yes. After a pause I added that it was interesting that such a memory of danger had followed my saying to him that he wanted me to feel 'on the edge' sometimes – that he was letting me know how dreadfully dangerous things sometimes felt for him and that it was right that we were both concerned.

He recalled a teacher at school, in car mechanics class, whom Matthew had asked something that implied how to hot-wire cars. The teacher had given him the information and not asked why he wanted to know. I said I thought he was letting me know about two things. Firstly, grown-ups may not be straight but collude with exciting illegal things, like the teacher giving him the information. [I was thinking of corrupt objects again.] How, then, could he possibly know to trust me and my concern? Secondly, perhaps he was warning me that he could be tricky – tricking the teacher and perhaps other grown-ups, like me. He gave me a very direct, straight look. Collusion, of course, is one of the major pressures felt in the counter-transference with psychopathic patients (Symington 1980).

There was a further pause. Matthew said, 'The bike engine's still running.' The bike, of course, had been stolen and hot-wired. His friends were second-time thieves, having come across it stolen and abandoned. They had by-passed the ignition and could not turn off the engine. They would have to cover the exhaust pipe, cutting off the air supply. [All endings, I thought, are traumatic – even for the bike.] 'Someone stole it last night.' I must have looked astonished. 'Yeah, when we'd gone home Dave had left it at his back gate and phoned to say it had been taken. We found Steve had taken it and had it at his place. It would have been pathetic if a nicked bike had been nicked – I mean we couldn't report it to the police, could we?' I said that I thought that was really interesting: that, when something has gone wrong in the past, the grown-ups will simply not take a young person seriously. Perhaps in some ways this was a little like Matthew – it is impossible for him to hope that the adults will be concerned *now* for his safety when they made such a bad job of it in the past. 'You mean Sean,' said Matthew, referring to his mother's abusive boyfriend. 'Yes, and everything that happened then. Now, as a result of that, you are making me into another of these grown-ups who hears very dangerous things but can't stop you. Sometimes it feels better to do that than for you to hope that it might be different.'

The following pause felt more thoughtful. 'I'll only go tonight if Steve has a crash helmet for me. I know he's got one. It *is* scary – but exciting scary.' ['Crash helmet' has become equated with me, interesting when one thinks about heads and minds.] I added that that was why he insists on driving, being in control: 'It's like not taking the risk that the adults won't protect you again, but it's also the same "on the edge" excitement of waiting for something to happen that was awful and too much for you when you were little.' Matthew nodded slowly.

It was almost time to stop. Matthew checked the clock and put on his jacket. He told me that he *was* careful as sometimes it could get too scary. Moreover, tonight they wouldn't be on the road but in a farmer's field. I said that he was taking on some of the adult bits about protecting himself but still being 'on the edge'. He was leaving me with something to worry about – perhaps he needed to do that. He gave a quiet smile and 'See you next week!' I thought it was a promise to stay alive.

A note on networks

There must be a functioning, communicating network that is able to create a safe, holding structure if therapy for the young person who is a risk to himself and/or others is to be considered a treatment of choice. We all recall Winnicott's exhortation that delinquents need placement, not psychoanalysis, after he had the clinic basement flooded, his car jump-started and his buttocks bitten – more than once – by his first child analytic patient (Winnicott 1956; 1963a). If there is not such a network, the issue is certainly placement. One could view this as offering practical 'containers' until the stage is reached where words can contain and anxiety be symbolised rather than enacted. This cannot be stressed enough. Our omnipotence – or pressure from the network – may take us into a therapeutic relationship that then fails because external containment and understanding are lacking, and we repeat and re-visit trauma upon a young person who unconsciously seeks it. In Matthew's case the problems of finding a good residential community did not arise. There was a functioning, thinking network: he was at a good EBD school, had a three-year Supervision Order from the court, which gave time to work, and had a good, involved social worker. His family moved a distance away but, with joint planning, Matthew stayed with his grandmother through the week, sustaining attendance at the same school, and went to his father at weekends. Issues arose about leaving school: this is often experienced by adolescents as the school's abandonment of them, although they cannot articulate this, and the temptation is to get oneself thrown out or to leave it before it leaves you. This Matthew tried – and the network contained. He completed his exams.

It is also important that the network be experienced as safe and holding as, in therapy, the young person will inevitably get in touch with the early feelings of victimisation and humiliation that led to the offending behaviour. Such a time may present a risk of suicide – as does the later stage when the adolescent begins to look at what he has done to others and guilt and shame arise – and a good support structure is essential. Equally, the defences, based on activity, may reassert themselves, as they did originally, to blot out such pain and the risk of further offending ensues. This has to be understood and *not* reacted to in a superego-ish way.

Networks suffer transference and counter-transference processes. All too often, this remains unconscious and damaging. It is *vital*, when working with young perpetrators, that a 'case manager' be appointed to work with the network and help the unconscious become conscious. This needs an experienced person.

When warfare breaks out in the network, or communication stops and unilateral decision-making appears, there seem to be three main processes at work (Horne 1999):

1   Individuals in the network identify with and take up the positions of different family members (Kolvin & Trowell 1996). Such identifications polarise – the young person is viewed either as a poor traumatised victim or seen as a dangerous perpetrator; the parents are said to be overwhelmed by their ungrateful evil child or perceived as dreadfully neglectful and abusive. Holding all views together and recognising the transference manifestations is vital.

2   The family system also gets re-enacted in the network – the myths, collusions and strategies for family homeostasis become replayed by all of us.

3   The internal world of the offender patient is realised in the network where we repeat the functions and attitudes of internal objects and 'willingly' reinforce unhelpful defences (Davies 1996), principally the drive to activity. This compulsion to act, to do something, is commonplace and, as therapists, we will enrage other services at times by refusing to do this but requesting space to think together. The process of by-passing thought and reflection, after all, is the delinquent and abusing adolescent's prime defence, and he unconsciously tries to make it ours.

There is a paradigm from Transactional Analysis that is very helpful when thinking of networks. It comprises a triangle:

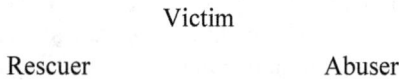

Victim

Rescuer   Abuser

We move around it, not at will but pushed by others, taking up all positions. It is a salutary blow to one's omnipotence to be brought in as a 'rescuer' but quickly to be defined by the network as an 'abuser' (of the child by keeping him in therapy; of colleagues by not being able to say that he is no longer a risk) – and one becomes a victim oneself.

Conclusion

Keeping grounded and keeping sane are the two main tasks for the worker with acting-out adolescents. Regular clinical discussion is essential, both for support and survival but also to ensure that we are not seeing only one part of the young person or complying with 'the dictates of the transference' (Wilson 1999). A colleague can provide an oedipal third for reflection, an antidote to primitive pre-oedipal defences and anxieties. Pace and intimacy are important technical issues, and the level at which to take up conflicts (Edgcumbe 1988) is an important aspect of judging these. The impact of developmental deficit, body-based defences and pre-verbal trauma should inform our assessment and work, and a developmental and psychoanalytic framework is essential. Most importantly, 'thought not action' is the key for patient and psychotherapist – creating space for thinking and reflection.

Epilogue

A year on, Matthew's 'delinquent group' is now a social group. All are in work and the group now includes girls – opening up issues of sexuality in therapy. A sense of responsibility is a strong feature of his functioning. He dared to ask if there might be any flexibility when he is in work – could I still see him but at a later time? – a big risk, to ask for something, and on my letting him know that this was possible he promptly missed the next session (a telephone call – 'I've lost my train fare!'). Intimacy still takes careful negotiation.

Note

1 This paper was presented at the ACP Conference in September 2000 and published in the *Journal of Child Psychotherapy* 27(1) the following year. Earlier versions were given at conferences in West London and Prague. Thanks to all these colleagues for feedback and ideas – and to the BAP colleague who invited me to write it to support the establishment of an adolescent service in her area.

References

Alvarez, A (1992) *Live Company: Psychoanalytic Psychotherapy with Autistic, Borderline, Deprived and Abused Children* London & New York: Tavistock/ Routledge

Alvarez, A (1996) Addressing the element of deficit in children with autism: psychotherapy which is both psychoanalytically and developmentally informed *Clinical Child Psychology and Psychiatry* 1(4): 525–537

Campbell, D (1994) Breaching the shame shield: thoughts on the assessment of adolescent child sexual abusers *Journal of Child Psychotherapy* 20(3): 309–326

Davies, R (1996) The inter-disciplinary network and the internal world of the offender. In C Cordess, & M Cox (eds.) *Forensic Psychotherapy: Crime, Psychodynamics and the Offender Patient* Vol. II: *Mainly Practice* London: Jessica Kingsley

Edgcumbe, R (1988) Formulation of interpretations in clinical work with adolescents. Unpublished paper given at the Institute of Psycho-analysis, London, October

Fonagy, P & Target, M (1996) A contemporary psychoanalytical perspective: psychodynamic developmental therapy. In E Hibbs & P Jensen (eds.) *Psychosocial Treatments for Child and Adolescent Disorders* Washington, DC: American Psychological Association

Freud, A (1936) *The Ego and the Mechanisms of Defence* London: Hogarth Press

Freud, A (1968) Difficulties in the path of psychoanalysis: a confrontation of past with present viewpoints. In *The Writings of Anna Freud* Vol. VII 1966–1970: *Problems of Psychoanalytic Training, Diagnosis, and the Technique of Therapy* New York: International Universities Press 1971

Glasser, M (1979) Some aspects of the role of aggression in the perversions. In I Rosen (ed.) *Sexual Deviation* 2nd edition Oxford: Oxford University Press

Glasser, M (1996) Aggression and sadism in the perversions. In I Rosen (ed.) *Sexual Deviation* 3rd edition Oxford: Oxford University Press

Glasser, M (1998) On violence: a preliminary communication *International Journal of Psychoanalysis* 79(5): 887–902

Horne, A (1999) Sexual abuse and sexual abusing in childhood and adolescence. In M Lanyado & A Horne (eds.) *The Handbook of Child and Adolescent Psychotherapy: Psychoanalytic Perspectives* London: Routledge

Hurry, A (1998) Psychoanalysis and developmental therapy. In A Hurry (ed.) *Psychoanalysis and Developmental Therapy* London: Karnac

Kolvin, I & Trowell, J (1996) Child sexual abuse. In I Rosen (ed.) *Sexual Deviation*, 3rd edition Oxford: Oxford University Press

Lanyado, M, Hodges, J, Bentovim, A et al (1995) Understanding boys who sexually abuse other children: a clinical illustration *Psychoanalytic Psychotherapy* 9(3): 231–242

Lloyd–Owen, D (1997) From action to thought: supervising mental health workers with forensic patients. In B Martindale et al (eds.) *Supervision and its Vicissitudes* EFPP Clinical Monograph Series London: Karnac Books

Loewald, HW (1960) On the therapeutic action of psychoanalysis *International Journal of Psycho-analysis* 41: 16–33

Parsons, M & Dermen, S (1999) The violent child and adolescent. In M Lanyado & A Horne (eds.) *The Handbook of Child & Adolescent Psychotherapy – Psychoanalytic Perspectives* London: Routledge

Symington, N (1980) The response aroused by the psychopath *International Review of Psycho-analysis* 7

Welldon, E (1988) *Mother, Madonna, Whore: The Idealisation and Denigration of Motherhood* London: Free Association Books

Wilson, P (1999) Delinquency. In M Lanyado & A Horne (eds.) *The Handbook of Child & Adolescent Psychotherapy – Psychoanalytic Perspectives* London: Routledge

Winnicott, DW (1947) Hate in the countertransference. In *Through Paediatrics to Psycho-Analysis* London: Hogarth Press 1975

Winnicott, DW (1956) The anti-social tendency. In *Through Paediatrics to Psychoanalysis* London: Hogarth Press 1975

Winnicott, DW (1962) The aims of psycho-analytic treatment. In *The Maturational Processes and the Facilitating Environment* London: Hogarth Press 1965

Winnicott, DW (1963a) Psychotherapy of character disorders. In *The Maturational Processes and the Facilitating Environment* London: Hogarth Press 1965

Winnicott, DW (1963b) Hospital care supplementing intensive psychotherapy in adolescence In *The Maturational Processes and the Facilitating Environment* London: Hogarth Press 1965

4 'Gonnae no' dae that!'

The internal and external worlds of the delinquent adolescent[1]

Introduction

There has over recent years been considerable reluctance in Child and Adolescent Mental Health Services in the UK to take on work with young people whose acting out is of a delinquent nature. One influence has certainly been that of the psychiatrist: 'delinquency' and its catch-all diagnostic category 'conduct disorder' were often viewed in the 1980s and early 1990s as problems that were socially based and not requiring the intervention of a doctor. This followed developments in criminological theory where there was through the 1960s and 1970s a backlash against what was perceived as the medicalisation of behaviour felt to emanate from social conditions – poverty, opportunity, environment, exclusion. In thus protecting the delinquent from being viewed as in need of mental health intervention, such a stance has paradoxically deprived mainstream thinking of the subtlety that a psychoanalytic perspective adds both to our understanding of delinquency and to our capacity to intervene on behalf of the young delinquent.

Delinquency plus: Matthew, Giorgio and Angus

It is still rare nowadays for a child to be referred to child and family mental health services simply for delinquency – unlike the experience in the pioneer days of

Child Guidance and when the specialist Portman Clinic was established in London in the 1930s. This seems due to changes in what concerns the environment outside. Sexually abusive adolescents form the bulk of referrals to the Portman, with those who download child pornography from the internet a growing category. However, there is a not insignificant number whom one finds are, in addition to the presenting problem, highly delinquent into the bargain. Three patients come to mind:

Matthew

Although Matthew at 14 came to the attention of the Youth Offending Team via an incident of sexual abuse of the 6-year-old sister of a friend, therapy soon revealed that his major occupations were risk-taking delinquent activities with a group of same-age peers and finding himself in situations where he was physically in danger from others. I have written of him elsewhere (Chapter 3 and Horne 2001) but briefly the salient factors from his childhood were warring and very young parents; a depressed father who had been admitted for in-patient psychiatric treatment as an adolescent; parental break-up when he was two; his mother's new partner treating him with great violence; his mother's death (query suicide) when he was 5, leaving him for two years with his abuser while his father fought for his custody in court, and possible sexual abuse by his natural mother's stepfather who had abused her when her own mother's death left her in his 'care' at age 13.

His relationship with his paternal grandmother, a reliable object, was an asset in his therapy. His containment in a network that included a good, thinking special school and an excellent Youth Offending Team social worker enabled therapy to be a treatment of choice. There, his delinquency could begin to be understood as being about a search for risk-taking, mindless states that both repeated the sensations of his early and terrifying abuse and sought to be in control of his helplessness. He remained in once weekly therapy for over two years and by the end at age 17½ had a job in which he was valued, a girlfriend and a non-delinquent group of friends.

Giorgio

I did not meet Giorgio but was asked to provide a paper assessment of his development, therapeutic and placement needs for a social work team that I had worked with in the past. Giorgio at 16½ was highly delinquent, highly sexualised in his acting out and put himself at risk sexually with his preoccupation with men's toilets. Incidents of self-consolation through masturbation when small had been followed by incidents of touching other children. At 13 there were a number of episodes of arson. At 14 he was deliberately seeking abusive situations, a predicament his foster father described dismissively as 'cottaging'. One wondered what more he had to do to get the environment to take note in an active, strong and protective way.

Following his progress through the chronology provided was not difficult, although depressing in the lack of concern evidenced from his environment. Parental violence and a father who served a prison term for sexually abusing several children; a toddlerhood characterised by fear, flight and life in women's refuges; pseudo-independence noted by the police at the age of 6; placement with a foster father whose female partners always left him and whose ambivalence about therapy undermined all attempts to help Giorgio; and a total paralysis of the professional network that could not challenge any of this in Giorgio's interests.

The response of the network was one of political correctness perhaps, but one always retains in mind the capacity of networks to enact the internal worlds of acting out, delinquent or criminal patients (Davies 1996). The consequence was that there was never a structure that was predictable, set limits, cared emotionally and could contain. The recommendation was placement. It was clear that without a good therapeutic community Giorgio's future was bleak, either leading to sexual assaults against others, or to heightened risk of harm through increasingly more risk-taking delinquency, or settling for a repetition of his abuse by making himself available for older men. Only once he experienced containment could any therapy be offered – and this would have to begin with the slow work of ego structuring, affect recognition, affect tolerance – the developmental therapy that has been part of the Hampstead Clinic's work for many years and is so well described by Anne Hurry (Hurry 1998) – before his emotional states could be entertained in mind by him.

Three months later, Giorgio was re-referred: his foster placement had broken down and he had now been moved from south west of the city to some 40 miles north east, placed in 'semi-supported living accommodation'. Could we give him therapy? The answer was no, holding out against the pressure to rush to action and to rescue, precluding thought and reflection, but I offered a time to meet together and think and plan. The network went into deep silence; then I received a letter from my social work colleague letting me know that a containing placement had finally been arranged and Giorgio had been delighted to move there, back to his known area south west of the city. Therapy will now be arranged locally, given the stability of his placement. Holding out for what is necessary does sometimes pay off.

Angus

Referred for sexually accosting his 5-year-old niece, Angus turned out not to be preoccupied in any way with paedophilic fantasy and, following the usual Child Protection meetings with Social Services, the Police and Education, no action was taken against him. A very high degree of delinquent activity, however, did emerge immediately, to the extent of making me wonder if he were breaking down. Some of this was directed against his family – returning home very late, attacking the front door with his boots and, finding it locked, gluing the locks, sleeping rough in the garden, lying, stealing from home. Irate letters from his GP urged us to 'do something' on the instant, the GP feeling pressurised by the family and by his own anxiety about Angus. The network was already acting out: activity and not thought was the emphasis.

Angus's history was appalling. The oldest of six siblings, he was eventually adopted at 9 years of age. Prior to this he had been treated with neglect, physical, emotional and sexually abusive behaviour that probably involved a paedophile ring, and had learned that lying, running away, stealing and shouting imprecations were important mechanisms to use in dealing with adults. Defecating in his room was also amazingly successful in keeping them at bay, a trait that continued on his arrival in the adoptive home. Recourse to the body and very early body-based defensive manoeuvres was very much a part of Angus's unsophisticated repertoire for coping with anxiety and with his objects. The ego was not, in any sense, mature.

Angus and the sister next in age to him were eventually taken into the care of the local authority when Angus was 6 years old. There followed 23 changes of placement before their adoption at 9 and 8 years of age. Some of these placements were abusive, both physically and sexually. In one, they were placed for adoption but, the adoptive mother finding herself to be pregnant, they returned from school one day to discover their bags packed and on the doorstep and the social worker due to call to move them on yet again. In Angus's recollection, this was the first placement they had been in where they were neither hit nor abused. Perhaps the rejection was too hard to think of as also part of an abusive response.

At referral, he was at the age of 16 in an exceptionally conflictual relationship with his adoptive parents. His father was distant – Angus described going with him to a climbing group that his father took and being shouted at for not looking out for the other members like a co-leader. Angus had hoped for closeness, an intimacy in sharing an occupation with his father and, hurt, he had stormed off. He had a close – perhaps over close – relationship with his mother who had found him the easier of the children to relate to. It seemed that, come adolescence, this closeness came with threat, without the possibility of an oedipal father to mediate the intimacy. His experience was compounded by his parents' marital difficulties. The separation necessary in adolescence was thus impossible to achieve and the overlay of sexual issues, especially for an abused young man, impossible to tolerate. His friends were younger (so he physically stood out amongst them), highly delinquent, verbally abusive to his parents (taking Angus's complaints about them literally) and physically confrontative with his father. A group pastime was to stand outside the community centre and lob milk bottles at passing cyclists – his parents were environmentally very aware, cycled and belonged to several community groups. The insult felt very personal.

Angus lied as a matter of course. While it was frustrating to experience this capacity to be economical with the truth, his capacity to lie almost automatically seemed both to indicate a return to mistrust of his objects and a need to keep them at bay, and an attempt to hold on to difference and separateness.

On the fringes of the group when one of them stole the handbag of a prostitute going about her business in the street, Angus was picked up by the police. The Youth Offending Team, to whom his social worker and I had already referred him with his and his family's consent, finally became involved. His family could no longer tolerate either his presence or his challenging behaviour and asked him to leave, having attempted this also the previous year. Meetings with his school (he is a talented artist who won a place at a specialist arts school) ensured co-operation, understanding and support. A foster-carer took him in and set limits on his activities. He settled briefly and kept away from his delinquent friends. Then he pushed the limits with school, lost his place and – on his last warning in his placement – drove off in his carer's car, damaging it before he returned it, and denied he had anything to do with it.

Angus was given a supervision order and managed to comply with the retributive aspects of it. His mother took him to a Retreat in his father's native country for a month, which he enjoyed. There he made good relationships with another artistic youth and his family, and with the Order's chef who offered to teach him catering. The magistrates agreed to shorten his supervision order and Angus went off to live and train at the Retreat. His mother reports he is doing well, interspersed with comments that 'He is mad, you know!' I have severe reservations. Now almost 18, Angus appears to have been managed by the rather arcane and archaic procedure of transportation.

I did a lot of work with the network around Angus – school meeting and contact, carer support, parent work – although strikingly I never saw the parents together. Their marital difficulties, which I think caused such unmentionable anxiety in Angus when compounded by his arrival into puberty, meant that the marriage just survived if they had some distance from each other. I refused to take Angus into psychotherapy with the network as unholding as it was, to the rage of family and GP, but did see him about fortnightly when he was about. He did not miss appointments although at times he cancelled the odd one, and we did a little work on ego functioning. The main message was his not being lost to mind. The family managed to keep in contact with me, too, and with them the main work was preventing them from acting in a retaliatory way without thought, addressing the way they tried to split the professional network, attempting some understanding of Angus's drive for activity as a defence against recollection and thought (especially in the context of his parents' marital difficulties) and holding firm to my resolution that therapy would not at this time be helpful for this young man. We survived.

Brief comment on the adolescent process and societal responses

> I would there were no age between sixteen and three-and-twenty, or that youth would sleep out the rest; for there is nothing in the between but getting wenches with child, wronging the ancientry, stealing, fighting.
>
> (Shakespeare *The Winter's Tale* Act III scene iii 57ff)

The shepherd, given life in Shakespeare's lines in the early 17th century, would speak for every generation since, identifying mid to late adolescence with promiscuity, lack of respect, delinquency and violence. There is in the adolescent – and in the delinquent – a capacity to elicit an extremely puni-tive societal superego, specifically from those with the power to make and enforce law, and therefore with the power to define what is and is not 'delin-quent' or 'anti-social' or 'criminal', and to initiate responses to such activ-ity. It seems generally accepted that adolescents should be getting on with life and with the developmental tasks of individuation, separation, ownership of the body, establishing a more mature identity and becoming an autonomous self-regulating 'self'. In one sense, delinquency may be viewed as part of an appropriate developmental process, part of normal separation, establishing dif-ference and experimentation – or at least as on this continuum. It frequently enables identities to be tried out in the group, albeit the risk involved is con-cerning. Most delinquents, however, do grow out of it: they form attachments and relationships, and these provide a further opportunity for intimacy and establishing identity on manageable terms.

'Gonnae no' dae that?' is less a question than a warning shot fired across the bows. One often hears it from a distracted parent to a boisterous toddler in the super-market, or addressed to the latency child who is bored in the company of the adults and seeking mindless activity. After the warning may come punishment. With ado-lescents, the phrase perhaps contains more venom and despair as the adults struggle, often impotently, with the developing potency of their young people, with their own aspirations and envy that inhibit the young from separation and autonomy, and with their fear of the world's perception of their failure when others view the actions of this 'work in progress' that is the adolescent. In this, while knowing the tasks necessary for the achievement of autonomy and intimacy, we are often com-pelled emotionally to pull the young back to us, necessitating greater and sometimes delinquent effort on their part to individuate: as Winnicott wrote, 'There is not yet a capacity to identify with parent figures without loss of personal identity' (Winnicott 1963b: 244). It is a cliché of child mental health work that the policeman's son may well be referred for theft or delinquency and the teacher's daughter for truancy – anything but identification with the parent. The urgency is to be different – and the fear is how this will be managed.

Paul van Heeswyk quotes Philip Larkin's 'a beginning, a muddle and an end' (van Heeswyk 1997: 4) as more relevant in its description of adolescent develop-ment as a confusing experience, rather than a stage-by-stage sequence. Indeed, part of this 'muddle' would include the ambivalence of the adolescent in rela-tion to the search for individuality and separation: fear of disentanglement from parental objects is as powerful an unconscious force as the drive for separation. This, too, is encountered by society as well as family and is a further factor in our responses.

The impotence and confusion we can be made to feel is vitally important as it affects us as parents, citizens and as therapists. We hold the projected anxie-ties about future and change, responsibility and progress, and swing as readily as adolescents between lauding their creativity and idealism while condemning their impulsivity and reliance on activity rather than reflection. The corollary is that we are pushed, in the transference, to respond equally actively and equally without reflection – as parents, citizens and therapists.

Margret Tonnesmann draws our attention to the earlier experiences which are also re-enacted by the adolescent – important to keep in mind when we consider how theory mainly focuses on oedipal (and consequent superego) matters:

> The adolescent not only acts out his oedipal conflicts, he also re-enacts his pre-oedipal and sometimes non-verbal and somatic infancy. He has therefore a second chance actively to master and integrate the privations, deprivations, traumatic distress, intrusions and neglect which he had been passively exposed to and suffered during his early life. Traumata of later childhood, in so far as they rendered the immature ego instantly helpless by the flooding of stimuli rather than causing an intra-psychical conflictual response, are re-enacted in a similar way. If, however, the damage has been too extensive so that sufficient intra-psychic organisational ego resources are not available, or if the environmental provisions are not good enough, this second chance is bound to fail.
>
> (Tonnesmann 1980: 39)

The role of the body-self, trauma and environment are particularly important in delinquency.

Theory and the internal world

In the legal sense, the delinquent is a young person who has committed an act that, were he an adult, would be defined as a crime. Here, I do not distinguish between anti-social, delinquent and conduct disordered behaviour – I think these are often on a continuum although the one need not lead to the next *if the environment gets its response right* – but I do think that to be called 'criminal' one has to have a more established psychological structure than early or mid-adolescence allows. The activities that we generally accept as delinquent include stealing, lying, vandalism and violence.

Psychoanalytic theories as to the roots and causation of delinquency must, inevitably, go back to Freud's 'Criminality from a sense of guilt' (Freud 1925) where he describes the individual who seeks punishment by reason of a harsh superego. In this the role of oedipal wishes and guilt form the core, and superego formation which is dependent on the oedipal resolution. In adolescence, with what we understand as the reworking of oedipal wishes, relationships and boundaries (the film would be entitled: *Oedipus 2 – the body awakes . . .*) it would seem helpful to keep this in mind when thinking of delinquency.

Aichhorn (1925), one of the earliest innovators in provision for delinquent or 'wayward' youth, points to two 'faulty developments' in the child's mental structure that establish a predisposition to delinquency:

a)   there has been no move from the pleasure principle to the reality principle, consequent on either too indulgent or too severe treatment in early life. This is similar to Mrs Klein's move from the paranoid schizoid to the depressive position or Winnicott's process of disillusionment. Although Aichhorn is writing from the theoretical stance of Freudian drive or instinct theory, the importance of object relationships is evident – the capacity of the carers to help the child leave behind the early egocentric, narcissistic way of being and engage with confidence with the real world.

b)   there has been a malformation of the ego ideal and hence the superego.

The ego ideal is an important concept: the sense of 'who do I want to be, how do I perceive myself?' arises from the introjection of and identification with key people in the child's environment and enables the development of the sense of shame when one falls short of this wished-for self. One could not quarrel with Aichhorn's theory, especially when one thinks of Angus whose lack of any sense of the 'other' was striking and such a factor in his lying. He remained rooted – as were the delinquents so well described by Peter Wilson (1999) – in a highly narcissistic mode of functioning.

Mrs Klein's approach in 'Criminal tendencies in normal children' (1927) echoes Freud but proposes that the superego works in a different direction, trying to 'reject the desires belonging to the oedipus complex' (Limentani 1984–1985: 388).

In all of these, the role of the oedipal resolution and superego formation is central. One might wish to extend ideas about the superego and its formation. As in perversion, one can with the delinquent and offending young person find the use of two superegos – one that is externalised onto society, that is anti-social and seemingly against law, and an internal one that is more linked to the ego ideal and more depressive. This internal conflicted superego is often unrecognised by society in its insistence on the use of the words 'offender' and 'perpetrator', often of very young children. The external one – as with Angus – may be the result of an ego ideal built on internalisations of delinquent peers and early abusive adults. It may therefore be corrupt.

In 1944 John Bowlby was already exploring the issues that led to his major work on attachment theory. In 'Forty-four juvenile thieves', published in expanded version in 1946, he not unsurprisingly focuses on early separation from mother as a key predisposing factor. This resonates with Winnicott in the 1940s: 'I cannot get away from my clinical experience of the relation of not being wanted at the start of life to the subsequent anti-social tendency' (Winnicott 1940s: 52–53),

This contrasts somewhat with Winnicott's later formulation of 'the anti-social tendency' where he is clear that the anti-social child has suffered deprivation (not privation) and seeks that which he once had, making a demand and claim on the environment for what is his by right (Winnicott 1956). This would seem to indicate a more integrated and functional ego than was available to Angus in mid-adolescence. Despite his abusive early years, Matthew might more readily be representative of this Winnicottian delinquent and this, perhaps, because of the availability of his paternal grandmother, a consistent object.

Especially interesting is Bowlby's category of 'Affectionless' children whom he says are evident from the age of 3 and who formed the bulk of persistent offenders in his Child Guidance survey, usually combining truancy with their delinquent activity. It is possible that these 'affectionless' children are those with whom, in therapy, one has to work on their victimisation and trauma before they are able to think of the predicament in which they place others – the conflict is in relation to the body, shame and humiliation in very early childhood, as with Matthew. Or they are the children for whom deficit and not conflict is the issue, necessitating long structural work on the ego, affect recognition and tolerance, and then the ability to recognise affect in the other, as advised with Giorgio.

In Anna Freud's contribution to a festschrift for Aichhorn in 1949 (Eissler 1949; Freud 1949) we find early object relations are also the key, albeit she writes within the construct of drive theory. She emphasises 'early disturbance of object-love' resulting from absent, neglectful, ambivalent or unstable mothering, or multiple impersonal carers, meaning the child cannot invest emotionally in parent figures, so retreats to the self, the body and its needs which 'retain a greater importance than normal' (Freud 1949). This absence of 'good enough mothering' is also problematic in relation to aggression, agency and potency, which are not met with understanding, and may manifest on a spectrum from 'overemphasised aggressiveness' to 'wanton destructiveness'. Her later comments on lying and stealing (Freud 1965) are also apt. Early childhood lying is 'innocent', dependent on the development of ego functions; it may lead to fantasy lying; delinquent lying requires greater ego development and has purpose in avoiding or distorting reality (Freud 1965: 115). Angus's lying probably served his survival very well as a boy; he uses it now in the same childish way. Likewise stealing, while reflecting initial infantile difficulties in distinguishing 'me – not me' and 'mine – not mine', responds to the developing urgency of the superego – not an achievement for Angus or Giorgio.

Edward Glover, working at the Portman, attempted to separate out those for whom a psychoanalytic approach might be necessary:

> if pathological delinquency is to be regarded as in the main an *object-relation disorder*, a view for which there is much to be said, we must really distinguish between transient crises of disorder due mainly to *functional stress* [Glover 1950], and *symptomatic* reactions to oedipal *conflict*. Here again many psycho-analytical observers fail to distinguish delinquencies due to pubertal stress from those which are due to Oedipus conflict and which develop from an organised symptomatic form that tends to persist well into the twenties. To be sure, unconscious conflict exists in all cases delinquent and non-delinquent, but it does not in all cases give rise to defensive *symptom construction*.
>
> (Glover 1956: 313)

This is important. In therapeutic terms it helps us distinguish those young people for whom we might best offer consultation to the network and environment, and those for whom therapy is a viable and necessary proposition. Glover is clear as to the normality of delinquency during the developmental process of adolescence and therefore clear that we should not pathologise it. His view, however, still locates the area of risk as early conflict, oedipal in origin, as does that of Kate Friedlander, another early Portman Clinic pioneer (Friedlander 1947).

Winnicott's delinquent – the child who flooded his clinic basement, jump-started Winnicott's car in the clinic driveway and bit him on the buttocks three times – roused him to plead for placement. In 'The anti-social tendency' (Winnicott 1956), however, he is clear that the issue is placement *first*. Only when the structure is secure – and by this he means 'the provision of an ego-supportive structure that is relatively indestructible' (Winnicott 1963a) – can we engage in an analytic process with the delinquent. He wished to continue with his acting out lad; his clinic forbade it. The clinic superego acted punitively, and a further loss was inflicted on a conflicted boy. This is the process that, in society, we find hard to resist.

One of the most useful papers on delinquency is that by Limentani, a former Director of the Portman Clinic, written in 1984–1985. At that stage in the Portman's history, more mixed presentations – or the uncovering of both delinquent and sexually deviant behaviour – were evident. Whereas Limentani rightly emphasises the importance of the body 'that will finally carry the responsibility and task of accepting, rejecting, or finding alternative solutions to the wealth of psychical experiences' (Limentani 1984–1985: 387) he also points to the sexual motivation that may be linked with offending. This, as in Cooper's understanding of perversion (Cooper 1991), involves a sexual object that 'has been dehumanised and transferred to an inanimate object' (Limentani 1984–1985: 386). With delinquents, we may see a process that seeks (but has not achieved) such a solution.

Where the early theoretical picture does not quite seem to be sufficient is in the area of trauma – and especially what Khan has termed 'cumulative trauma' (Khan 1963). Pre-verbal trauma, especially through an experience of severe physical and/or sexual abuse, would appear to be a feature of those young people referred to us today. In the absence of any attentive object – and the presence of corrupt objects – the child has only recourse to the primary body-ego, which remains a solution and resort when anxiety later appears. As Khan reminds us, later traumata may appear minor but to the child traumatised early, there has been no development of a protective function that reduces the impact of these. The impact of such an on-going experience of trauma, moreover, on the integration of the violated body into the psychological sense of self is frankly enormous and leaves the young person, conflicted at puberty, with problems resulting in a constant use of activity, the repetition of bodily based experiences that replay the sensations of early trauma, and a hyper-sensitivity to the intentions of adults. In Australia a long-term sociological study recently found 'that child sexual abuse is an independent risk factor for offending and delinquent behaviour' (Swanston et al 2003: 729) and, unsurprisingly, that it also correlated with aggression. I think those of us who work primarily with young people have actually known this for a very long time and find hope when the adolescent process frees up the psychological structure and makes the material available for work.

I wonder if Winnicott had it partly right, that some delinquent or conduct disordered children are in search of something. This would indicate a certain ego development and strength and a real capacity to make demands on the environment, and I would, as noted, see Matthew as a Winnicottian delinquent. I find greater psychopathology and cause for worry in the delinquent who, like Angus and Giorgio, has a poorly functioning ego, a patchy ego ideal and a superego that dare not be accessed, where deficit reigns and activity both blocks out memory and feeling and reminds one that one is alive. All too often referrers comment, 'He has no sense of victim empathy or remorse.' This is very true of both Angus and Giorgio. But then, there is not a functioning ego at a state of maturity where a sense of the other and so remorse might enter the frame. For many of the young people whom we see, we should not expect remorse: developmentally this has still to be achieved. Such young people, moreover, have most certainly never been in receipt of empathy as victims themselves.

The external world

We have known of the prevalence of delinquency in normal adolescence for many years – even if we may have forgotten our own. West's study of the young offender (West 1968) alerted us to this almost 40 years ago, citing research across Europe and in the States.

It means that we have to be careful about whom we label and how, and with what intent. If an element of delinquent functioning is a common part of the adolescent process, aiding separation and individuation, we need a safe but light touch, a structure that holds but wherein we do not respond with purely punitive action. The one-off incident of sexual abuse by a 13-year-old surely need not lead – as it did with a patient of mine – to his being put on the Sex Offenders' Register for 2½ years and to his school's banning him for ever from any involvement in group activities that in practice would have encouraged equal peer relationships and a more appropriate use and experience of the adolescent body. We need far more sophisticated, less crude responses.

Adolescents are creatures of extremes: there is little middle ground (although in psychoanalytic psychotherapy we seek to create this) and we must not respond ourselves with parallel extremes, either by being harshly punitive or, at the other pole, by failing to be concerned. Given the tendency to activity as a defence against anxiety in adolescence, above all we need to avoid knee-jerk policy making and retain *our* capacity for thought and reflection – the functions that so often are at risk of being lost in the adolescent process and in the adolescent's interactions with family and environment. At the start of this paper I referred to the case of Joseph Scholes who killed himself in a Young Offenders' Institution, caught in the Home Secretary's knee-jerk reaction to the rise in mobile phone thefts. In the months following this, a range of advertisements appeared, reminding the reader that stolen mobile phones will no longer work – the non-knee-jerk reaction, making society and the mobile phone business partners in a *thinking* response to juvenile crime. In the interim, however, Joseph Scholes suffered both from a harshly punitive legal injunction *and* from a failure of concern once he was in custody.

When does delinquency become defined as criminality? We must assume that it is when a psychological mindset is established (i.e. is not in process of develop-ment but is there). This impinges upon legal concepts such as *mens rea* (the guilty mind, the capacity to form intent) and *doli incapax* (applied to children with the assumption that below the age of 13 they are incapable of harmful intent) – which latter the government recently abolished for 10–13 year olds. Yet the adolescent is in the throes of character development; we know that the superego in Glasser's explication is not formed until the end of adolescence (others might say it contin-ues to alter well in adulthood); and we hesitate (or ought to), in the psychoanalytic world anyway, to use of young people terminology that would indicate an estab-lished structure. They are engaged in a process and we must be careful neither to foreclose on it nor to find only rigid responses.

With the expectation that the young person *will* act out, the structures we develop require flexibility if they are to enable psychoanalytic work to be a treatment of choice in the face of such inevitable challenge. It was, therefore, disappointing to hear a few years ago that the Probation Service (before the deci-sion to amalgamate the Probation and Prison Service into the National Offender Management Service – another unthinking response) has been required to breach offenders (i.e. bring them back into court) if they missed two appointments. The same pressures are felt by the Youth Justice system. The disinterested observer might think that it is the healthy adolescent who misses an appointment, and the compliant or unindividuated one who attends faithfully – but that would be to think, and to think in developmental terms. This is *mindless* policy; and with adolescents who offend, who act, we must above all retain our capacity to think and to seek space for thinking. All in the network also need to be allowed to use judgment and to exercise that judgment without fear of censure.

Finally, we desperately need to address policy for the young offender who is imprisoned or sent to alternative secure establishments. We fail in the duty of care for youths like Joseph Scholes when we do not persuade penal and secure institu-tions of the risk of self-harm in young people like him. His history of risk was well known. There is a great need for trained staff in such institutions – and probably specialist officers rather than, as at present in the UK, staff who work in both adult and youth penal fields and are moved from one to the other – for on-going consul-tation, and for psychiatric assessments to be taken seriously. Staff members, who experience the 'all or nothing' quality of the adolescent, need support in keeping *both* aspects in mind and in not being seduced or angered into denying the vulner-ability. Equally, there has to be a more integrated approach to the young person on release. Although policy guidelines require Social Services, Youth Offending Teams or Probation Services to liaise with the institution, this is an often chaotic and last-minute process – at the very time of his abandonment by the institution, the young offender is left not knowing his next step. This need not be so – but it requires resourcing if it is to be done in any meaningful and containing way. It is about providing that 'degree of structural strength and organisation' emphasised as essential by Winnicott (1963a) and Wilson (2004).

Implications for intervention

When Glover writes of the first 15 years of the work of the Portman Clinic (Glover 1949), he describes a fully functioning multi-professional team engaging with the network around the young offender, providing assessments in particular for court and above all helping other professions to think about the nature of the delinquent and the meaning of the delinquent act. Therapeutically, however, he bemoans the absence of much analysis (by this he means four or five times weekly psychoanalytic sessions). Limentani wonders if analysis is the right approach at all, serving more to give clinicians knowledge and insight as 'there must be some doubt as to our therapeutic effectiveness' (Limentani 1984–1985: 384). I would question this. Perhaps in a world where four or five times weekly work was the analytic norm, it was difficult to see once weekly work as other than a poor compromise. Today, once weekly work is often the treatment of choice, if individual treatment is offered.

Within this framework for exploring delinquency, there is a clear implication that the analyst/therapist requires flexibility as part of his repertoire. Peter Wilson (2004) took psychoanalysts to task in the Glover lecture for being too enthralled to their analytic superegos and not being prepared to be creative in technique. This may be true of more classical analysts; my own experience is that we have the adolescent processes clearly in mind, the variety of approaches one would use with the adolescent patient, then set this in a frame that also keeps *both* risk in the present *and* the traumatised early self in mind. For the child who has not only been abandoned by his objects but been attacked by them, the active presence of a therapist is both essential and threatening – we must also hold both in mind.

The power of the delinquent act, as Don Campbell has said (2004), forces a counter action. In policy, it tends to be the societal superego that is called into unthinking play. In the family, it may be 'Gonnae no' dae that!' followed by physical retribution. In therapy, it may be that we hit back with an interpretation or we refer on, as Don noted. In this, we are not reflective but simply retaliating, falling in with the 'imperatives of the transference' (Wilson 1999). Not complying with the provocation of the transference, monitoring our counter transference, creating space for thinking, firstly for therapist and then, if lucky, for the delinquent – all are technically essential in the work. Equally, with the delinquent in therapy we have to pay especial attention to the problems of intimacy and detached concern. Fear of closeness makes the delinquent – like Angus – need real flexibility and a kind of contained freedom. It is vital that our concern is known, that we do not drift into not caring and letting them go. Angus came up with reasons to cut his sessions short – he would arrive early, when I could not see him, and claim that he had hoped for his session early as he had an appointment at the Youth Offending Team that necessitated his leaving early. One could comment, with a smile, on his capacity to regulate just how much he felt he could manage of the old bat up at the Portman, and he would relax and often stay.

It is inevitable with adolescents, never mind delinquent ones, that there will be acting in and acting out. One's own commitment will be challenged in the therapy room but, even more importantly, the network will be driven to mirror the delinquent's internal world (Davies 1996). This takes a great deal of containment and one usually needs a colleague to case manage this part. Matthew, in time honoured adolescent fashion, tried to get his school to expel him before his exams and leaving date. He caused a further violent fight with a peer. The network got together, thought, and contained him. He completed his exams, was successful, and managed a 'good' leaving and a move into the adult world. Many networks do not think, and the young person is lost. In the early 1970s there was a great deal of concern that the peak age for juvenile delinquency coincided with the last year of school: when the school leaving age was 15, the peak age was 14; when the school leaving age was raised to 16, the peak age for juvenile delinquency moved to 15. There was a strong correlation between truancy and delinquency, much of the latter happening during the former. Teachers were castigated for making the last year neither relevant nor interesting for these young people. Yet the issue is one of identity and crisis, not teaching skills: when faced with the fundamental shift from 'me-in-school' to 'who am I after school?' many young people find it unbearably traumatic and attempt to leave school before, as they feel, it leaves them. This needs understanding, clear holding boundaries and thought if the young people are to be able to make the transition creatively and not self-destructively.

Anna Freud's great contribution of the analysis of the defences and of the ego has had an important impact on work with adolescents and especially adolescents who offend. With many, there is a long period of ego structuring work – 'naming of parts' as a colleague, Dorothy Lloyd Owen, has called it, articulating and naming emotions and emotional states, helping the young person recognise these and regulate them, gaining control. The violent young man is often as overwhelmed by the sudden precipitation of his violence as is his victim. He needs practice in recognising anger, in predicting when it may occur, and in how to articulate justifiable annoyance and aggression. Only once this is done can more insightful work take place.

Importantly, Limentani focuses us on the role of the body – and this means care in technique where we have to avoid humiliating the young person with our interpretations. It is possible to split off issues to do with the body (and with sexuality which is also a theme), almost make it a third person in the room, and so make it safe to discuss, and engender curiosity and thought about what it gets up to. The prime defence, after all, is activity – and that is body-based, pre-verbal, recalling the somatic experience in infancy.

The first 'technical' decision, however, is not what to do in the room – it is whether the environment available is the right one in which to help the development of the young delinquent. Context is the first issue – as with Angus and Giorgio – and we need to be aware of the variety of supportive schemes that are available to the forensically vulnerable youth, like Youth Offending Teams and their new Youth Support projects where physical activities, educational support and mentoring are excellent features. Issues of how to approach individual work must follow such wider considerations: a therapeutic package is essential involving a resilient and facilitating environment where the capacity for thought mirrors a good oedipal experience.

What should the relationship of psychoanalysis to delinquency now be?

There are three key areas for the psychoanalytic psychotherapist to keep in mind:

1   The issue of environment and placement remains prime. One could say that 'containment' with understanding provides a developmental experience that enables some delinquent adolescents to move on safely to more normal development. This may mean a therapeutic kind of containment in a residential institution where the early deficits can be addressed and the pressure to retaliate punitively can be both resisted and understood. However, it also means involvement with the network, engendering a shared understanding and a common approach to providing a robust and safe environment. Psychotherapy may well not be a treatment of choice and it is important that we can explain this while being involved and helpful in other ways: as with Giorgio, getting the setting right is an essential first move. If we do not do this, we may take into therapy young people whose acting out becomes uncontainable and, in stopping therapy, we add further loss and abuse to their life experiences.

2   The provision of psychoanalytic psychotherapy remains an essential resource. Although this is patently not the treatment of choice for every delinquent, as Glover (1956) and Limentani (1984–1985) remind us, for those who are in a stable setting and for whom there is conflict and an otherwise troubled career, it remains vital that we continue the provision. Our capacity today to think positively in terms of once weekly psychotherapy, being flexible as to the young person's tolerance of intimacy and being aware of those young people where initial structuring work is necessary, gives us greater scope and hope in our psychoanalytic approaches. For those young people for whom delinquency is a defence or a response to deficit, and where there is conflict, this seems important.

3   The dissemination of understanding is perhaps the most important function for child psychotherapists in the future. Prevention of unthinking reactions – by clinicians, other professionals, network and politicians – is an important part of that process and it is essential if networks are to be resilient enough to be of use to the young delinquent.

Perhaps where we have retreated somewhat from a higher profile is in the area of challenging and influencing policy. We do engage with particular issues, are invited to participate in think-tanks and provide briefings – and *must* respond to such invitation. We have as a profession been reluctant, however, to be more public about what we do with patients who offend and what our particular understanding offers. There are many reasons for this. The climate in which psychoanalysis found itself in the early days of analytic interventions with delinquent and offending youth was very different – psychoanalysis was becoming valued as having something to offer and engaged the minds of more than those trained in its treatment methods. Today we experience at best ambivalence, at worst attack. It is remarkable that, despite this, we find the demands for psychoanalytic understanding growing and it may be a feature of interest in or despair about young people who are driven to action. There is also the urgent problem of confidentiality with a patient group that is often disparaged and marginalised. Finally, we have the advent of media of a very different kind from the more deferential press of the 1920s and 1930s. Driven by sensation, polarisation, competition to publish what could not previously be published, the media can seem driven by action not thought (both adolescent and delinquent, then) and an often very corrupt superego. Yet this is the climate in which we hope to help the superego development of our delinquent young patients.

Note

1 Earlier versions of this paper were given at the 70th Anniversary Conference of the Portman Clinic, London, March 2004 and at the 52 Club in January 2004. It was published in the *Journal of Child Psychotherapy* 30(3) 2004.

References

Aichhorn, A (1925) *Wayward Youth* London: Viking Press 1935

Bowlby, J (1946) *Forty-Four Juvenile Thieves: Their Characters and Home-life* London: Bailliere, Tindall & Cox

Campbell, D (2004) contribution from the floor at the Glover Lecture, London, January 2004

Cooper, A (1991) The unconscious core of perversion. In G Fogel & W Myers *Perversions and Near-perversions in Clinical Practice – New Psychoanalytic Perspectives* New Haven & London: Yale University Press

Davies, R (1996) The interdisciplinary network and the internal world of the offender. In C Cordess & M Cox (eds.) *Forensic Psychotherapy: Crime, Psychodynamics and the Offender Patient* London: Jessica Kingsley

Eissler, KR (ed.) (1949) *Searchlights on Delinquency: New Psychoanalytic Studies* New York: International Universities Press

Freud, A (1949) Certain types and stages of social maladjustment. In KR Eissler (ed.) *Searchlights on Delinquency: New Psychoanalytic Studies* New York: International Universities Press

Freud, A (1965) *Normality and Pathology in Childhood: Assessments of Development* New York: International Universities Press

Freud, S (1925) Criminality from a sense of guilt. In Some Characters met with in Psychoanalytic Work *SE* 4

Friedlander, K (1947) *The Psychoanalytic Approach to Juvenile Delinquency: Theory, Case Studies, Treatment* London: Routledge & Kegan Paul

Glover, E (1949) Outline of the investigation and treatment of delinquency in Great Britain: 1912–1948 with special references to psychoanalytical and other psychological methods. In KR Eissler (ed.) *Searchlights on Delinquency* New York: International Universities Press

Glover, E (1950) On the desirability of isolating a 'functional' (psycho-somatic) group of delinquent disorders *British Journal of Delinquency* 1(2): 104–112

Glover, E (1956) Psychoanalysis and criminology: a political survey *International Journal of Psycho-Analysis* 37: 311–317

Horne, A (2001) Brief communications from the edge: psychotherapy with challenging adolescents *Journal of Child Psychotherapy* 27(1): 3–18

Hurry, A (1998) Psychoanalysis and developmental therapy. In A Hurry (ed.) *Psychoanalysis and Developmental Therapy* London: Karnac

Khan, MMR (1963) The concept of cumulative trauma. In *The Privacy of the Self* (1974) New York: International Universities Press

Klein, M (1927) Criminal tendencies in normal children. In *Love, Guilt and Reparation and Other Works* London: Hogarth Press

Limentani, A (1984–1985) Towards a unified conception of the origins of sexual and social deviancy in young persons *International Journal of Psychoanalytic Psychotherapy* 10: 383–401

Swanston, HY, Parkinson, PN, O'Toole, BI, Plunkett, AM, Shrimpton, S & Oates, RK (2003) Juvenile crime, aggression and delinquency after sexual abuse: a longitudinal study *British Journal of Criminology* 43: 729–749

Tonnesmann, M (1980) Adolescent re-enactment, trauma and reconstruction *Journal of Child Psychotherapy* 6: 23–44

van Heeswyk, P (1997) *Analysing Adolescence* London: Sheldon Press

West, DJ (1968) *The Young Offender* London: Penguin

Wilson, P (1999) Delinquency. In M Lanyado, M & A Horne (eds.) *The Handbook of Child and Adolescent Psychotherapy: Psychoanalytic Perspectives* London & New York: Routledge

Wilson, P (2004) The delinquent and the psychoanalyst. Unpublished paper given as the Glover Lecture at the Portman Clinic, January

Winnicott, DW (1940s) The delinquent and habitual offender. In DW Winnicott *Thinking about Children* Eds. R Shepherd, J Johns & H Taylor Robinson London: Karnac 1996

Winnicott, DW (1956) The anti-social tendency. In *Collected Papers: Through Paediatrics to Psychoanalysis* London: Hogarth Press 1975

Winnicott, DW (1963a) The psychotherapy of character disorders. In DW Winnicott *Deprivation and Delinquency* Eds. C Winnicott, R Shepherd & M Davis London & New York: Tavistock Publications 1984

Winnicott, DW (1963b) Hospital care supplementing intensive psychotherapy in adolescence. In *The Maturational Processes and the Facilitating Environment* London: Hogarth Press 1965

5 From intimacy to acting out

Thinking psychoanalytically about dangerousness[1]

Prologue: a referral arrives

This paper describes the referral of a 14-year-old boy to a specialist London clinic, the responses engendered by it, and expands on the transference and counter-transference phenomena arising from a presentation of violence and a history of cumulative trauma. As the referrer, a Consultant Forensic Child and Adolescent Psychiatrist working in 'Townsville', a specialist service quite far from London, expressed in her request:

> We would like an assessment of Martin to be undertaken to provide us with a psychodynamic formulation which we can use to help our continuing efforts to understand Martin and manage his case.

This sounded good – a colleague, non-psychoanalytic, who thought that psychoanalysis had something to offer in understanding a patient. She continued:

> We envisage that assessment leading on to a consultation process for the team at Townsville on a regular basis while he remains with us.

Even better: the Trust that employed me would be very happy at the prospect of ongoing paid consultancy work in a forensic setting.

That letter was written two months after Martin's 14th birthday. The Home Office, who financed his placement at Townsville, had agreed to fund a specialist assessment jointly with the local Health Authority but the Health Authority took time to accede to this. By the time that funding was finally clear and negotiations as to just what we would undertake had been completed, five months had passed. The logistics of Martin's care had changed by then – not unexpectedly, really, as the referral itself indicated a crisis in both understanding and caring for him. Martin was resident in a specialist containment and treatment facility for children whose offences were serious. Two weeks after this letter was written, the government announced a consultation on future plans for the Centre, including possible closure, and the staff was informed a week before we visited that it had to close – deeply unsettling both for staff and for Martin. He had arrived there 2½ years previously, some 3 months before his 12th birthday, having been given a five-year sentence for two counts of arson and two further counts of arson with intent to endanger life. He was 11 years old when he committed the offences. In addition, four months before this referral, he had attacked a staff member, a woman to whom he was close, with a plastic cricket bat. The attack was said to have 'come out of the blue' (as the referrer's assessment states: 'he has behaved in a very violent manner, including a serious unprovoked attack, when he was apparently calm and content'). The alarm system failed and no-one else was in the Unit at the time. Martin shouted, 'Die, bitch, die!' amongst other things during a prolonged attack. He received an 18-month Conditional Discharge[2] for this offence and is said to have 'shown no remorse'.

Martin's original sentence – minus the usual remission – was almost over. The staff team at Townsville was inclined to keep him on, feeling him to be both a risk and at risk. What did we think?

Several assessments accompanied the referral – we received one that had been prepared for the original court case 2½ years earlier and two others compiled very recently, within the four weeks preceding the referral's being written, and patently arising from the crisis of the attack. One was by one of only two specialist in-patient units in the country. The consultant there would not admit Martin as he was not psychotic although he was perceived to be at high risk of developing formal mental illness (one would have to continue to have the concept of violence as a defence against psychosis in mind, however). Furthermore, he was deemed to 'fulfil the criteria for the legal definition of psychopathic disorder' – as well as fulfilling the criteria for conduct disorder – but the hospital was unable to provide treatment for this so could not detain him. The final report had been written a week earlier by Dr A, the referrer, for the Centre and for the Home Office, and included the recommendation of a specialist assessment.

One could argue logically that Martin should *not* be seen yet again; rather, a consultation to the staff would be more appropriate. I have no problems with this logic; indeed, I argued it at the time. But for me, it also resonated in an embarrassing way with memories of my time in a London Child Guidance Unit where, with an abundance of Psychiatric Registrars and Senior Registrars in training, it was possible when – in my case – an encopretic child was referred to propose, 'This would be a *very* good case for the Registrar! We don't see too many of these! S/he should really have the experience!' So I was also aware of my capacity to opt out of certain cases – and of anxiety informing my response to *this* request about *this* child. The more purist response of 'not another assessment' was diluted by my guilty wish not to see Martin. (For those of you who might be wondering about the soiling, I got my come-uppance when I saw – for seven years – a lass who was encopretic at the start of therapy and who, one day, arrived car sick into the bargain – the child in the next chapter. My list of 'what Ann can tolerate' has altered . . .)

Why bring this case to this conference? Is this bravado – see, we *do* work with very dangerous children at this clinic! Is it an externalisation of the anxiety I felt when the request came my way via an analyst colleague who is very experienced in court work and with whom I often worked closely? Perhaps. There is certainly the opportunity to think with colleagues about the roots of violence and the few choices open to Martin in relation to his world and his perception of his objects – and I would argue strongly that, with the early and severe damage we find in so many of our young patients today, it is essential that we embrace a range of ways of thinking about and working with potential violence. Martin is at the far end of a scale, but we see daily in child and adolescent mental health settings children who appear to be progressing unstoppably along this continuum. But also, importantly, there is a very simple basic message. We can find ourselves in the NHS today struggling to hold on to the value of the psychoanalytic method and the particular understanding that psychodynamic theories bring. Sometimes it feels as if we are pressed to be anything and everything other than what we are – should we be family therapists, cognitive therapists? While an understanding of other modalities is essential for the child psychotherapist, the core that we bring in our specialism must neither be lost *nor should we apologise for it.* It is what we bring and what we do well. As with Martin, when the chips are down, it may offer a vital means to reasoned, reflective insight and a way forward. This paper, therefore, also seeks to stand up for the unique and specialised understanding that psychoanalysis can bring to complex cases.

I mention all this because decisions on the consultation/assessment continuum are often not clear-cut, however much we believe we have unambiguous principles and try to apply these. I also put it in because I don't usually experience any difficulty in saying, 'No I *don't* think we should do an assessment – but can we help in *this* (other) way instead?' It has become so necessary, especially in work with delinquents or young people whose defences are action-based and whose environment does not allow therapy to be a treatment of choice. I further include it because we all have limits and must allow ourselves to recognise what we can and cannot manage – without a superego that makes us doubt whether we are then 'proper' psychotherapists. We *have* to work in a fashion that allows us to continue to think, where our own anxiety does not preclude reflection. And with Martin, I was not sure that this was something I could manage.

Martin's history

I *was* resistant to seeing this child. I had to think for quite a while about the meaning of my reluctance: what did it reflect in me and in the child? How does one deal with an ever-increasing daily deluge of inhumanity, as was reflected in Martin's life experience? I will return to the counter-transference later. As the weeks passed, it became apparent that a meeting with Martin was not only desired by the referrer but required by the Home Office[3]. One is then in a very different ballgame where institutional approval and survival become factors. I felt that I was being gently bullied as a consequence of great anxiety that appeared to permeate quite high up the network. Some of that anxiety was certainly getting into me. Martin, moreover, was now expecting me and had said, rather imperiously, that my colleague and I might visit!

There was sufficient in Martin's history to give one pause. He is the younger of two full brothers born to parents who separated when he was 17 months old, his father maintaining contact. His very early developmental history and milestones are not available and although his early development was described by his natural mother as 'normal' there are no corroborating reports. Certainly, Martin was said by the Health Visitor to have been beyond parental control while still under 2 years of age. It was also known that his birth father was a violent man, the violence towards Martin's mother continuing after their separation. A year later, Martin's mother met Mr B who moved in within the week. They married within 3 months and had three further children. Concerns from the outside world coincide with this: at 2 years 9 months Martin was showing problems in playgroup with oppositional behaviour and aggressive behaviour towards peers. Both boys were put on the Child Protection Register for physical neglect when Martin was 4, but then removed as a result of Mr B's 'aggressive and uncooperative attitude' . . . Aggression in men is already a feature. Mr B was charged with arson of the family home when Martin was 4 years 4 months old; both boys were accommodated 8 months later at their parents' instigation as they could not cope with them. At this point, the marital violence in that relationship came to light, as did Mr B's predilection for locking the boys in their bedroom at night. Once more on the Child Protection Register, the boys were separated, going to different foster families, and full care orders were gained. Martin experienced the breakdown of several placements – as the court report put it: 'it became impossible for any foster family to cope with Martin' and he was admitted to a Children's Unit age 6.

Here, he used to telephone the fire brigade, watching them arrive together with the police, and he visited the fire station with his mother as a treat. A failed attempt was made to rehabilitate him to his natural father. Once he had settled in the Children's Unit, he was assessed for psychotherapy and over the 18 months before he was fostered Martin attended once weekly. The Unit reports describe him as exhibiting sexualised behaviour towards adults and children. He had nightmares and sleep problems, was distrustful, destructive and ran away frequently. He was enuretic by night – a symptom that only cleared up after the move to his adoptive parents. The possibility of ADD was explored; it was thought that his presentation was consequent on the abuse (physical and emotional) that he had suffered. Therapy reports comment that he viewed adults as persecutory, had jealous and murderous feelings and fantasised about omnipotence – not surprising, really. Martin's sexualised behaviour arose in relation, he himself thought, to feelings of being controlled. However much the professional teams suspected, Martin remained resolutely silent about his past. The containment of a good placement, a good specialist school for children with emotional and behavioural difficulties, regular psychotherapy and a coherent care plan allowed him a settled period.

He moved to live with his adoptive family aged 8 years 2 months, exactly two years after arriving in the Unit. This entailed a considerable geographical relocation for Martin and the loss of his therapy. A family group of several children in Martin's Children's Unit had been fostered and then adopted by Mr and Mrs D;

Martin had kept in touch and was also adopted 14 months after his move there. His older brother began to visit and moved in when Martin was 9, being adopted too when Martin was 10½.

I am very aware of giving considerable detail in this story. With this kind of child, one seeks reasons and possibly a sense of containment and control in the exactness and logistics of things because the feelings are unbearable. Or one seeks, in the detail, an avoidance of the whole.

It was only when Martin was living with the Ds that he disclosed severe physical, emotional and sexual abuse to Mr D. It is important to keep in mind that it was to his foster (later adoptive) *father* that he felt able to speak about this for the first time. The details are gross and I will summarise what was later recorded in a psychology report when Martin was 10: his mother forced Martin and his half-sister to simulate sex; he witnessed adults (including his mother and Mr B) having sex; in the presence of another woman he engaged in sexual behaviour with his mother; he was involved in sexual activities with his mother and Mr B (being digitally penetrated by both and penetrated anally by Mr B whom he also had to fellate). In addition, there was severe physical maltreatment including being hit with belts and punched. The children were utterly convinced that they would be killed if they told anyone about this.

Perhaps a comment on the D family, the adoptive parents. Mr and Mrs D had been married for over 20 years and were in their 50s and 60s. It was a second marriage for both and there were children from the previous relationships. Over the years they had fostered and often adopted over 20 children, the majority from very terrible backgrounds. Family was important – there was little external socialising – and they lived in a large house in the countryside. Visiting professionals have unanimously praised the quality of care given to children and the progress they have made there.

Offences

Some three years after moving to live with the Ds, Martin began to set fires. He links this to having watched a firefighting demonstration just before his 11th birthday and thinking 'it would be fun' to see the real thing. Although there were four episodes with which he was to be charged, at least five occurred, the amount of risk to others increasing each time. After the first two fires – to clothes on a washing line and to a school – he thought that his family 'would dump me and not care about me. I was trying to get away from home and thought they would hurt me. They never had – though I lied to the police that Dad had hurt me.' In this conversation with Dr C, the exceptionally experienced Forensic Child and Adolescent Psychiatrist who prepared the court report, he added that he had set more fires 'because I'd ruined everything and I wanted to get away from home.' He had gone into locked placements, pending sentence, where he felt 'safe'.

The school had been empty, but Dr C was struck by Martin's persistence here and at a later fire – particularly for a child whose attention span was brief and whose distractibility was legend. The third fire was a summerhouse where again, after pampas grass and a sack of hay failed to ignite, he persisted until they did. He could see a rabbit and two guinea pigs in cages inside: the risk of harm is getting higher. The last two fires were in a porch where homeless people often slept and at a petrol station. Martin knew there was white spirit in the porch and had been told it could explode; the petrol station is sadly a magnified version of this escalation of severity.

Thinking about violence

Let's take a break to think about what the theory has to offer us here and the sense we can make of Martin's position.

Of prime importance is Mervin Glasser's concept of the 'core complex', the vicious circle in which there is a search for an idealised intimate narcissistic relationship. On gaining closeness, the attendant anxieties of merging and loss of identity, of being consumed, arise with fears of annihilation and the infant reacts with self-preservative aggression against this engulfing mother – violence in the service of protecting the ego. This soon results in a sense of isolation and fear of abandonment that, in turn, provokes the search for closeness – and the journey around the circle continues (Glasser 1996b). The violence in the Unit was an attack on a woman Martin was fond of and with whom he appeared to work particularly well. In the meeting with Martin, we will see attitudes to his adoptive mother that also recall core complex phenomena. If we think about the exacerbation of the incidents of arson, we have to note that Martin was then in a family where he had found a benign father to whom he was able, for the first time, to disclose his abuse. There was, in Martin, a capacity to hold on to hope in relation to men, despite his abuse by Mr B. We recall the summoning of the fire brigade in the Children's Home – the fireman with the hose, the phallic male who is creative and not abusive, who rescues rather than destroys. It seemed that Martin was able at that point to have a place in his father's mind – the necessary process of dis-identifying from the mother and being separate from her, aided by the father – but that this could not be sustained.

Interestingly, reports comment that Martin talks of his adoptive and his natural mother in a muddled, confusing way, conflating them (when distressed) seemingly into one malign maternal imago. *Any* key woman might then be drawn into being a part of this.

The laid back, big family may have enabled him to negotiate intimacy better than in a more intense nuclear family – but eventually the intimacy becomes too much. He seeks help – summons the firemen – firstly in a way that is less dangerous to others, then he has to up the ante to get any notice taken. Dr C noted in her report that he told her: 'I wanted to get into trouble – into a mixed load of trouble – I knew the police would be involved and a lot of other things – I felt that I needed to be away from home – that's exactly what I felt – I was fed up at the time, being around the house – it gets boring when you live there a long time'. It sounds very much as if the core complex issues were becoming too hard to manage and, I suspect, his father was probably not available as antidote to the internal devouring/abandoning mother. 'I kept saying, "Fire brigade, you're going to be out all day today!" as I was hiding in the bush': such a need of an all-day man who has Martin in mind. Without the antidote, identification with the aggressor (Freud 1936) perhaps becomes both a resolution and a fear. His internal fantasies of violence, in response to the core complex fear of loss of self, made him afraid and feel he had *already* 'ruined everything' – the thought was the deed. His arson was both a desperate search for help with his growing feelings of violence and a seeking of punishment as Freud describes (Freud 1916).

Glasser reminds us of the importance of the admixture of internal world, internalisations and real experience:

> A . . . shortcoming in many of the discussions of dangerousness is the absence of attention given to the contribution by the offender's inner world: a man's deprived background, his broken family, his violent parents and so on do not in themselves make him behave violently or in a sexually criminal way, although such factors may help both to structure his potential violence and to determine the triggers to his violent behaviour.
>
> (Glasser 1996a: 273)

Sinason has alerted us to the particular vulnerability of boys who are sexualised by their mothers (Sinason 1996). Martin was used – treated as a part object – by his mother with devastating impact on the essential development of the protective sense of shame (Campbell 1994). His vulnerability to the engulfing internal mother, and the split internal humiliating and abandoning mother, causes his acting out to be directed against women and it is the need for and dread of closeness to them that triggers his rush to violence. Verbal abuse, often with very sexually disparaging language, is a common way of Martin's expressing anxiety, but the symbolisation is not sufficient *when the anxiety is not recognised as such* – and he has to act.

The nature of the violence is also important. This – at present – is violence in the service of the protection of the ego, Glasser's self-preservative violence (Glasser 1998). One of the most helpful articles in this area is that by Marianne Parsons and Sira Dermen. The authors argue

> the limitations of an exclusive preoccupation with aggression in working with violent youngsters. We suggest instead that violence be understood as an attempted solution to a trauma the individual has not been able to process, and we define this trauma as helplessness in the absence of a protective object . . . . The youngster is both a perpetrator (in the external world and in his ideal image of himself) and also a victim (having been failed at a point of maximum helplessness and lacking an internalised protective membrane). He enacts this disjunction, causing harm to others and inviting punishment unconsciously from the law.
>
> (Parsons & Dermen 1999: 345)

The 'unprocessed trauma' is akin to Hyatt Williams' 'psychically indigestible experience' (Hyatt Williams 1997: 104) and Boswell (1997), in a review of children detained under section 53 of the Children & Young Persons Act 1933 (the legislation under which Martin was detained), found that 72 per cent had suffered abuse of some kind or kinds.

The unhooking of 'violence' and 'aggression' allows us to think of what might be helpful in therapy. When we think 'defence' and 'anxiety' we tend to find very different phrasing from when we think 'aggression' and 'attack'. That is not to argue for therapy here; simply to remind us that 'the appropriate therapy has to be directed to the neglected, defective side' (Freud 1947: 42). We are into the realm, then, of structuring and attention to the ego, as Anne Hurry has so well elaborated (Hurry 1998). As Parsons & Dermen add:

> The job of the child psychotherapist is to resist collusion either with the values of his ideal self (violence) or the demands of his harsh conscience (sadistic punishment); rather it is to understand his predicament, something he cannot do himself.
>
> (Parsons & Dermen 1999: 345)

The authors have found that this approach – and internal understanding on the part of the therapist – enables emotional contact with patients who 'find it singularly difficult to communicate effectively with others, or indeed with themselves, without resorting to violence' (*ibid.*).

When one thinks of trauma, deficit and lack of an internalised protective membrane, it gives one pause technically. Interpretations can be used to attack, retaliate, defeat and distance our patients as well as to heal. Edgcumbe is clear that interpretation alone is not sufficient for violent children (Edgcumbe 1971) and I find it encouraging that, at the Colloquium on Violence hosted by the Anna Freud Centre in 1995 (cf Perelberg 1995a) one workshop group raised the important question as to whether modification of classical technique was inevitable in work with violent patients. For those of us working already with that adaptation of classical technique that is Child Psychotherapy, flexibility perhaps comes with less questioning.

Recent and current functioning and further thoughts on theory

My colleague Dr D examined the Day Logs of the Unit and previous records while I met Martin. There she found a rather different picture from the 'out of the blue' description of Martin's attack on his worker. On arrival at the Centre, he had been placed in S Unit where he made some progress and seemed fairly settled. However, his peers here were older, and he resisted education. He was moved to T – the Unit on which the attack happened. There it was decided to engage him in work on his past abuse – despite clear warning in Dr C's court report that such work should only be done if Martin requested it, with staff whom he selected and at his pace. 'Life work' was also attempted. The records note incidents of verbal violence, then threats to other people; the threats became threats to kill. He began to talk about fires – he would hurt others or destroy property with fire. On one occasion when he had to be restrained, he was confined to his room. The knowledge that he had been locked in and abused by Mr B seemed to have been forgotten, as were the reports of his being locked in while awaiting sentence and urinating in and trashing his room. He destroyed walls, floors and carpets. Sexualised derogatory remarks to women followed and occasional kicks and punches at staff members. The attack with the plastic bat seemed the culmination of this. His victim was off work for a week and sustained quite serious injuries.

Transferred to a third unit, from his arrival there he had been thinking and speaking of hurting staff. An Art teacher in the Education block, with whom he had no current contact, reminded him of his father and he offered financial rewards to other young people if they harmed her. One-to-one special observation was instituted on a daily basis; Martin's activities and mobility were severely curtailed. During the period leading up to the assault Martin had attempted to secrete cutlery and to adapt furniture (which he had broken) into weapons. His threats to kill staff since then have been taken very seriously and reported to the police. He has also talked of sexually assaulting staff and spent long periods of time in the lavatory with pictures he had torn from a catalogue – pictures of knives and chainsaws. He was thought to masturbate to these. He talked of killing himself, cut himself superficially, pushed things into electrical sockets and threw water over the TV, hoping it would blow up and he would die.

It is not hard to see the serious decompensation resulting from Martin's being induced to recall and review the trauma and humiliation of his past. The tight regime led to some settling – for the month after the attack there was a violent incident each day. This settled during the following month with the close monitoring and lessened even more thereafter. Martin was allowed to choose who would monitor him as his escort each day and managed to develop a working relationship with Martina. Interestingly, the doctor who assessed him for the psychiatric in-patient unit felt that this increased his omnipotence and should be discontinued. Fortunately, the staff disagreed. His presentation to the psychiatrist had been remorseless and omnipotent; it seemed impossible to note the anxiety beneath it and recall the possible move from Townsville that was the reason for that interview.

When thinking of Martin and his masturbating to a catalogue, one concludes that the only position available to him at this lowest point appeared to be identification with objects of violence. He had become one too – the internal 'ideal image' as perpetrator mentioned by Parsons and Dermen (1999). In the Colloquium, the workshop group chaired by Veronica Mächtlinger and Marion Burgner offered a list of elements for conceptualising the descriptively violent individual: these included 'inability to feel human about the other and the self' (Perelberg 1995b: 165). Ferenczi first alerted us to this reaction to abuse: 'The [abused] child changes into a mechanical obedient automaton' (Ferenczi 1933: 163).

This is reminiscent of Cooper's comments on the core trauma in perversion and 'dehumanisation', which he defines as a strategy to protect against human qualities of loving, vulnerability and unpredictability: '... the core trauma in many if not all perversions is the experience of terrifying passivity in relation to the pre-oedipal mother perceived as dangerously malignant' (Cooper 1991: 23). Martin had just been reminded – in a persistent way – of the dangers and terror of feeling human. His violence had become something to cathect and to identify with. He was on the cusp of its becoming sadistic.

When thinking of his decompensating, one must also have in mind violence as a defence against psychosis and have grave concern as to his future.

Encountering Martin

Before arriving at Townsville, I had suggested that Martin be consulted as to whether we should meet alone or with a staff member whom he trusted. He had chosen Martina, his key worker who was also a group worker on his Unit. (I did wonder if Martina's groupwork role helped de-intensify her key worker role in Martin's mind.) Our meeting lasted just over 40 minutes. He had been aware of our arrival in the Centre and our presence on the Unit (we met with Martina and Dr A, the referring psychiatrist, initially before seeing Martin) and it is to his credit that he managed a meeting of this duration. We introduced ourselves so that he knew just who was where and when. He had been sedated – it emerged that this was the current way of coping with his destructiveness and a trial of anti-psychotic medication had been recommended by Dr C – and he asked Martina to stay with us when Dr D left with Dr A.

Martin chose to sit at the far end of a settee, nearest the door, on the arm of the settee, with Martina next to him. I was in a comfortable chair on the other side of Martina. Let me make a diversion. There is an interesting piece of 'Portman lore' – ideas refined over the years by the psychotherapists and psychoanalysts who work at the Portman Clinic with a patient group who are always difficult and often dangerous – that helps us think about danger. If a therapist is working with a violent patient, the tendency in many therapeutic settings is for the therapist to sit in the chair nearest to the door: if the situation feels unsafe, there is a quick exit for the therapist. Seemingly paradoxically, but actually faithful in psychoanalytic terms, Portman lore says that the psychotherapist should allow the patient the seat nearest to the exit. For most violent patients, the anxiety aroused by a suddenly perceived threat to the ego leads to a violent reaction in the service of protecting the ego (Glasser 1998). Having an exit available thus frees the patient *not* to have to attack, but to preserve the ego by escape. Martin was astute in his choice.

Needless to say, there was very little in the way of explicit information to be gained from this encounter but a great deal in terms of how Martin interacted with new people (especially those outwith his control and on whom he, in some sense, relied for the future).

He was able, in some detail, by talking to Martina but darting glances at me, to describe a crucial telephone call to his adoptive parents in which he had succeeded in letting them know that he did not wish contact at home at present. Martin spent some time on this and it became apparent that, in not wishing to go home, he was protecting both himself and his family from the possibilities of his violence. He had rehearsed saying 'No' with Martina who waited within earshot while he telephoned. The call had mainly gone well and his father had been sad but understanding. However, in the background his mother had constantly shouted that he should come home, saying how much they missed him and wanted to see him home. Martin had experienced this, in his words, as 'totally winding me up!' He was – to me in the recounting – verbally extremely abusive and denigrating of her, a verbal version of the violence. It hardly seemed the time for interpretations in the transference . . . I commented that he had managed to get his message heard and that his anger with his Mum really appeared to be about her not being able to hear him like his Dad had managed. He paused, and I got a glance – he did manage to hear the positive – then he turned back to Martina. I was struck that his mother's stance was about her needs and wishes while his father appeared to be able to hear Martin's needs.

Martin is said, in all reports, to lack concentration. In this meeting, he showed a very practised capacity to divert from the matter in hand by changing the subject or by affecting a state of not listening – almost a dissociated state – and then requesting that what had just been said be repeated. I could see how it could be enormously provocative and I am certain that, should he get a reaction, he would enjoy continuing to do it consciously. I simply survived it: I felt that, were I even to do one of my mild interjections ('You're very good at not hearing! That's important!') I would lose him. He was performing in my presence and I was the audience, but the performance was showing me how he kept himself safe in relation to his objects. Interestingly, it did not feel sadistic or aggressive and that arose from thinking 'defence' and not 'aggression'. Again, it was one of these behaviours on the cusp.

When talking about school, Martin took great pride in his ability in Maths. In this he likened himself to Martina and joshed her like an equal about it but also with pride in the identification. Such identifying removes difference, so removes separateness and danger. He liked the similarity of their names. He agreed when I said he might well feel at the mercy of the grown-ups, when he insisted in not knowing why I was there. Finally, he could not dare admit strong emotion. My comment about sadness at the closure of Townsville elicited a denial of ever feeling sad. It was not to deny any weakness; rather, a need to exclude affect or it would overwhelm.

Martin's identification with Martina might be seen as adhesive by some. It did not seem to me to be the deceptive 'simulation' Glasser has commented on (Glasser 1996a) nor yet to lie in the area of true/false self. Certainly, issues both of separateness and of intimacy were vital. I wonder if, in seeking the ideal almost merged relationship of Glasser's 'core complex' vicious circle (Glasser 1996b), one also needs to think about Martin seeking an idealised relationship as a way of ablating difference and separateness as the latter means harm and danger. Being the same also precludes the need for thinking – one knows because one is the same.

What psychoanalytic understanding specifically offers Martin and his carers

It is sometimes necessary to be made to experience what others experience to aid their belief that we do, in fact, comprehend it. It happens often with children and we are used, in the clinical situation, to putting this into words for them. Where events are overwhelming to the mature, professional adult, and when nothing seems to be available to dilute the intensity of the stressful experience, it is likely that whatever one offers will not suffice. With Martin, I think the process of dealing with *my* anxiety by planning a joint interview with Martina was important – for me, certainly, but also in modelling the necessity of taking on only what one could manage and still be able to think. Dr D's taking time to trawl through the Day Logs was similar – there *is* information to hand, but you need to be given time and develop procedures to collate it and put it in the context of the young person's history and trauma. Above all, having a perspective to *add* to the staff's understanding but not having *the* expert answer allowed us to join in thinking together and offer a report that summarised this reflection.

Finally, there is the initial matter of my reluctance to see Martin, enveloped in the question of an assessment too far or too intrusive. In work with violent young people, the counter-transference is a key tool and one finds this in most of the writing about technique. My counter-transference reaction was both the old-fashioned Freudian one of 'what belonged to me' (no, I don't want to be hit, and I don't know if I can manage this) and the Paula Heimann one of what is created by both analyst and patient together. When one thinks in this latter way, the emphasis moves from simply being what I feel *I* can manage to what Martin might feel *he* can manage in the face of *his* anxiety – hence offering him the choice of how we met. The shift is – as often in technique – from thinking 'attacking me' to 'anxious and needing to defend against me'. It matters.

Recommendations

When we provide recommendations it is, of course, important that these are clear, comprehensible and *can* be used and understood – they must have meaning to the recipients. The recommendations in Martin's case you may wish to discuss:

1   Martin will require a secure environment for several years to come. He is a risk to others and is likely to increase the behaviours that indicate he can be a risk to himself. [I make no apologies for being so blunt – dissembling is not clever in complex cases.]

2   The most dangerous points arise for Martin when he develops a relationship of closeness and intimacy with others – his arson attacks began when he was settled with his adoptive family and had a sense of wanting to escape this; his attack on a staff member occurred when a good, close relationship had been established. Staff will have to be aware of the risks in this – he has a need to protect himself, by violent means, from a sense of over-closeness, and is

trapped in a cycle of needing intimacy and then fearing the consequences of this – consequences that, in the past, have included losing his identity as a human little boy and being severely abused. It is important that staff have good consultation available to help them handle this aspect of Martin's functioning.

3   Offering programmes to explore his early experience is not wise – I note that Dr C in her report stressed that any such work should come at Martin's pace and follow his need to talk. I would agree very strongly with this. He has, so far, chosen two people to do this with – his adoptive father and his present key worker, Martina. He must not be pushed on this – the memories are overwhelming and humiliating and his only protection from these, at present, is violence. He will select his own person in his own time. Being available for this will be important, as will ensuring that the dangers of intimacy are recognised, catered for in the timing of sessions, and in having consultation available.

4   There must be a senior person holding an overview of Martin's functioning and a group aware of the detail of his day to day 'going on being', sharing information and responsibility. This is essential not only for Martin's progress but for staff safety. The overview should be in the context of Martin's history which should be known by staff – the escalation of violence in the past has both been predictable and is directly related to this.

5   Staff with whom Martin has developed a good relationship will need to keep alert to his feelings of abandonment at the closure of Townsville and his anger at this, and to the potential for his acting out these feelings against staff (especially women to whom he feels close), himself and property. His difficulty in expressing emotion must not lead to thinking that he has no feelings on the matter.

6   Therapy should be offered to Martin. This, however, should focus on the deficits in his psychological development and on strengthening his ego functioning or sense of self. It will be long and very slow! Flexibility in the therapist will be essential, as will flexibility about length of sessions, timing of sessions etc. Martin will need to be allowed to feel more in control of the pace, to feel safe enough about approaching emotions and emotional states. This should be discussed with him, otherwise he may turn it into a perverse control. A male therapist would be preferable.

7   Education has been a problem area for Martin. His lack of concentration is probably not due to any deficit (but I support Dr A and Dr C in their recommendations about a neurological examination: one would not wish to miss anything). Thinking is often, for young people like Martin, equated with remembering and flashback memories of childhood. He is overwhelmed by what comes into his mind and is therefore practised in 'switching off'. Approaches that offer desensitisation could be explored. In class, a focus on areas like Maths, computers and IT might help as he can deal more readily with material at an abstract level.

8   Martin's violence seems, from the records, to show a pattern of escalation – and this also happened with the arson attacks. Detailed notes on his emotional state need to be kept and any pattern spotted as early as possible, otherwise he ups the violence. When such behaviour is seen to be beginning, Martin should be helped to see that people recognise that he is *anxious* and that his anxiety is rising, and he should be involved in plans about what he feels would be helpful. It is important that, in alerting him to his changing anxiety level, care is taken not to humiliate him but to choose a form of words per-haps agreed in advance – a signal.

9   This links to his inability to recognise emotional states. At present strong feelings of any kind are experienced by him as simply overwhelming and his sole repertoire for dealing with them is to be violent, to protect himself from them. Slow work should be done on naming emotions – as one would with a toddler e.g. 'Gosh, that must have been annoying' or 'That was really pleasing' – as a first step in gaining control. Again, careful wording is needed. Feelings, if they cannot be named and recognised (and he has no way of rec-ognising feeling states until they become overwhelming) take on enormous and terrifying proportions and must then be decanted outside the self onto the outside world.

10 Martin has appreciated Martina's support in asking his family for some dis-tance at the moment. This is important, as it seems to be the first recognition that intimacy is a complex issue for him and the distance protects his family from his possible violence as a way of dealing with it. He also felt listened to in this. It is vital to keep in mind when thinking about family contact – we often assume contact is 'a good thing'. It is not necessarily so when close-ness is the issue that causes violence, and great care should be taken to listen to Martin. It is also important that his family is helped to understand this central, core complex issue: Martin's mother, in particular, should be given time to think through her strategy with him and how she can be caring but not consuming.

Conclusion

I am not proposing anything ground-breaking or novel here. It is a simple story about a very difficult boy and those who worry about and are burdened by his future. For many seemingly impossible children psychotherapy comes a long way down the list of interventions one might recommend – we can, at times, punish ourselves with a sense of omnipotence about our skills, a sense that we should be able to work with any kind of case. Other – especially at times more diluted – interventions may well be more appropriate choices in particular situations; but psychoanalysis has a huge amount to offer in *understanding* the origins of and approach to such behaviours, in consultation and the creation of space for thought and reflection. It is, in this, a prism for viewing the internal world and its impact on the external world that is second to none. And when we don't want to work with specific cases, and where it is because we cannot sustain a capacity for thought in the face of anxiety, we should give each other permission to take up a different role and view this as a creative response and not a failure.

The closure of Townsville, the last specialist centre, did happen. The new Youth Justice Board refused to purchase places in this establishment and the government's stance *before the consultation even began* was that local authority Social Services Departments were now well provided with secure accommodation and 'have become skilled and experienced in dealing with many young people needing secure care' (DoH 1999b). This ignored the announcement earlier in the year, by the DoH, of serious deficiencies in the first of the privately run Secure Training Centres (of which we now have four dealing with the under 17 age group under Home Office contract), focusing on problems in

a)   managing instances of bullying;
b)   managing suicide avoidance and self-harm prevention;
c)   maintaining good order;
d)   achieving satisfactory educational attainments;
e)   overcoming criminogenic attitudes and behaviours.

The need for better management to support a 'committed but largely inexperienced group of staff' was especially singled out in these deficiencies (DoH 1999a). It felt more than hypocritical to the experienced Townsville staff.

Current changes mooted in the youth justice sphere involve the development of a specialist staff working in juvenile establishments and able to move between custodial and community sectors – a welcome emphasis on the child as central and not the custodial task. For boys under 15 and girls under 17, Local Authority Secure Children's Homes and Secure Training Centres will be the primary establishments available and there is a plan to develop 'intensive fostering' (Youth Justice Board 2004:10). As a profession, we have already made good contacts with local authorities in relation to looked after children, adoption, fostering and Sure Start, and are attempting to have an impact on Youth Offending Teams and forensic services. We must remember that with secure facilities, too, we need to have a voice or Martin and other seriously troubled young people will be left to enact violence on those who seek closeness.

Notes

1 This paper was first given at the annual conference of the ACP in June 2005. It was published in 2009 in *Through Assessment to Consultation: Independent Psychoanalytic Approaches with Children and Adolescents* eds. A Horne & M Lanyado London & New York: Routledge.
2 A Conditional Discharge means that the offender must be of good behaviour for the time period set down (here 18 months). If he offends in any way during that period, he will be returned to Court where he will be sentenced for both the original and the new offences.
3 The Home Office is a ministerial department of Her Majesty's Government of the United Kingdom, responsible for immigration, security and law and order.

References

Boswell, G (1997) The backgrounds of violent young offenders: the present picture. In V Varma (ed.) *Violence in Children and Adolescents* London: Jessica Kingsley

Campbell, D (1994) Breaching the shame shield: thoughts on the assessment of adolescent sexual abusers *Journal of Child Psychotherapy* 20(3): 309–326

Cooper, AM (1991) The unconscious core of perversion. In G Fogel & W Myers (eds.) *Perversions and Near-Perversions in Clinical Practice – New Psychoanalytic Perspectives* New Haven & London: Yale University Press

Department of Health (1999a) Report calls for action to improve conditions at Medway Secure Training Centre DoH press release 1999/0027

Department of Health (1999b) Future plans for [Townsville] Youth Treatment Centre DoH press release

Edgcumbe, R (1971) A consideration of the meaning of certain types of aggressive behaviour *British Journal of Medical Psychology* 44(4): 373–378

Ferenczi, S (1933) On the confusion of tongues between adults and the child. *Final Contributions to the Problems and Methods of Psychoanalysis* New York: Basic Books 1955

Freud, A (1936) Identification with the aggressor. In *The Ego and the Mechanisms of Defence* London: Hogarth Press 1968

Freud, A (1947) Aggression in relation to emotional development: normal and pathological *The Psychoanalytic Study of the Child* Vol. 3–4 New York: International Universities Press

Freud, S (1916) Some character types met with in psychoanalytic work III Criminals from a sense of guilt *SE* 14 London: Hogarth Press

Glasser, M (1996a) The assessment and management of dangerousness: the psychoanalytical contribution *Journal of Forensic Psychiatry* 7(2): 271–283

Glasser, M (1996b) Aggression and sadism in the perversions. In I Rosen (ed.) *Sexual Deviation* 3rd edition Oxford: Oxford University Press

Glasser, M (1998) On violence: a preliminary communication *International Journal of Psychoanalysis* 79(5): 887–902

Hurry, A (1998) *Psychoanalysis and Developmental Therapy* London: Karnac

Hyatt Williams, A (1997) Violence in adolescence. In V Varma (ed.) *Violence in Children and Adolescents* London: Jessica Kingsley

Parsons, M & Dermen, S (1999) The violent child and adolescent. In M Lanyado & A Horne (eds.) *The Handbook of Child and Adolescent Psychotherapy: Psychoanalytic Approaches* London: Routledge

Perelberg, RJ (1995a) Violence in children and young adults: a review of the literature and some new formulations *Bulletin of the Anna Freud Centre* 18: 89–122

Perelberg, RJ (1995b) Report on the Colloquium *Bulletin of the Anna Freud Centre* 18: 165–167

Sinason, V (1996) From abused to abusing. In C Cordess & M Cox (eds.) *Forensic Psychotherapy: Crime, Psychodynamics and the Offender Patient* Vol. II: *Mainly Practice* London: Jessica Kingsley

Youth Justice Board (2004) *Strategy for the Secure Estate of Juveniles: Building on the Foundations* London: Youth Justice Board for England & Wales

6   Entertaining the body in mind

Thoughts on incest, the body, sexuality and the self[1]

To begin at the beginning ...

There had been several years of concern about the Long family. Mrs Long, whose first marriage had been to an older, cruel, violent and sexually abusive man, had a son (Robert) from that marriage. It was suspected – indeed, disclosed by Robert then retracted – that Mrs Long had sexually abused him and it also seemed to be a matter of local knowledge that, following the death of her husband, she had frequently entertained a group of young adolescent boys in her house. The first contact the clinic had with the family was a consultation about Robert whose compulsive sexualised actions had become extremely hard for his care staff and social worker to manage and understand.

Married again – to a man of her own age who, like her, had learning difficulties – Mrs Long had two further children and was pregnant with a third when *she* was referred. The assessment led the diagnostician to conclude that psychotherapy for Mrs Long was not at that point a treatment of choice; however, the first child of this second marriage, Katiebelle, had begun to act in a sexually inappropriate way with her younger brother, being compelled to intrude repeatedly into his bedroom in the middle of the night for this sexual encounter, and a referral was made in relation to this. She had learning difficulties – global developmental delay, functioning on the 1st centile – was encopretic, still in nappies at night, neglected and waif-like.

Katiebelle had been sexually abused from the age of 18 months by Robert, then 14. The abuse ceased when he was finally taken into care, some two years on, although his mother remained unable (some thought unwilling) to keep him apart from her other children. Katiebelle came for her assessment a week after her seventh birthday. I saw her weekly in therapy for over seven years.

Introduction

I would like to explore several themes in this paper with the help of Katiebelle:

a)   the child and young person's relationship with the body, especially how this is integrated into the psychological sense of self, notably when it carries damage. Winnicott's term 'personalisation' is of help here (Winnicott 1945,

1949, 1972), a term he devised to counterpoint the defensive position of depersonalisation, as a positive developmental form:

> The term *personalization* was intended to draw attention to the fact that the in-dwelling of this other part of the personality in the body, and its firm link with whatever is there which we call psyche, in developmental terms represents an achievement in health.
>
> (Winnicott 1972:7)

A little further on he simplifies: 'personalization' is 'an in-dwelling of psyche in soma' (Winnicott 1972: 10).

One interest, therefore, is the developmental process while being aware of the insult to it. If the mind is extant throughout the body as Gaddini reminds us (Gaddini 1980), then the body becomes complicit in the inability of the traumatised child to process what has been overwhelming to the immature ego and complicit in the mind's constant state of alertness to intrusion of memory or re-enactment of the trauma. For Katiebelle, the 'S word' ('sex') constantly lurked, awaiting an opportunity to bound into her mind, and had to be kept at bay. Indeed, I would posit that the body itself merely functions and 'is'; it is to be *not* thought about at all times. Part of the therapeutic process is to enable the child to entertain the body in mind, to have a body image and a concept of body in which she then can belong.

b)   the child – and the body and sexuality of the child – in the eye and the mind of the mother, especially when there has been an incestuous relationship. The meaning of this in the therapy – how it emerges and how progress is gained – has an impact on our technical approach.

c)   sexuality. I take the view that infantile sexuality is proto-sexuality, the capacity for passionate, sensuous and wholehearted relationships with both sexes, but is a long way away from adult sexuality. Indeed, we must learn greater exactness in our use of concepts in relation to the developing child to ensure that we simply do not elide the one idea to take on equivalence to the other. The intrusion of adult – and perverse – sexuality has to be considered in relation to the nature of the trauma and the defences engaged against this; to the developmental thrust (in Winnicott's terms 'the general inherited tendency that the child has towards integration', Winnicott 1945: 8) that is halted or diverted; to the developmental stage of the child at the time of the trauma; and to the capacity to regain a pathway to 'normal' development – of which sexuality is a part.

It is not unusual for child and adolescent psychotherapists to work with children where sexual abuse has been an element in their very early childhood: indeed, it is all too common a feature of the work. Less frequently, we engage with children and young people who are driven to enact past abusive and sexually abusive experiences, or to decant the anxiety and shame arising from their memories of such events onto others. This repetition-compulsion, identifying with the aggressor in order to relieve one's mind and body of memories of humiliation and victimisation, arrives in the consulting room in a variety of ways – invitation to abuse, seductive overtures, perversion of normal verbal intercourse and terror of a potentially abusive object. Of course, sometimes sexuality makes its way into the consulting room and is prominent in its absence but with our awareness of the 'shadow of the object' (Bollas 1987) in the counter-transference.

Katiebelle arrives

A tall, extremely thin, fey looking child sat apart from her heavily pregnant mother in the waiting room. She had fine, mousey brown hair and a tremendous sense of lightness about her as if somehow she was not certain about having substance. Her grubby NHS spectacles sat aslant her face and were held together with elastoplast. Nevertheless, she placed herself before me as I introduced myself to both and stared, head on one side, with very direct curiosity. She hesitated as we came down into my basement room – possibly the due anxiety one would expect at a first encounter but I felt it more to be an uncertainty about what one did. Very soon the session theme of 'how do you get things right?' emerged. Already, it seemed, there was a child who was concerned about the state of mind of the object rather than in any way egocentric.

Katiebelle flitted carefully around the room as if she could not bear to stop and settle to play with any one thing there. I showed her the locker that would be hers with bits and pieces in it – the usual 'kit' of paper, felt pens, sellotape, scissors, string, a small doll family, a few farm and wild animals. She was overwhelmed that something had been done with her in mind, that the adult might anticipate her presence. I was reminded of Anne Alvarez's injunction that the good experience can be as overwhelming as the traumatic one and require time to recover in order to integrate it (Alvarez 1988). She stood in the middle of the room and looked at me. She offered that she was wearing a sweatshirt that she liked. It was a nice sweatshirt, very well washed and rather aged. We were wearing similar colours. She came across to me and compared the tones, then beamed. This seemed to give her the courage to explore. While placing people in the dolls' house, she was insistent that the parents shared a bedroom but then she seemed a little uncertain about the children sharing a room. I said, with the referral in mind, that she might be finding it awkward when people shared but she did not respond. Finally, she drew and volunteered to draw me. The picture was exceptionally primitive. A circle represented the head and she added two eyes and a smiling mouth. Two long lines came down from this, each ending in a foot. Somewhere in the middle she drew a circle. I was just beginning to feel a sense of relief that it might be a body representation when she said informatively, 'That's the belly button!' Looking at me quite carefully, she added, 'I think I'll give you arms.' This small sign of hope felt hugely affecting in the counter-transference. At times she drifted into another place in her mind, coming back and reminding herself where she was. We talked of her possibly coming every week – a radical but entertaining idea – and she asked about the time, how to know how long we had, packing up when the big hand on the clock reached 10. In the waiting room her mother sat eating biscuits and drinking cola, wearing a huge pair of headphones. She shrieked at Katiebelle who stood like an arthritic crane in front of her, forearms and hands twisted together and one leg wrapped around the other.

In the second assessment session Katiebelle came cautiously downstairs with me. She showed great anxiety, questioning 'Are these your stairs?' 'Is that your kitchen?' She seemed to recognise nothing. I gently drew her attention to her locker and the pictures she had drawn. There were instances when she stood in bizarre, contorted postures, as if the awkwardness of the body position was an attempt to contain anxiety and the discomfort served to remind her of her exist-ence. She peered in the dolls' house, returned to the table and, about 10 or 15 minutes into the session, suddenly looked straight at me and said, 'You're *Ann* – I *know* who you are!' It felt once more that she'd had no expectation of a reliable, attentive object: Katiebelle thus struggles to gain any sense of herself, or of the self reflected back from the object, from any of her adults.

In brief, the session was not unlike the previous one, flitting and alighting briefly, living in the moment with no sense of continuity and little sense of 'going-on-being'. I made simple connections and at one point she darted to me, hugged me and drifted off once more. She did ask to go to the lavatory where I waited for her outside a little way off. The odour that accompanied her back to the room made me wonder about her encopresis and its relation to anxiety and abuse. I was left feeling that this child was like a series of atolls surrounded by sea, not joined. There was some glimmer of hope about attachment – the com-parison of our clothing, the eventual delighted memory of her previous session, her sense of pride when I noticed her good efforts and that she could consider that arms could be a good thing. At the end her mother was very ambivalent about returning which made Katiebelle come very close to me, lifting her head with her lips puckered, silently asking for a goodbye kiss. The discomfort of this episode lay not in the refusal but in her need for a sexualised approach to mitigate a crisis.

Thinking about Katiebelle's arrival

In initial sessions the themes of a whole analysis are often suggested. This was no exception. The issues that preoccupied her, the meaning of her objects in her internal world, the defences available to her, despite our apparent paucity of con-versation, were there in outline. Her preoccupation with her compulsion to abuse – and the great difficulty in thinking about this giving rise to primitive defensive manoeuvres of denying, ignoring; her constant attendance to the object and how to be acceptable to this, indicative of the lack of any internalised capacity to think of herself as tolerable and the lack of a good-enough reflection of the self back to the child; the absence of any sense of substance and any sense of 'going-on-being'; the immaturity of representations of the body; dissociation and 'switching off' as a way of dealing with the possibility of stress; the good experience as a source of engulfment; the use of sexualisation as a way of gaining mastery over anxiety – all were there.

One could also begin to create a theoretical frame – find the theoretical bricks that would enable us to assemble an understanding of her experience and the internal sense she made of it. In this we think of the child as a part-object to the mother, not a sentient being with integrity and individuality, and recall Estela Welldon's formulation of the perverse female who turns inwards, to the body and the body products, in her annihilation of *her* internal, abusing mother (Welldon 1988). For the child of such a parent one revisits Winnicott's comments on the development of the self:

> The self essentially recognises itself in the eyes and facial expression of the mother and in the mirror which can come to represent the mother's face. Eventually the self arrives at a significant relationship between the child and the sum of the identifications which (after enough incorporation and introjection of mental representations) become organised in the shape of the internal psychic reality.
>
> (Winnicott 1972: 16)

We recall Mrs Long, headphones firmly attached, mouth filled with biscuits. Winnicott goes on to emphasise the role of parental expectations in modifying the emerging self – and we recall Mrs Long's ambivalence about her daughter, her exposing her to the son whom she had abused. In therapy, throughout the first months Katiebelle played very repetitively at hide and seek, longing and not longing to be found. In the counter-transference, hunting behind chairs, under the couch and in her favourite place beneath my desk (from which I often thought she emerged, brought into life, into a world where she was able to be perceived differently from the reflection she saw in her mother's gaze) I felt she was revisiting the dangerous drama of being found by her abuser. Heightened anxiety and adrenaline rush repeated the prefatory body sensations of her infant self. Interpretation centred on the fear that I might be abusive, the wish that this now might be different, and the need constantly to repeat the good experience of being found by a good-enough object. As with a small child, the emphasis was on the joy of finding – '*There* you are! How awful it felt not to find and see you!' – and the process of internalising a normal developmental engagement between adult and child. It is such a developmental achievement to know one can make the object pursue and seek one; how much more so when that object can also begin to be internalised as 'benign'.

Who the child is in the eyes of the incestuous and incest-permitting mother and of the incestuous partner becomes an important question. The absence of any stage of primary narcissism must be part of our construct – there is no experience of the omnipotence that should be part of normal development. Nor is there the straightforward affirmation through gaze between mother and baby:

> Of course, the baby does see the mother's smiling face, but this, which is in reality her response to his smiles, reflects back to him his own aliveness: 'The mother is looking at the baby and what she looks like is related to what she sees there' (Winnicott 1967: 112).
>
> (Wright 1991: 12)

Dio Bleichmar emphasises the look of the seducer which 'inhabits the body' and results in an absence of any safe or secret place: looking 'in the mirror or when she bathes, there is always another detached pair of eyes looking at her body through her own "sexualised" eyes' (Dio Bleichmar 1995). There appears to be little respite from the internalised view of the object – and dissociation (used often by Katiebelle in our early days) would seem an obvious defence against exposure and the absence of privacy. Indeed, we should also consider the impact of the loss of shame as a protective function in development.

The very young child is body-centred; the first ego is a body ego.

> Experiences of being-next-to or being-in, characterised by softness and continuity, give rise to what Winnicott describes as going-on-being ... The lack of such experiences, or the experience of impingements at skin level, threaten the infant/child with a feeling of annihilation
>
> (Grand & Alpert 1993: 332)

This body, Krueger reminds us, 'is often the narrator of feelings [patients] cannot bear to hold in conscious thought, much less express in words' (Krueger 2001: 239). Laufer develops this a little farther: 'Within such a safe space the infant can begin to feel its own body as having the capacity to protect itself from the "bad" experiences intruding into its own body ego boundaries' (Laufer 1991: 63). She finds that the risk inherent in the distorted body image – the mental representation of the body – lies in that 'it forms a psychotic core to the personality in that it must affect the person's relationship to external reality' (Laufer: 1991: 71). Entertaining the body in mind thus becomes of the essence.

Given Katiebelle's family history, it is not surprising that I had Fairbairn in mind. As the Independents emphasise, the drive of the child is towards relationships. In Fairbairn's construct, the child will split off the bad parent in an attempt to hold on to an illusory good parent, in the process defining herself as bad, rather than risk loss of the object (Fairbairn 1952). The process of the therapy, then, with luck enables the child to find and perceive herself to be motherable.

Finally, there is the place of identification with the mother and 'how the mother responds to her daughter's sexuality is of crucial importance for the girl's future relationships' (Klockars & Sirola 2001: 233). Mrs Long's attitude to Katiebelle's body and sexuality was perverse. The child was treated as a part-object, not a separate human being who might be seen as such, and that part-object was offered for abuse to the already abused son. Reliant on the early body-self, Katiebelle then evacuated the humiliating memory of abuse onto her little brother via the body. Thought plays no part in such an early process. Developmentally, there is still a struggle to establish an ego ideal, this being dependent on the objects available, and the role of shame in that process is important. Don Campbell reminds us of the protective function of shame – it takes us out of humiliating situations when, for example, we cover our faces, and once more it is about 'seeing' and 'being seen' – and he points to the absence of this protective shield in abused and abusing young people (Campbell 1994). Katiebelle could not bear to talk of her body, what it got up to, nor the overdetermined 'S' word, for many months, such was the shame she felt. Oedipal resolutions – far ahead in psychological development – are thus unsurprisingly few with abused children like Katiebelle and identification with such a mother as Mrs Long – part of the normal oedipal resolution – also carries its complexities.

Reflecting on technique after the assessment: 'first you have to build the house'

Winnicott's comment that 'there are no brakes on fantasy' (1945: 153) always comes to mind when I think of Katiebelle, and reminds me of the tricycle I was much attached to when I was 3, a hand-me-down from my big brother. The pedals were built into the front wheel. There were no brakes – to brake, you had to keep your feet firmly on the pedals and stop pedalling, very difficult to achieve when you were speeding downhill. Fortunately – perhaps – I lived in a small village with little traffic. But it required an active *not-doing* and a resistance to *doing*. For the child whose immature ego has been overwhelmed by invasive trauma, there are no brakes on memory or fantasy – indeed, the fantasy of assaulting another child comes hard on the heels of the intrusion of memory with its attendants, humiliation and shame. It operates equally outwith control. One aim is thus to interpose 'thought' between 'fantasy' and the compulsion to act. Thought becomes the equivalent of 'not-pedalling', enabling 'not-doing'.

For Katiebelle, this would be part of the therapeutic process, but it was evident from these sessions that the earlier stage of recognising emotional states would be the first essential, before she would be able to think about such states and gain some control over action. This takes us into the arena of fluid and sensitive interaction between a developmental stance and an interpretative, analytic stance – work on the lines of Anne Hurry's 'developmental psychotherapy' (Hurry 1998). Where the capacities for thought, curiosity, feeling and emotion are limited, whether this be due to conflict (when it appears as a primitive defence) or deficit, 'the analyst's task is to engage inhibited or underdeveloped processes within the analytic encounter' (Hurry 1998: 67). And technically ' . . . it is important that the analyst be prepared to move between the developmental/relational stance and the interpretative, as Anna Freud described. . . . Both developmental relating and understanding are necessary; each can potentiate and reinforce the effects of the other' (Hurry 1998: 71–72).

Hurry's concept of the analyst as '*developmental* object' was to be important in work with Katiebelle. Recognising and naming affects was a large part of the early sessions – 'Gosh! That was a good goal! You must have felt really pleased!' or equally: 'Ouch! That was a sore kick. I think your foot was feeling terribly annoyed with me!' and the emotional states were named before they could be explored.

As a corollary of this, the therapist has a difficult task with the child whose thinking is still concrete: to talk of what might be in mind can be to seem to give it actuality. In situations like this, work in the displacement gives access to externalised affects and defences. It is, as Anna Freud said, 'a way of approaching threatening mental content gradually' (Sandler, Kennedy & Tyson 1980: 165). So we played with the doll families, and reflected on their experiences, thoughts and feelings, until Katiebelle herself could say, 'I feel . . . '

Every abused child is hyper-sensitive to the actions and intentions of the object. This requires the therapist's acute awareness of issues of intimacy and distance, what can be verbalised, what is likely to be experienced as intrusion – and, as Khan reminds us, for the child traumatised early, there is no internalised protective sense and later impingements may well take on traumatic proportions (Khan 1963). Intimacy becomes a key therapeutic issue. Indeed, I often find myself waiting when a new child comes for therapy to see where he/she will sit – or I say that I am going to sit over there, by the window, away from the door, leaving a good space in which the child may feel safer. I have found this initial process of finding a manageable distance to be the first indication in the counter-transference of traumatic intrusion and psychological safety. With children where a sense of hope may still lurk, the core complex difficulties with intimacy, obliteration, rage and abandonment are all too readily summoned (Glasser 1996).

Equally, there is the role of hate and the impact of this in the counter-transference. Reading Winnicott is essential:

> . . . an analyst . . . must be able to be so thoroughly aware of the countertransference that he can sort out and study his *objective* reactions to the patient. These will include hate. Countertransference phenomena will at times be the important things in the analysis.
>
> (Winnicott 1947: 195)

> Sentimentality is useless . . . as it contains a denial of hate.
>
> (*ibid.*: 202)

In this paper, Winnicott also alerts us to the need for us to hold on to our experience of hating – for some patients, there comes a point when the process can be discussed; for others it cannot as 'there may be too little good experience in the patient's past to work on' (*ibid.*: 198). Therapy then becomes even more a parallel expression of the 'good-enough' experience.

Four years on

In the clinic where I saw Katiebelle, one had permission to engage in treatment for four years, after which the therapist presents the work to the clinic team for joint consideration of 'what next?' There had been times in the four years when I had discussed Katiebelle at clinical meetings – the staff group was not unacquainted with her and had been enormously enriching of the therapy in the understanding they offered. During the four years Katiebelle shifted from dealing with her object through activity although her bizarre poses took a little time to be abandoned and she would run and climb around the room. Her encopresis, after one dreadful session when it was combined with car-sickness, slowly vanished, seemingly in parallel with a capacity to contain – contain feelings and think about them, contain body products and contain the impulse to enact her abuse. Gradually games of hide and seek were initiated by her, controlling finding and being found, and helping the internalisation of an object who would seek her at her own pace. Those who have read Juliet Hopkins' paper about Paddy, supervised by Winnicott, will recall the slow ego-structuring work necessary before the child can face conflict and conflictual feelings (Hopkins 1996). Katiebelle tried out ego strengths and competencies, especially rehearsing with the body in physical struggles at football and rounders where she had enormous determination and persistence. In this, there was a gradual sense of integration, a body that could function as a whole. This integration was aided by her respite carer who taught her basic hygiene and self-care and who dressed her appropriately – very different from the often dirty clothes provided by her mother. Splitting off her body for our joint consideration allowed it to begin to be entertained in mind: 'Wasn't that interesting what your body did!' encourages the thinking part of the child to ally with the therapist and thus both can observe together the infantile part. She allowed curiosity about me to emerge in endless games of 'school' where I was often set the writing topic of 'What I did at the weekend'. For a spell, she would leap onto the couch and sing, and a strong, deep tuneful voice emanated from this slight body, as if she had a total sense of self-in-body while singing. Experiences of being bullied were mastered in games of Ludo where her generosity in helping me was matched by her aggressive attacks and humiliation of the other two players, in fantasy her two persecutors in school.

Importantly, Katiebelle got in touch with anger, aggression and hate. Ludo could equally be an arena for wiping out my pieces, relishing sending them back to the start. At times, this felt like appropriate rehearsal of the aggression that becomes agency and potency; at others it was deliberately controlling and bloody-minded. The counter-transference gave the clue as to which. Waiting while she took turn after turn, manipulating the dice until she threw a 6, I could feel distressed for her but equally there were many times when I felt furious, frustrated and excluded. This extended to the clinic environment. Katiebelle had noticed that, if she lingered on her arrival at the top of the stairs, a teaching group would emerge at the bottom from the room next to mine. Arms across the stairwell from wall to wall, she chose her moment to declare loudly, 'I'm coming DOWN!' and watched the adults retreat, leaving her triumphal pathway clear. Endings of sessions could be times of high anxiety, delaying, panic and opposition. Despite always having warning of the advent of the end of our appointment time, Katiebelle often tore around the room, desperately seeking something to take with her, at times shouting and swearing at the top of her voice in order to let any colleagues know how bad a therapist she felt me to be. For most of the therapy, I dreaded such endings. Although practical steps guaranteed some containment (I ensured that the next appointment was always 20 minutes after Katiebelle, giving time to focus on the ending, to tidy the room – often in chaos – and for my recovery) I knew that in my counter-transference being available to the degree of fury and despair that she felt would mean that I would be drained at the end. Surviving this mattered; resilience in the therapist (who does need ways of becoming available to the next patient) depends greatly on the availability of listening, thinking colleagues and one wise colleague often came to my room after Katiebelle's session offering coffee and a processing ear. All therapists have to survive and still think, even when the thought is about the inability to think.

Her abuse emerged from time to time, as much as she felt she could deal with, and we thought together about Robert's abusing her in the bath – being regularly sent by their mother to bathe Katiebelle – and about her body's memories of this resulting in its trying to do the same to her little brother. She was overwhelmed at the idea that one could explain why she behaved in this way and it led her to develop the concept of her mind as a third person in the room (as I had with her body): 'My brain tells me this . . . ' became a useful introduction to themes that might have felt infantilising or shameful.

Equally her greater certainty in relationships had led to her telling me that she had a boyfriend, Ruben, who was 'Nice. He helps me in class and gives me answers.' This was minus any sexual overlay, a very latency relationship. That session continued with 'What I did at the weekend' written by Katiebelle and illustrated with a drawing of her playing football in the park with another girl. Katiebelle explained that the circle in their middles was a belly button. She thought that other people had them – but perhaps they didn't. I thought that bodies and differences were in her mind today. 'Do you have one as well?' I said that she was thinking about other bodies, about what everybody had and about differences between bodies, especially my grown-up body and her girl's one. 'I'm thinking about sex now.' I wondered what she might be thinking about, but she drank her cola silently, big-eyed, looking at me. I said that sex had jumped into her mind again with the talk about bodies and belly buttons. She laughed. She shouted 'Freeze!' in a loud, harsh voice. 'On you go – you're the teacher – you say "Freeze!"' I said that the teacher didn't seem sure about the muddle about bodies, other bodies and sexy thoughts. 'Go on, *freeze!*' I said that she wanted me to stop thinking about the worrying thoughts about sex, and how these can still pop with surprise into her mind, so she was freezing them out.

This led her to remember her respite carer and she told me that she didn't see her any more. I wondered about that. She said that her Mum hated Irene and had an argument with her. I said that must be extremely difficult for Katiebelle when grown-ups don't get on and make muddles for children. 'I hate Mum.' There was a pause, a sense of shocking despair. I offered that it was hard to love *and* hate people – like she hated me when she thought about breaks and holiday times. She looked at our calendar: we were approaching the Christmas break. 'Christmas Day. I couldn't come here on Christmas Day! Ho, ho, ho.' I agreed but added that sometimes we wished we could. She stared and nodded. I said she was thinking about losses today and how angry they can make us feel.

The clinic team supported continuing work with Katiebelle until she had achieved puberty, anticipating that the advent of potent sexuality might well be a source of conflict for her.

The last years

During these next three-plus years, Katiebelle became, at her own instigation, Kate.

Finally, her social worker accommodated her following grave concern about her mother's neglect and her incapacity to cope with an adolescent whom she, ever more strongly, saw as a sexual rival and with whom she engaged in adolescent fights. Kate moved into a permanent foster home where the foster mother was older, a grandmother, and in her age easier for Kate to love without fear of hurting her mother. Kate also made her transfer to a mainstream secondary school with good special needs staff, such was the improvement in her functioning.

This led to two important sessions:

> Kate, almost 12 years old, in foster care with access visits home, played at 'parents and children' – several games, all involving the life-size baby doll. The theme was giving birth to a baby – a fairly straightforward and untraumatic event as she played it – followed by 'how to grow it properly'. She fed and changed it, then settled it carefully to sleep. The mother became ill, had to go into hospital, and the father had the dual worry of being with his wife but also needing to care for the baby. How could these two demands be resolved – does father choose wife or child? That both could be managed was what she sought. In the next session the extended theme was clearly 'How to be a good parent' with the emphasis on which needs of the parents would be forced upon the baby. The baby was dealt with rather roughly as father and mother wanted 'to cuddle'. Father tried to get mother to put the baby down. 'He wants to sex her,' said Kate flatly. I wondered what the baby was thinking. Kate looked startled that the baby might have an opinion that could be solicited or inferred. She began to play out both parents trying to have intercourse and the baby being squashed, in the way or otherwise a nuisance. As she looked at me for a reaction I felt I was being asked to intervene: perhaps the baby would be better in her room, sleeping, and the adults could keep grown-up sexy things just for the grown-ups? She nodded. The baby was settled elsewhere. Darkly, she told me that she hated hearing her parents 'sexing'. Then – 'And I wish they wouldn't go into my bedroom to do it!' This was said very seriously and despairingly. I commented that she had been thinking a lot about what was grown-ups' business and what children weren't ready to know about yet. 'Yes.'

Later, in school it emerged that Kate had made threats to harm herself and the staff were worried. She entered a group programme of Drama Therapy – which she enjoyed – and in the setting of this could explore issues around adolescence and relationships. One could say that Kate was still articulating distress through the body (the threat had come on the heels of her mother's insisting that Kate should return home, an eventually ineffectual insistence) but at least one could point to her talking of what her feelings were impelling rather than acting it out.

Endings

My informing Kate of my retirement had been delayed for several months by the onset of her menstrual periods. I did not want the potential for her as a woman to become aligned with my perceived rejection in ending. When finally I told Kate that we would be stopping work in 9 months' time, she gave an anguished whisper, 'But you *know* me!' She tore off to the lavatory. I felt utterly hopeless and inept. On her return she told me that she had been upset in the toilet. I had a small sense of relief at the maintenance of her capacity for verbalising emotional states. It was not surprising that she began to wonder in subsequent meetings if I had become an abuser, too. (In a sense, I had.) The story of a man who wished to be her boyfriend emerged. He pursued her home. He was her brother. He was everywhere. He was her husband. He would break in – how on earth could she be safe? The tenor was of terrifying fear of rape; thought had become impossible – panic reigned. Words, for several weeks, could not be heard when this theme came into her mind. It felt to me like a film without sound where little was delineated and the depiction was dark and unformed; and Katiebelle had lost any expectation of a listener able to hear, think and begin to process such deep anxiety. Interpretation, when it became possible, was of me as the man, my seduction of her, my abuse of her sense of hope and intimacy, my abandonment of her. The strength of the primitive affect was more than startling; delusion and reality together informed an almost psychotic fantasy. The marked difference was that she could actually attempt to articulate it: somewhere in her mind there *was* the concept of an object who heard even while she thought she could not imagine such a person.

The theme of changing, potent, sexual bodies continued in a later session as she let me know, with her back to me, that she was going shopping for a sports bra with her foster mother. After a pause she said in a low voice that it was because she was being teased in school. I wondered aloud about this – it sounded as if the other girls might be teasing her about her breasts because theirs hadn't grown much yet. Maybe they were jealous that she needed a sports bra. Kate slowly turned round and stared at me. A grin appeared and grew wider.

There was much repetition of earlier play – recapitulation is quite usual in child work. This included 'Do you remember when I did singing?' She leaped on to the couch to sing as she had when a lightweight 7-year-old. The leg of the elderly couch gave way. My counter-transference feelings were mainly bound up with the couch. 'Do you remember when . . . ?' frequently appears in normal parent-child interaction and is part of the process of internalising a sense of going-on-being. There was more work on the intrusion of her memory. 'I'm thinking the S word again!' 'And I notice that you can think about it and not have to do something!' She nodded seriously – 'Yes, I don't *do* things any more.'

In one session she noticed my hands. A finger came out and almost prodded them but drew back – the loss of elasticity in the skin was evident and she knew of my retirement. 'Yuck! You're OLD!' It was as if in this moment she realised that I had changed – not into an abuser but simply old. This was a new adaptation and an appropriate use of aggression in separation. It allowed her distance, while dealing a small blow to my narcissism.

Endings of sessions, while still fraught, became different in two ways. First, Kate had become able to articulate her feelings of let-down and anger, along with her occasional wish to STOP NOW (shouted at me) as a way of dealing with the pain of ending. She no longer resorted to the frantic use of her body, rushing around and hiding. In addition, she developed a ritual for ascending the stairs at the end, the two of us side by side like a three-legged race, and Kate stretching over two then three then four and more steps with each pace. It was a laborious ascent that allowed her the physical contact of leaning on my arm as she demonstrated her physical growth and capacities and allowed her to triumph over me as she became the competent one. Colleagues would often encounter this somewhat bizarre sight and would wait until we made it to the top.

Towards the end, during one session she walked slowly up to the door. My raincoat hung on the hook. There was a long mirror on the wall to the left of it. She reached out – again slowly as if ready to comply with any prohibition. I watched, not feeling any aggression in this move. She put on the coat. It fitted her perfectly at age 14½. She struggled to fasten the belt but persisted – her own containment – and looked in the mirror. We both felt great sadness. I found myself unable to speak, tears in my eyes. When I could find words, I commented that she was trying out being me and having me wrapped around her in that way; perhaps, though, we both would miss each other but have each other inside our minds.

Conclusion

Technically, the work could be said to have depended mainly on an approach that owed much to Anna Freud and to Winnicott. One can see the adoption of a very Winnicottian position – beginning with the mother who survives the infant's aggression and continuing to the resilient but containing environment he describes especially in work with delinquents. The parallels between the process of therapy and the process of the good-enough developmental experience are evident. Within this one also needs access to the thinking of Anna Freud and her successors on the development of the ego ('First you must build the house before you can throw anyone out of it' is Anna Freud's reference to the need for ego structuring in order later to be able to address a mature enough ego in the therapeutic process). And, of course, both these theoretical-clinicians emphasise the necessity of the defences, however apparently maladaptive, and the need to acknowledge and evince curiosity about them rather than immediately to confront.

It is also in the writings of Anna Freud and Winnicott that one finds such an emphasis on the adaptation of psychoanalysis that is psychoanalytic child psychotherapy. The capacity to be responsive to the child – and to develop themes at the child's pace – starts with the in-tune good-enough mother: Katiebelle could gradually risk engaging with curiosity and learned that she could be met and 'known' in this process. Anna Freud equally allows a freedom of therapeutic interaction, an absence of any absolute sense of 'right' and 'correct' approach that can only be freeing for the therapist: 'There is no absolute psychoanalytic technique for use with children, but rather a set of analytic principles which have to be adapted to specific cases' (Sandler, Kennedy & Tyson 1980: 199).

Perhaps the only argument with Miss Freud at this point would be to note that technique is not 'adapted *to*' specific children; rather, it is created in the dyad, in the therapist-child relationship, in the transformational space between, while drawing its import from the understanding that psychoanalysis brings.

This freeing the therapist from institutionalised positions is, for me as a child psychotherapist, the most evident sign of an Independent: 'The key to an understanding of the Independents is their avowed openness to learning from any psychoanalytical theories' (Rayner 1991: 4). Or, like Winnicott, 'I aim to be myself and to behave myself' (Winnicott 1962: 166).

Writing papers, it must be acknowledged, is as much for the writer as it is for one's colleagues or indeed the patients on whom one is reflecting. Kate has been often in my mind. She is left with many issues that will cause struggles for her and probably necessitate the life-long involvement of a wider network. Whether one thinks a mature sexuality will ever be available to her is an open question. To have reached some sense of 'an in-dwelling of psyche in soma' and 'going-on-being' is an achievement and perhaps merely the foundation.

Note

1 This paper was given at a BAP conference in 2006. It was subsequently published in 2012 in P Williams, J Keene & S Dermen (eds.) *Independent Psychoanalysis Today* London: Karnac

References

Alvarez, A (1988) Beyond the unpleasure principle: some pre-conditions for thinking through play *Journal of Child Psychotherapy* 14(2): 1–13

Bollas, C (1987) *The Shadow of the Object: Psychoanalysis of the Unthought Known* London: Free Association Books

Campbell, D (1994) Breaching the shame shield: thoughts on the assessment of adolescent child sexual abusers *Journal of Child Psychotherapy* 20(3): 309–326

Dio Bleichmar, E (1995) The secret in the constitution of female sexuality: the effects of the adult's sexual look upon the subjectivity of the girl *Journal of Clinical Psychoanalysis* 4(3): 331–342

Fairbairn, WR (1952) *Psychoanalytic Studies of the Personality* London: Routledge & Kegan Paul

Gaddini, E (1980) Notes on the mind-body question. In A Limentani (ed.) *A Psychoanalytic Theory of Infantile Experience: Conceptual and Clinical Reflections* London & New York: Tavistock/Routledge 1992

Glasser, M (1996) Aggression and sadism in the perversions. In I Rosen (ed.) *Sexual Deviation* 3rd edition Oxford: Oxford University Press

Grand, S & Alpert, J (1993) The core trauma of incest: an object relations view *Professional Psychology: Research and Practice* 24(3) 330–334

Hopkins, J (1996) From baby games to let's pretend *Journal of the British Association of Psychotherapists* 31(1 Part 2): 20–27

Hurry, A (1998) *Psychoanalysis and Developmental Therapy* London: Karnac

Khan, MMR (1963) The concept of cumulative trauma. In *The Privacy of the Self: Papers on Psychoanalytic Theory and Technique* New York: International Universities Press 1974

Klockars, L & Sirola, R (2001) The mother-daughter love affair across the generations *The Psychoanalytic Study of the Child* 56: 219–237

Krueger, DW (2001) Body self: development, psychopathologies and psychoanalytic significance *The Psychoanalytic Study of the Child* 56: 238–259

Laufer, E (1991) Body image, sexuality and the psychotic core *International Journal of Psychoanalysis* 72(1): 63–71

Rayner, E (1991) *The Independent Mind in British Psychoanalysis* London: Free Association Books

Sandler, J, Kennedy, H & Tyson, R (1980) *The Technique of Child Psychoanalysis: Discussions with Anna Freud* London: Hogarth Press

Welldon, E (1988) *Mother, Madonna, Whore: The Idealisation and Denigration of Motherhood* London: Free Association Books

Winnicott, DW (1945) Primitive emotional development. In *Collected Papers: Through Paediatrics to Psychoanalysis* London: Hogarth Press 1975

Winnicott, DW (1947) Hate in the counter-transference *Collected Papers: Through Paediatrics to Psychoanalysis* London: Hogarth Press 1975

Winnicott, DW (1949) Mind and its relation to the psyche-soma. In *Collected Papers: Through Paediatrics to Psychoanalysis* London: Hogarth Press 1975

Winnicott, DW (1962) The aims of psychoanalytical treatment. In DW Winnicott *The Maturational Processes and the Facilitating Environment* London: Hogarth Press 1965

Winnicott, DW (1967) Mirror-role of mother and family in child development. In DW Winnicott *Playing and Reality* London: Tavistock 1971

Winnicott, DW (1972) Basis for self in body *International Journal of Child Psychotherapy* 1(1): 7–16

Wright, K (1991) *Vision and Separation: between Mother and Baby* London: Free Association Books

7 Rhythm, blues, affirmation and enactment

It's tough soloing without a rhythm section[1]

Prelude: the context

The theme of the conference for which this paper was written was 'Rhythm and Response: the dance of psychotherapy', the stimulus being the film *Rhythm is it!* – part of the BBC Imagine series. Several groups of young people, varied in background, education and opportunities, rehearse separately and are brought together to perform a vibrant dance to Stravinsky's *Rite of Spring*. Often overcoming early adverse experiences and present disaffection, many gained a genuine sense of self and worth. Numerous metaphors emerge from such a framework: the reader will perhaps forgive when they become over-extended.

Scene setting

It is often, in jazz, the rhythm section that establishes time, pace, beat and melody at the start of a piece – usually piano, bass and drums. They declare the broad territory, lay down a structure, and expect the soloist to develop from it in as individualistic way as he or she can with lively continuing interaction – rhythm and response. My knowledge of jazz is minimal, narrow and deeply self-indulgent but it seems to me that the rhythm section provides both foundation and texture – and, like John Donne's 'stiffe twin compasses' in 'A valediction forbidding mourning', allows glorious exploration outwards with (or because of) the safety of the home base to return to.

Of course, this is not unlike human development – 'first you give your children roots, then you give them wings'. We've always known what children need at the start: we are simply not such an untroubled species that we can always recognise and provide it in a good enough and timely manner.

Those of us who work as child psychotherapists find ourselves encountering a variety of tunes, rhythms and responses, the work usually taking us not simply into the internal world of the child but also to the family and the outside world. There we may encounter frantic and isolated solo dancing at a pace and tempo that must inevitably burn the dancer out; dreamy self-indulgent dancing that ignores all others on the dance floor and cultivates its own corner; brisk gestured movements that indicate practicality and common sense – and still keep an eye upon the handbags in the centre; showy strictly egotistical virtuoso dancing demonstrating much flair and style – usually over a short distance; old fashioned mannered two-steps that are contained, regulated, limited in their breadth and scope but always aware of where others are and careful of them; or even at times – I am particularly remembering the head of a school for children with emotional and behavioural difficulties where I worked when I first came to London – a remarkable Palais Glide, swan-like and elegant, utterly detached from the pace and requirements of life outside, and not often seen even in those days.

We need thus to be aware of other people's motives and concerns, capacities and strictures, dissonances and rhythms, while still trying to hold a sense of the individual crescendos and silences of our young patients. The ambition of the childcare network may be to create a harmonious team, a system working together to enable a child to have sufficient ego growth, insight, self-regulation and self-esteem to go solo, to find himself back on a positive developmental track; but we may find ourselves rather more often being the caretakers of the hall in which the performance should happen, struggling to ensure that, as each professional does it 'my way', each part of the network at least does not damage the others or the would-be soloing child.

The end

'Robertson' was, I think, relieved to be preparing to go to a residential school for troubled and troubling children when we met for what turned out to be the last time. Coping in secondary school – it was secondary transfer time – would have been impossible and he could well have joined a long line of intelligent black boys simply viewed as disruptive and finally expelled. The network, including me, had proved to be not good enough as a rhythm section for him, perhaps all of us finding it difficult to negotiate the startling dichotomy between his brittle, charming, vulnerable, omnipotent ego and his driven compulsion to abuse, split and deceive. It was further typical of the therapy that his foster father did not manage to bring him to our planned final session, a rail strike intervening. The foster father had, over the 20 months of our contact, often been caught up in what Peter Wilson has called 'the imperatives of the transference' (Wilson 1999), unable to avoid being drawn into yet another stand-off with the 11-year-old over who was in charge, and somewhat rigidly unable (or unwilling) to plan creatively for other means of arriving at the clinic. Robertson, interestingly, had spent the previous, penultimate session carefully photographing the clinic and our therapy room, as if he knew that this would be our last encounter – having equally painstakingly managed to remember to bring his camera with him on his very long train journey and having anticipated the strike – and was especially meticulous in taking several shots of the front door. He had his own rhythm; not always in tune with the rest of the world, he could rarely perceive any other position to adopt, especially in his family, but in therapy he could talk of regretting this uncomfortable and unsatisfying disjunction. We hoped that the stability, the boundariedness and the Winnicottian understanding to be offered by his new therapeutic community would enable him to find other positions – other rhythms – and so let him eventually access his undoubted intellect and take off solo.

I always find I write about children who have moved me, made me think about them, about what happens in that space between therapist and patient where rhythms can be challenged, expectations explored and where new rhythms sometimes emerge. Robertson has also been in my mind because of my awareness of failing him – really from the very first engagement with the referrer – and because of the experience of 'mis-steps in the dance' (Stern, 1977) that ensued, mainly mis-steps in the dance of the network. His story encourages us to reflect on the processes that unconsciously stimulated this.

Beginnings

Beginnings – as we all know – matter. They both establish and confound expectations. The rhythm one meets – and that greets one – on arriving in the world, indeed from the womb onwards, is a rhythm that establishes our potential, the spontaneous gesture of the curious child that is met or ignored and so sets in train dependence on particular neural pathways or expectations of particular human interactions and responses. We are aware of the effects on the foetus and the newborn infant of the mother's pre-natal depression (Field, 2004), especially in the inhibition of dopamine and serotonin production, and we know the impact of the pregnant mother's stress level on cortisol levels in the foetus and infant. We could delineate such difficulties as 'bodies out of rhythm': indeed, Graham Music reminds us that current research shows the drama of the struggle between mother and developing foetus as the foetus seeks control of nutrients at the potential cost of its host body (Music, 2009: 58). We recall Winnicott's remarks concerning the later stage of the growing infant whose mother has to be able to survive his ruthlessness (Winnicott 1958). Let us, then, keep the body in mind.

Sue Gerhardt in 2004 focused the attention of the intelligent general reader when she wrote accessibly of the physiological concomitants of parental nurture, particularly of the chemicals released as a result of loving interactions and feelings and those like 'corrosive cortisol' which emanate from stress and more negative experiences. It could have been subtitled 'attachment theory and the brain'. That early experience affects mood, expectation and potential is certainly not new to psychotherapists. We would all accept that attunement is important in establishing the rhythms of life and it matters that mother and child can to some extent sing from the same song sheet and very roughly in tune (children have forgiving ears for parental singing). Working with children like Robertson, however, makes one particularly alert to the role of the body – the first ego; to predispositions established early for the body to be relied upon as the only available regulator of affect, the projector of what cannot be tolerated, and the medium (rather than that of thought) for seeking a primitive psychological balance.

Robertson

Robertson missed out on attunement. It was useful to read what could be gained from the Social Services chronology extracted from their files. Robertson is his mother Ms B's first child, born when she was 17 and named after his father who was mainly absent. His father's violence towards Ms B and her family led her to ask for social work help in getting an injunction against him at a time when Robertson was 20 months old and she was five months pregnant with his younger brother. We might, then, assume violence in Robertson's early environment. Ms B had moreover been referred a number of times to the Community Psychiatric Nurse for depression: the second pregnancy, at the age of 19, was by a white man whom she had met while a patient on a psychiatric ward and who had a history of arson. It was much later that it emerged that Ms B had suffered depression from the age of 10 and that in earlier adolescence she used to cut her arms. When we encounter children who *act*, where the body is cathected in the absence of an attuned adult, we are wise to hold in mind at least three generations of the family history. Here was a mother, not really out of childhood, whose own childhood experience had left her vulnerable and self-harming.

Before he was 2, Robertson had been seen twice by a psychologist due to the lack of development of expressive language which was said to cause him to be frustrated and over active. We can make fairly solid assumptions about the non-availability of the adults for verbal engagement and understanding, and especially for containment. He saw the psychologist over the next year. The notes return to this when Robertson is 4 years old, when the psychologist re-refers the family to Social Services as he has begun to start fires, still has language difficulties and exhibits severe behavioural problems. These are written in the notes as somehow of equal inconsequence, yet he is said to have started a fire that led to the family's being temporarily rehoused two days after his 4th birthday. His mother had at times talked of fears of losing her sanity and, when her mood was low, was preoccupied with the death of her own father which occurred when Robertson was 2 years old. She found it impossible, however, to sustain contact with mental health services and was said to be very detached from the children and absorbed in her own needs.

Many aspects of the history are familiar yet shocking. This is a conjunction of responses, a sense of contradiction that was to continue throughout my experience of Robertson. Particularly noteworthy was the short-term nature of each intervention and that the family was dealt with on a duty basis and the case closed each time as soon as Ms B failed to attend the office. It seemed that Social Services viewed the task as offering brief responses to Ms B's requests – it was hard to engender a concept of long-term intervention, perhaps because of the entrenched nature of the difficulties. Over the eight years of Ms B's contact with social work prior to the crisis that generated the referral for psychotherapy for Robertson, referrals and written expressions of concern came in from adult mental health workers, health visitors, clinical psychologists, a childminder and school staff, including one from the psychologist that described the family situation as 'dangerous' and informed social work staff of a suicide attempt by Ms B during Robertson's first year. This is important when we think about the dance of psychotherapy – in child psychotherapy there is often a significant network expressing concern, albeit not necessarily centrally involved. It becomes important to invite – in an insistent kind of way – the members of the network to participate in the dance, or at least to attend the dance practices even if they cannot join a major performance. Otherwise there is around the edge a chorus that should have influence but is often left impotent, not incorporated into the joint understanding and planning that such a family really needs. The alerts they offer simply become thorns in the side of social workers who can in turn be dismissive of the concern expressed. Ms B was offered a range of help – childminder, Home Start, family support. She could engage with none. Each request is met by an action – but there is no space for gathering the information together and for thinking. Actions thus become the defence against thought and against having to think, particularly about the concern of others. Robertson's defence mechanisms, as we will see, thus became those of the network.

When I was studying Criminology in the late 1960s, it was fashionable to say, in rather a throw-away manner, that arson was a sexual offence. I find it interesting that, although by that time psychoanalytic theories of criminality had generally been abandoned, superseded by structural and socio-political critiques, this remained an accepted truth. I have not come across a child who sets fires who has not suffered sexual abuse, usually of a persistent and grossly intrusive kind. To hear of fire setting in a child of 4 should have set off warning bells in any attentive professional.

The family grew – two brothers and two sisters arrived. The father of the girls married Ms B but refused to live with her, Robertson's bad behaviour being cited as the cause. It was observed by others that the boys were active, unsupervised and thus often in danger and that they were always perceived by their mother as blameworthy, particularly Robertson. The fifth pregnancy prompted the hospital to inform Social Services that Ms B always suffered post-natal depression with her pregnancies, a fact astonishingly not communicated in the years prior to this.

With that information one might have been alert to the absence of conversation and response, of the early maternal containment of emotional experience, leaving the infant with only the body to rely on. There is no reciprocity in such a developmental scenario. When this continues into latency, we often find a child who has never been able to develop a sense of an interested adult and so been able to internalise the protective function of the adult. Such a child will put himself in positions of risk – or use externalisation as the only recourse in ridding the self of what is psychologically unmanageable. Much of this will be negotiated through the body, the primary basic self.

Concern, minimal action, rejection by Ms B and seemingly consequent heightened activity by her sons are the feature of the rest of the records. Ms B seemed to arrive at the social work office to complain but not to pursue. She had a partner who dealt drugs and who, she complained, once hid his drugs down Robertson's underpants and slept with underage girls. School referred once more on account of neglect and Ms B's depression only a fortnight before Tara (now 4) told her mother that Robertson had put his penis 'in my fanny'. Robertson was just over 9 years old. Ms B managed to inform Social Services within four days which was, given her state, pretty good going.

The therapeutic dance

The beginning of the 'dance of therapy' is of course the referral, the invitation to become partners. Here we may find we are already standing on each other's feet, shouting to be heard above the music – or dancing a totally different dance. I was approached by a community child and family mental health clinic to see if I would take Robertson into twice weekly work, it being felt that he needed more than once weekly. The team was in the process of assessing the family, referred to them by the local social work team, and Robertson was living with a foster family.

At this time, it was explained that there were no spaces for very long-term therapy amongst the child psychotherapists in the specialist clinic where I worked. I would moreover be retiring in two years' time (a further rhythm of life and not without its influence). We thought about it together and decided I could offer twice weekly therapy in conjunction with the local clinic's continuing to hold the case and their undertaking family work with Robertson's family of origin and support work for the foster carers. However, we awaited the results of their initial family assessment before exploring with Robertson and his foster carer whether psychotherapy might help. This assessment arrived three months later, supported Robertson's continuing placement with his foster parents and reiterated the request for therapy in relation to the sibling incest and Robertson's challenging behaviour. I asked for a network meeting, very conscious that working across clinics and agencies might well add difficulty, although I had a very good experience in the past of joint work with the psychiatrist in that service. Previous experience also offered that there can be advantages in an incestuous family being seen in different clinics as it makes a statement about 'separate beds'. In the meantime, appointments were sent to Robertson and his foster carers. The clinic registered him as 'James Robertson', reversing his name. It took a considerable time to get our system to change this. This continues to preoccupy me: it seemed impossible for Robertson to be himself.

As I state in the paper that now forms Chapter 10:

> It is also important that we think about the context of the therapy – in terms of the clinical space but also with young people in terms of the supportive network that allows therapy to become a treatment of choice. Too often I have heard of therapists who engage with children when the environment is neither supportive nor able to withstand the impact of the therapy, and the therapy is stopped when the children act out. This is abusive and thoughtless.
>
> (Horne 2006: 234)

It was rather salutary for me to be caught up in getting it wrong. The mis-steps in the dance involved

a)   the referring clinic did not attend reviews, Professionals' Meetings or conferences. The network meeting did not happen. Family work *was* offered to Ms B – who had attended two of the four assessment interviews and gave permission for Robertson to attend therapy – but it could not be sustained. Ms B also declined an offer to meet me as Robertson's therapist. On reflection, I find the rhythm of my retirement to have been a major factor here: without the import of a limited timescale which now meant only 18 months of twice weekly therapy for Robertson, I would (hopefully) have waited, insisting on the meeting first and requesting clarity about the total therapeutic package;

b) the discovery of the involvement of a further agency, a specialist private fostering agency, that was responsible for the foster carers but had not been involved in the referral process;

c) Don, the foster carer, was to turn down parent work once Robertson's sessions were established; the referring clinic worker neither pursued this nor passed on the information, nor did Don;

d) Social Services continued to deal with the family on a duty basis for a considerable number of months, having decided that the involvement of two specialist clinics sufficed in the circumstances;

e) only with a change of social worker at the fostering agency several months later did it come to light that little was being offered to the foster father, it being (mis)assumed that as a youth worker himself he would cope well with Robertson. This was despite the clear recommendation in the assessment report that 'Robertson needs to be living in an environment where his behaviour can be monitored and challenged constantly by carers who can engage with the bit of him that very much wants help. We think the carers will need regular professional support to withstand the demands of providing this kind of therapeutic placement.'

f) finally – as if we needed it – we were some seven weeks into twice weekly work when there was a serious rail accident and trains stopped altogether for about five weeks. The travelling difficulties were a nightmare; the fearfulness that trains might crash an extra terror. Don proved intractably unable to think flexibly about getting Robertson to the clinic and we often did not know if he would make it.

One could envisage more robust structures for a therapy.

When such misunderstandings, let-downs, fragmentation and confusions happen, it is important to think of the role of projection onto the network of the internal world of the individual patient as Richard Davies has written (Davies 1996). Izzy Kolvin and Judith Trowell in 1996 pointed to a mirroring process that takes place in networks around abuse: different agencies or different professionals will find themselves adopting the position of different family members and identifying with them. While such identifications can be very helpful in bringing transference feelings into the discussion, this is only when it is clear that it *is* transference that is being experienced and when there is a forum for discussion. One can, for example, see in the referring clinic's position – and the early position of Social Services – something of Ms B's depression and difficulty in focusing on her sons and her wish to be rid of the nuisance of them.

I have a personal view that one can also see the processes in the network as being a reflection of the dysfunctional family system itself – the system being more than the sum of its parts. The defences, unconscious expectations and positions adopted invade the network and too easily become part of our own functioning. I often felt impotently enraged at the lack of availability of indispensable colleagues and their essential input – and frustratingly impotent in remedying it. My identification here was often with Ms B's hopelessness and sense of being abandoned to it by the men in her life.

The referrer's assessment did bring to light some very important information, especially in relation to family patterns around sexuality and sexual relationships. Robertson was extremely controlling of his siblings. In the interview he claimed his sisters were responsible for his sexual assaults (all the children, it seemed, were involved) and insisted that he had only once watched a sexy film at night. Ms B thought it possible that the children had witnessed the adults having intercourse. Adults often wandered around the house naked, she said, and the children's favourite game was 'mothers and fathers'. Indeed, she described Robertson more like a partner than a son: he checked up on her relationship with her current partner and advised on what she should do – thus he was explicitly involved in her sexual life.

Robertson comes for assessment

Robertson and Don arrived 15 minutes late for the first of four assessment sessions. This should have warned me. Lateness was to remain an issue. Simone, Don's wife, was not with them. I was to meet her later when she occasionally brought Robertson to his therapy – a slim, quiet woman who seemed naturally to take second place to her husband. Don was a tall, handsome black man, well-dressed, warm and engaging, about 30. He had the hint of a South African accent. Robertson looked up at him constantly as if he would devour him with his eyes and as if he could not believe his luck in having such an admirable foster father.

Robertson himself was a good looking, solidly built lad of average height, wearing his school's bright red sweatshirt top. He greeted me politely, gently prodded in the back by Don. He looked a little embarrassed. I asked if we might meet for a little time together so that I could hear something of how they saw things; then I would like time with Robertson on his own. After that Robertson and I would have two further meetings before we all met once more to plan whether and how therapy would happen.

Don pointed out that it was he who was Robertson's carer. Trained abroad as a youth worker, he had undertaken this fostering work as a full-time task, being available for Robertson. His wife Simone worked as a solicitor specialising in child work. Oh, and his mother in the States was a psychologist. Despite this jousting for professional space, he came across as capable, insightful about things that were about being a boy and missing home, and able to be clear – with warmth – about expectations and boundaries at home. Robertson got into trouble mainly through not bathing, being loud and telling lies. Sadly, Don said that it was hard to help when he told lies and they did not know what was true. I was reminded of Winnicott and the child who can change external reality through a lie, confusing the adult, and therefore begin to construct and believe a different internal reality. Robertson told me proudly that Don was a lay pastor at the church – and that he was glad he was helping him with the lies. 'Sounds as if they just arrive suddenly, these lies?' He nodded, a little shame-faced. 'They just come out.' 'Perhaps they helped when you were little,' I offered, 'but now that you're nine they do get you into trouble a bit?' He looked curiously at me.

After a useful joint session, Don returned to the waiting room and I met Robertson. The assessment highlighted three main issues:

– for Robertson activity was the only negotiator of pain, his body an immediate recourse when frightening affect approached. His gymnastic demonstrations on the couch began at our first meeting and he was proud of beginning to learn to play African drums;

– while he strived to present himself as the most popular boy in the school, Robertson was realistic about what he was good at and what took more exertion. He was in fact well above average but was seen to be increasingly struggling. He had a certain charm and fluency in his descriptions of himself, making me think both of deception and vulnerability. This reminded me of his difficulties in expressive language early on. I wondered about the absence of depth of meaning in his language: that with Robertson his fluency might conceal that deficiency. He had not experienced language as a container or clarifier of affect;

– he *could* think for spells about his situation and about what he had done to his siblings. He didn't blame anyone else, simply expressed how sad he was that he had done the sexy things with his sister, and how he wished he hadn't.

There is what I call a 'rhythm of recognition' sometimes when working with child patients – I'm sure it comes into adult work too. It isn't always possible to say just why one decides to take on certain young people. I know that my retirement certainly played a part – I felt guilty about leaving and wanted to be pulling my weight in the team; at the same time, I didn't want to go. But there is also the 'nevertheless' factor[2] – despite contradictions, one engages in the work. And Robertson could say that he was sad and wished he had not done what he did.

Gymnastics come before thinking: the themes of therapy

In order *not* to replicate the mis-shapen dance that the troubled child expects and replays in his object relationships, one has to keep in mind Winnicott's injunction that psychoanalysis offers an intimacy, like the early infant-mother relationship, in which the curiosity of the child – and the 'true self' – may be called forth. We are therefore always seeking space in which the child's defences and affect are held in mind, yet curiosity becomes possible. So active defences often have to be connoted positively first before we can then explore them with the child. Some of Robertson's defences could not possibly be out of mind – each somersault on the couch tolled his activity – but the more subtle ones could be lost and his use of the couch as a trampoline could hide shame, pain, seduction and fear of abuse.

One can experience a desperate impulse with such children to tell them what they should do to keep out of trouble. It is the imperative to 'do', to adopt the child's defence and be active, as being passive, reflective, receptive feels intolerable. Indeed, to be silently reflective can feel like being vulnerable, open to attack as was the child. The capacity for thought is vital. With Robertson, it was possible to let him demonstrate his latest gymnastic tumble for a bit – a re-establishment of his rhythm and a way of his re-finding his object at the start. That he generally needed to repeat it was interesting: I felt that it represented a structured, formalised and healthy use of his body – like Dr Kellogg's physical hygiene – but also was a test of me to see if I was still a non-abusive, non-intrusive, not perverse grown-up. A little, too, was what Billy Connolly has inimitably described in: 'Look at *me*, mammy – Ah'm dancin'!' While I mentally recalled Winnicott's comment that every infant needs an experience of omnipotence, I was very aware that Robertson's omnipotence and controlling at home stemmed from high anxiety and the absence of such affirmation, and that a delicate line was required here to affirm the sense of potency and agency as a developmental need but not to reinforce the enactments at home.

A typical session several months into therapy

It was Wednesday morning. Robertson arrived 20 minutes late. I went to collect him from the waiting room. Don was already deep inside a very large bible, reading. He raised his head to say, 'Sorry. We set off late.' Interesting dilemma – how to take this up. I asked if travel was becoming difficult again: 'No – it was me and Simone this morning, sorry.' Robertson was nowhere to be seen. I raised my eyebrows. Don's eyes indicated the stairs outside. In a raised voice I told Don that it was a pity Robertson had made the long journey yet somehow wasn't here to meet. That must be *very* frustrating for him. A bundle of energy leapt down several steps, landed in front of me and grinned. 'Hello, Robertson – you're here all the time!' [Sometimes with early deficit, it feels very mother-toddler.] He darted around me, along the short corridor and downstairs towards the therapy room where, arriving somewhat in the rear, I couldn't see him. A game of needing the adult to seek him ensued, and needing the adult to find him. I interpreted his ability to make me search for him, and keep doing it, and not let him be lost. He jumped out from his hiding place. I commented that he had been wondering just when I *would* look for him with the late journey, so he was making sure I did. It was awful, that feeling of being lost. He smiled. I wondered about the excitement of it – he was good at making it exciting and that was a good way of covering up being fed up at being late. [This was an old conversation.]

He told me he had learned a new move in gymnastics. 'Ann, I'll show you!' – and he promptly did. It took three or four turns before he did it to his satisfaction, somersaulting on to the couch and standing up, arms wide. He told me that it had been OK – that was the right way to do it. I nodded. Like many children who need to control rigidly, he has no middle ground between 'right' and 'awful', no sense of 'good enough'. I asked if I should make my usual comment, that he was telling me he needed to do *good* body things to help with the feelings? He sat back and waited for the end of my sentence.

In a sudden panic he looked at the clock. 'Oh, no! I wanted to . . .' He couldn't remember what he wanted to – anxiety flooded him. 'There are still 15 minutes,' I said. He sat, then looked at me, holding onto my gaze and breathing deeply. 'Fifteen minutes,' I repeated. There was a pause. I was aware it would be a long gap until his Monday evening session. I just commented that he was thinking about missing things – the minutes – and when that happened it was terribly difficult to get his mind on to what he had wanted to do. Things that are missing matter and can make us stop thinking. He nodded and breathed in. Proving to himself that he was once more in control of affect and situation, he altered reality: 'I *was* going to ask you to do my Maths,' he smiled mischievously. He spent the rest of the session attempting to build an elaborate and undefined construction out of paper, sellotape, plasticine and Lego. As happened frequently, he 'inadvertently' destroyed it in the process. Painful – but controlling it.

Shame and humiliation

Robertson was by no means the first child I had met who had abused a sibling. There is no template – but there is often an experience of early pre-verbal trauma that has been overwhelming to the immature ego. It is the flashback memory of this that has to be externalised, projected onto another, to dull the memory of humiliation and shame that comes with the flashback and to locate that in another child. The role of shame and the nature of the defences that may be marshalled against it then becomes extremely important and we have to think on it both theoretically and technically (Campbell 1994; Lampl-De Groot 1949). It belongs early, with the development of the ego ideal, that toddler sense of 'who I am and who I would like to be seen to be.' Falling short of the ideal causes shame and we normally take ourselves out of it, cover our faces. We know that Robertson at the least was exposed to adult sexual relationships and violence at an extremely early age, if not abused. Whatever the experience, it seems to have been persistent and overwhelming. The on-going driven nature of his need to externalise the feelings shows that it had – unsurprisingly – not been possible for him to process them. Don reported finding him under a quilt with a 2-year-old whom he was minding on one occasion: it continued in the placement.

To be careful about 'shame' and 'humiliation' (and the vulnerability of the ego ideal) need not mean avoiding anxiety or avoiding interpretation; it does mean actively taking great care about wording and timing. Anne Hurry, describing the work of assessing troubled adolescents (Hurry 1986), writes of using neutral words – 'strange' feelings, for example, rather than fearful or shameful ones – as one important way of being sensitive to the vulnerable ego. I have found it a great help for the child or young person who acts with the body, who might be viewed as functioning at a level of what I think of as 'body-based defensive manoeuvres', to address the body itself as a separate entity that cannot itself think but which does operate as a source of memories and at times acts on these. One can then comment, 'Isn't it interesting what your body gets up to' and address the thinking part of the child as an ally in reflecting on the infantile, acting part. Then joint curiosity becomes possible.

I noticed that, even towards the end of our work, Don still spoke of Robertson as showing no remorse. Remorse requires a sense of self and other that is more sophisticated than Robertson had managed to acquire. It is developmentally quite far on and the rhythm of Robertson's growth had not allowed him a mature emotional position. I always find with abusing boys that their victimisation must be heard first. Only with a sense that there is indeed a real self – rather than simply the perverse reality presented by their victimisers – can they *then* think of the other and, for most, realise with horror that they have treated others as they were treated. Robertson still had to firm up an ego ideal; superego functioning was miles away.

Pace, timing and intimacy

Equally pace, timing and intimacy are fundamental issues. Where intrusion has been such a part of the child's life that he is driven to evacuate his thoughts, fantasies and memories – as Robertson was – we have to find a pace that suits the child. Not rush, not provide an interpretation because we know that interpretation produces shift. And not intrude our need to know or our need to do. I found the brevity of the 18 months available to us for therapy remarkably difficult – the pressure was to *do*, a pressure not simply from the outside world where we are used to 'Is he not cured yet?' after two months, but from inside me with my rhythm of retirement. I find it interesting that we now have evidence that at times of acute stress, times of fight/flight reactions, we are actually using the oldest, reptilian part of our brains. Complex interpretations of anxiety made to an aggressively attacking child, or to one who uses constant activity and who feels threatened, will have no impact. Creating safe space will have an influence: as with Robertson's panic about not having enough time, one can offer simple reflective comments until the capacity to think returns. It is this ability to think that we seek, after all, for the abusing child – if we can help insert 'thought' between memory and the impulse to externalise onto another, we will have done good work. For the retiring therapist, it was also important to find a forum, with thinking colleagues in the clinic, where reflection could reign rather than action!

Reciprocity and its environmental requisites

Rebecca, a new social worker at the fostering agency, made contact, apologising for the considerable delay in replying to my request to meet due to her colleague's leaving. She would like to take on the case. Could we meet? We did.

A psychotherapist as well as a social worker, Rebecca understood the unconscious processes involved. She hinted at an earlier difficulty in the agency's working normally with Don who had been treated as a co-professional (which certainly needed to be acknowledged) in a way that did not enable him to admit difficulty and seek help. All difficulties were expressed in terms of Simone, his wife. I found this extremely interesting as it was noticeable that, on the few occasions that Simone brought Robertson, they arrived in good state and in good time – always, even in the aftermath of the rail accident. Don was studying to become a pastor – was already a lay preacher in his church. I could see him being very effective in this, with his warmth and charm. I felt it also helped explain that his mind was no longer fully on Robertson and his needs. Rebecca undertook to try to get a shift in Don's attitude to punctuality for Robertson's sessions. It seemed that – like Robertson – he had a tendency to lay blame outside himself.

Finally, Social Services allocated a social worker, Doreen, who also wanted to understand our joint struggles and Robertson's dilemmas – and who was able to be thoughtful about his future needs and placement. It emerged at this point that Don and Simone had agreed to take Robertson only while he was in primary school which would end in nine months' time – they wanted to start a family. This felt the ultimate deception. It would mean that my ending work with Robertson would coincide with his moving placement. That this had not been communicated to the assessing clinic nor to me seemed once more the consequence of the fragmented discourse and rhythm in the network – we were all, Robertson included, having to go solo when being in a band was essential. It was a relief that this unknowable reality could now be acknowledged and unsurprising that it could be articulated only once we had begun genuinely to work together in the network. Robertson's mother continued to dissemble with him, telling him on the phone and at access visits that he could come home whenever the family was rehoused. Robertson was tantalised but not convinced. Having been more contained, his behaviour again became difficult in his foster home and his sexualised behaviour reasserted itself in school and at church. Women became the targets of sexualised intrusiveness and attempted denigration. He tried to build a dyad with Don, man to man, excluding Simone. In school his bullying, kicking, sexualised swearing and attacks on others meant being banned from the playground and he had several within-school exclusions. The school noted that he could be opportunistic in his attacks, perceiving when he might be unobserved, and expressed concern about secondary transfer. The uncertainty was reaching us all.

Special educational statementing was undertaken; a recommendation of a residential therapeutic community was made. Ms B managed to explain to Robertson that she supported this: she could not offer what he needed at home; he would gain more from boarding school. He was saddened but also extremely relieved. Don and Simone undertook to keep him until his residential placement started. Our work continued on the main themes as before, but with an emphasis on loss and losing, mourning and anticipation.

Conclusion

You know the old jazzmen's joke – what is a piano trio? Two musicians and a drummer. Robertson's story is one of very many that demonstrate the importance of the good drummer – a drummer who listens to what is being created, underpins, upholds and contains and does not simply impose his own rhythm. It is subtle, this life business, and our task is simply to be good enough, to allow our patients to resume a developmental track that is more creative in its possibilities and far less constrained by the narrowness of expectation and defences than has previously been available. If we are failing in this we need to find another setting for the child where the boundaries can be sustained, a more subtle beat can be provided and the band can play on. With children like Robertson, we do need a whole band.

I do have hopes for Robertson, especially as his new setting provides therapy and an approach to his needs and deficits held by all staff in common – a staff group who sing and dance together, who can tolerate the strains and sacrifices that are necessary to bring in Spring and new growth. This makes me recall Winnicott's confession in 'The anti-social tendency' about his first child analytic patient – the lad who famously flooded the clinic basement, jump started and drove Winnicott's car in the clinic driveway, and who bit Winnicott on the buttocks three times. After the Institute of Psychoanalysis refused him permission to continue treating the boy there, Winnicott noted: 'It can easily be seen that the treatment for this boy should have been not psychoanalysis but placement. Psychoanalysis only made sense if added after placement' (Winnicott 1956: 307).

Not that psychoanalysis in itself was wrong – but the timing and the organisation of the psychoanalytic dance certainly was.

Notes

1 This paper was given at a BAP conference in York in 2009 and published in the *British Journal of Psychotherapy* 26(1) in 2010.
2 I recall watching Muriel Spark being interviewed on television. The interviewer challenged her conversion to Catholicism, offering a prolonged, insistent series of arguments. At each line of reasoning she agreed as to the illogicality of her position. When he finally ran out of points there was a pause. Then Mrs Spark said, 'Nevertheless . . .'

References

Campbell, D (1994) Breaching the shame shield: thoughts on the assessment of adolescent sexual abusers *Journal of Child Psychotherapy* 20(3): 309–326

Davies, R (1996) The inter-disciplinary network and the internal world of the offender. In C Cordess and M Cox (eds.) *Forensic Psychotherapy: Crime, Psychodynamics and the Offender Patient*. Vol II: *Mainly Practice* London: Jessica Kingsley

Field, T (2004) Prenatal depression effects on the foetus and neonate. In J Nadel & D Muir (eds.) *Emotional Development: Recent Research Advances* Oxford: Oxford University Press

Gerhardt, S (2004) *Why Love Matters – How Affection Shapes a Baby's Brain* Hove: Brunner-Routledge

Horne, A (2006) Interesting things to say – and why. In M Lanyado & A Horne *A Question of Technique* London: Routledge

Hurry, A (1986) Walk-in work with adolescents *Journal of Child Psychotherapy* 12(1) 33–45

Kolvin, I & Trowell, J (1996) 'Child sexual abuse'. In I Rosen (ed.) *Sexual Deviation* 3rd edition Oxford: Oxford University Press

Lampl-De Groot, J (1949) Neurotics, delinquents and ideal formation. In KR Eissler (ed.) *Searchlights on Delinquency* New York: International Universities Press

Music, G (2009) Neuroscience and child psychotherapy. In M Lanyado & A Horne *The Handbook of Child and Adolescent Psychotherapy: Psychoanalytic Approaches* 2nd edition London: Routledge

Stern, D (1977) *The First Relationship: Infant and Mother* London: Fontana/Open Books

Wilson, P (1999) Delinquency. In M Lanyado & A Horne *The Handbook of Child and Adolescent Psychotherapy: Psychoanalytic Approaches* London: Routledge

Winnicott, DW (1958) Psychoanalysis and the sense of guilt. In *The Maturational Processes and the Facilitating Environment* London: Hogarth Press 1965

Winnicott, DW (1956) The anti-social tendency. In *Through Paediatrics to Psychoanalysis* London: Hogarth Press 1977

8   Oedipal aspirations and phallic fears

On fetishism in childhood and young adulthood[1]

Introduction

This paper focuses on work with a young man who cross-dressed, wore nappies in bed and was preoccupied by pregnant women. When we engage with young people en route to a perverse solution – what used to be called 'the perversions' but now more delicately attracts the title 'paraphilias' in DSM IV, the American Psychiatric Association classification system, or 'neosexualities' in Joyce McDougall's understanding (McDougall 1995) – we encounter early insult, primitive defences and real fear of the oedipal constellation. Within 'solutions' such as fetishism there is also an element of deception – the need to conceal the phallus to protect it, and the desire to triumph over the object in so doing. Technically, it is important to keep a developmental and psychosexual frame-work in mind, to be aware of the subtle invitation to collude with the deception and to maintain close observation of one's counter-transference (Baker 1994; Carignan 1999; Renik 1992).

Stanley

Stanley is his mother's only child. At the age of 19 he was referred for psycho-therapy following anxiety that he might be paedophilic. Amongst other behaviours, he was constantly drawing mothers, babies and pregnant women, download-ing similar pictures from the internet and videoing advertisements for nappies and sterilising fluid for babies' feeding bottles. This behaviour, according to his mother, had become increasingly obsessive over the past year. He had admitted to the referring psychiatrist that he also dressed in women's clothes but now did so rarely. These activities, he maintained, did not give him any sexual arousal. The psychiatrist thought that Stanley was not a paedophile but that he could use and needed psychoanalytic psychotherapy.

It emerged at Stanley's assessment interviews that the family's impulse to refer him had occurred since his mother had accepted a new partner, Jim, into the home. Neither Stanley nor his mother had expressed any deep concern prior to this: it was Jim's view as an outsider that enabled them to perceive something not quite right in Stanley's preoccupations. The presence both of a man, and of an oedipal third, was therefore the precipitant. It may also have been the precipitant for increasing his obsessional behaviours. Interestingly, I found myself meeting with Stanley's mother and Jim without Stanley at one point during my assessment – as I would with a young child but as I very rarely do with an adolescent or young person. I have reflected on my thoughtlessness here, and on what must have been my focus on 'Stanley-the-child' rather than on 'Stanley the young man of nearly 20'. It has been vital to retain in mind that there is a strong counter-transference pressure *not* to see Stanley as a potent male – and a need to recognise behind this his anxieties about being phallic and being perceived to be so.

During the pregnancy Stanley's mother developed pre-eclampsia and Stanley was delivered by Caesarean section four weeks premature. He spent several weeks in an incubator in the hospital's intensive care unit. Throughout his childhood he suffered from a number of physical illnesses and a pituitary deficiency was treated over many years with growth hormones. He had an operation on his back for scoliosis, entailing long periods in hospital, and he was an in-patient for a whole year between the ages of 12½ and 13½ when he had the surgery. All his developmental milestones were delayed: he walked at 19 months, talked when he was 2½ years old, was not properly clean (i.e. still soiled himself) until 5 or 6, and occasionally there was bed wetting until age 9–10 when Stanley finally achieved being dry at night. He attended a normal primary school but transferred to a special school for children with learning difficulties at 11. This was both to provide for his learning difficulties and to give him a more sheltered experience as his physical difficulties made it impossible for him to survive the rough and tumble of a mainstream secondary school. He left school at 18 and completed a special foundation course for young people with learning difficulties at college. He did not want to return to college and, at referral, was at home, unemployed.

Stanley's mother, in her late 40s at the time of referral, was a local government official. She had been depressed at his birth, worried about his physical health and survival, and in a marriage that did not survive beyond Stanley's third birthday. His father, an ex-soldier, had since the divorce worked at a number of jobs with no great tenacity and often borrowed large sums of money (which he would 'forget' to repay) from his ex-wife. Stanley could see him 'When I want to' but had not done so for over a year. The possibility of identifying with a weak and uninterested father might, therefore, be problematic for Stanley.

The arrival of Jim caused major change in the family. He was divorced from his wife who continues to live with their daughters elsewhere in the UK. An ex-policeman who was once very active on the folk-singing scene, he entranced Stanley with his tales of and friendships with well-known entertainers. At times Stanley could not help but enjoy this contact with the famous; at others, he remembered to dislike Jim as he had altered the mother-child dyad irremediably. Jim had a heart condition, was awaiting a heart bypass operation, and was probably Stanley's best ally at home – but Stanley could not quite bring himself to see this at the time of the referral. Jim was concerned about Stanley's social isolation and encouraged his involvement in a local drama group, both performing and writing.

Thoughts on theory

In 'Three essays on the theory of sexuality' (1905) Freud outlined his view of fetishism:

> What is substituted for the sexual object is some part of the body (such as the foot or hair) which is generally very inappropriate for sexual purposes, or some inanimate object which bears an assignable relation to the person whom it replaces and preferably to that person's sexuality . . .
>
> No other variation of the sexual instinct that borders on the pathological can lay so much claim to our interest as this one . . .
>
> The situation only becomes pathological when the longing for the fetish passes beyond the point of being merely a necessary condition attached to the sexual object and actually *takes the place of* the normal aim, and, further, when the fetish becomes detached from a particular individual and becomes the *sole* sexual object.
>
> (Freud S 1905: 153–154)

The process of repression and idealisation, and the splitting of the ego in the service of the defence against castration anxiety, are fully elaborated in 1915, 1919, 1927, 1940/38a and 1940/38b. In 'An outline of psycho-analysis' we find the clearest statement:

> The creation of the fetish was due to an attempt to destroy the evidence for the possibility of castration, so that fear of castration could be avoided. If females, like other living creatures, possess a penis, there is no need to tremble for the continued possession of one's own penis. Now we come across fetishists who have developed the same fear of castration as non-fetishists and react in the same way to it. Their behaviour is therefore simultaneously expressing two contrary premises. On the one hand they are disavowing the fact of their perception – the fact that they saw no penis in the female genitals; and on the other hand they are recognising the fact that females have no penis and are drawing the correct conclusions from it. The two attitudes persist side by side throughout their lives without influencing each other. Here is what may rightly be called a splitting of the ego. This circumstance also enables us to understand how it is that fetishism is so often only partially developed. It does not govern the choice of object exclusively but leaves room for a greater or lesser amount of normal sexual behaviour; sometimes, indeed, it retires into playing a modest part or is limited to a mere hint. In fetishists, therefore, the detachment of the ego from the reality of the external world has never succeeded completely.
>
> (Freud S 1940/1938a: 203)

In a very clear and helpful clinical chapter, Campbell (1989) describes work with 'Charles', an adolescent who first came for help at the age of 16 and who finally managed to sustain three years of five-times-weekly work from age 19.

He outlines a history of abandonment and intrusion by the mother, an absent father, the development of a fetish for big-breasted women (phallic women) as a defence against castration anxieties and suicidal wishes consequent on the sense of abandonment. Charles's phallic-oedipal conflicts centred around rage with the father for leaving him with his mother, and anxious competition with this father. The combination of early anxieties (abandonment, merging), castration anxiety and phallic aggression appear as key features.

A similar finding of the centrality of castration anxiety underlies Kohon's (1999) view and, of course: 'In psychoanalytic theory, the castration complex is indissolubly intertwined and integrated with the oedipus complex' (Kohon 1999: 34).

The implication is similar in the case of a 6-year-old girl described by Hopkins (1984). Fetishism is found in males; this little girl believed she was a boy; her fetishistic interests abated in tune with her acceptance of being a girl.

Sperling, unlike Freud and Campbell, does not connect the fetish object with the fantasised penis of the mother (Sperling 1963). It is striking, however, that in her overview of fetishism in children there are many descriptions of what we would now call 'transitional objects' (Winnicott 1951) and not fetishistic objects. The same, indeed, is true of Wulff's paper (1946). Where a sexualised or displaced erotic relationship (e.g. with the mother's feet or shoes) is actually involved, there appear to be very few case examples of children in print. Sperling states:

> It seems to me that the need for a fetish has something to do with the reality of the child's experiences. In the lives of these children there has been real seduction and actual over-stimulation of these component instincts in the relationship with the parents, especially with the mother.
>
> (Sperling 1963: 381)

This comes close to the role of trauma, perceived by Khan (1979) in the formation of perversions and by Hopkins (1984) in the formation of a foot and shoe fetish in her young patient with gender dysphoria. To Khan, the intrusion of the environment is a reality in the histories of many perverse patients, rather than the fantasy expressed by most neurotic ones, and this has often been a sexualised and sexualising environment. Hopkins' little girl had been abused by her father.

The absence of the oedipal parental couple, whose task is to maintain the boundaries between the infantile and the parental, between the adult sexual relationship and the passion of the child for both parents, is in such cases compounded by a trauma wherein the adult perverts those boundaries, takes the child as adult partner, and renders the child's proto-sexuality both adult and corrupt (Horne 2001).

Issues of separation and aggression also feature in the writing on fetishism. Siskind (1994) presents one of the few child papers, working with a 3½ year old who will not give up his nappies. Although one would not assume that resistance to nappy removal was a prelude to fetishism, there are valuable comments in Siskind's work. Becoming a separate, autonomous person and gaining a safe capacity to use the aggressive drive were key themes in the work with child and parents. The role of aggression also features in Gillespie (1940, 1964),

Coopersmith (1981) who describes aggression subsequent to separation, Anna Freud (1965, 1966; 1972), Parens (1989) and in Campbell (1989); and difficulties with phallic aggression. The need to keep the powerful maternal object at bay is also a theme, by dehumanisation (Cooper 1991), as a defence against aggression or against merging and being engulfed (Rabain 2001). Managing the transition of separation is key to Rabain's paper.

The role of the absent or passive father in relation to the establishment of perversions has been noted by several commentators (Mancia 1993; McDougall 1995). The role of parents is an interesting one psychoanalytically and has been connected to theories about the development of a faulty superego in perversion. Gillespie summarises it succinctly:

> The kind of parental model that is likely to be found in cases of sexual perversion in the child is one which prohibits normal heterosexuality above all else, and treats pregenital and perverse activities with relative leniency, or even encourages them . . .

> (Gillespie 1964)

Finally, Glover (1933) first drew our attention to the link between perversion and the development of the reality sense and so to perversion as a defence against psychosis. Coltart's case study, first written in 1967, also explores fetishism as a defence against psychosis (Coltart 1996). I have found this to be the case with many adolescent gender dysphoric patients (Horne 1999). With Stanley, it is noticeable that, in a somewhat polymorphous presentation, he also cross-dressed at one time but that this appears not to have contained his anxieties.

When we think about Stanley's history, we see a child for whom the development of a sense of muscularity and body-self, the precursor in Winnicottian (1950–1955) and psychological terms to positive aggressive affect, was grossly inhibited. Indeed, his functioning at present indicates great inhibition in aggression. Separation, for Stanley, was both enforced in an untimely manner (by hospitalisations and his mother's depression) and paradoxically also impossible to achieve. From the age of 3 he had no functioning oedipal third who might protect against merging or offer opportunities for identification, directing the child – in the classical role of the father (Colarusso 1992) – to the external world, away from the over-closeness of the mother and infant dyad. This continued in adolescence when issues of intimacy and sexuality must have required Stanley to seek a safe position away from this revival of closeness, when the potency of adolescent sexuality became an issue. The absence of the oedipal third, the father or adult sexual partner of the mother, appears to have left Stanley at adolescence with only the desperate manoeuvre of adopting a perverse solution. To keep the phallus safe, it became hidden in the merged pregnant mother dyad; to exercise his aggression and rage, he triumphed over the object by becoming it; in order not to deal with separation and mourning, he denies the need of an object. Work was patently not going to be easy, nor would it be swift.

Themes from the therapy: progress and process

Stanley is a short, slightly bent young man with brown hair that often sticks up in an unattended kind of way. He has poor articulation in his arms and finds shaving and combing his hair difficult. The hair on the back of his head has a very fine, baby-like appearance. He dresses quietly but appropriately and can have a very lively look in his brown eyes. When he moves, he does so at speed, scuttling from one place to another like a crustacean on the seabed. The large backpack that he brings (containing many drawings and folders of his main and symptomatic pre-occupations) adds to this shell-like look. He does look rather strange and, to Jim's fury, strangers have commented on it in the street.

Amongst the preoccupations expressed during his assessment appointments, apart from very large numbers of drawings of the pregnant mothers and babies mentioned in the referral, have been witches and magic. He told me that witches were, contrary to popular belief, good women and he had done a project on this in college. A favourite television programme concerned a young witch, Sabrina, who had magical powers passed to her by her witch mother (her father was a normal human). There was in this an enormous idealisation of powerful women – indeed, with their magic these witches could be seen as the Freudian phallic woman in displacement. Space for the fear of this phallus-seeking woman, or for the adult oedipal couple, seemed lacking.

He had three individual assessment sessions; I met his mother and Jim two weeks later, then had a final meeting with Stanley to discuss our way forward. At this meeting he seemed eager – spontaneous and quite definite – about coming for therapy but when I asked gently what he would hope for from it, he could not answer. He pointed dumbly to his portfolio of pictures. I wondered aloud if there was, in the preoccupation with mummies and babies in his drawings, something about himself – who am I and what happened when I was growing bigger? He looked but could not answer. I also wondered to myself if there was, in his choice of therapy, less a collusion with his mother and Jim, or a wish for change, but more an aggressive attack – see, I have a therapy mother now and do not need to think about you. I noted that he always called his mother, when he mentioned her, 'mother' in rather a cold fashion. This would mean that change in therapy might be resisted: the fact of having therapy could become important, rather than any change it might bring. Thus as 'subjective object' (Winnicott 1962) I might further become a fetishistic object (Renik 1992).

Brought by his mother or Jim at the start, after eight weeks Stanley began to travel to therapy on his own (quite a distance from outside London by bus, train and underground) and has done so ever since. The work has been slow. Early themes were of being both mother and infant – a pregnant mother – so there was no need for an object and, crucially, no need to be angry or to mourn separation. He brought sheaves of drawings of pregnant mothers and a recurring dream of being a pregnant woman. Although he occasionally brings dreams, Stanley is unable to associate to these, stating them almost as concrete facts. His many drawings can go through several incarnations: he keeps his 'originals' and often copies them, then sees how they can be developed. I have taken up this idea of how things were in the beginning (his 'originals') and what can creatively be made of them.

A little of his history emerged from time to time but mainly he was in the here-and-now – or in the fantasy of his drawings, which to him appeared to have a reality. He had NO recollection (he was very firm in this, so firm as to be totally unbelievable) of his times in hospital. Eventually he was able to tell me a little of his school experience where there was a good male teacher whom he could appreciate and who he felt liked him, too, but also, swiftly, a recounting of a bad male teacher, as if the first were too much to hope for. It had been hard to contemplate male identifications. Later, he did say that he had been unwell from time to time throughout school and I could connect it both to his spells in hospital and to a worry, perhaps, that therapy might make him unwell – i.e. challenge the homeostasis of his defences. He added that he has asthma and tires easily. In the transference, I took this as a warning about pace.

The pictures of mothers and babies continued to appear, brought in large folders in his heavy backpack. The mothers, initially, were well-known female personalities whose glossy sexuality was important in their presentation and I wondered about this switching of interest from 'adult-sexual' to 'infantile-mothering', almost like a sleight-of-hand deception: 'I have actually drawn this (a sexual picture) but I make you focus on that (a mother and baby).' Soon a new version appeared, Tanya and her son Luke, Stanley's own invention, whose story centred mainly on their feeding and nappy-changing relationship. Tanya had blond hair, long red fingernails and a tendency in his drawings to look outwards 'to camera', even when ministering to Luke. Here was a narcissistic mother, with her nails potentially predatory. There was a striking lack of fathers, which I commented on. Then Tanya's home appeared – almost a mediaeval castle, impregnable and guarded by one armour-clad soldier outside a solid door. I asked, rather mischievously, if this were Luke's father, but no. There was no external oedipal third, protecting the male infant from being merged or damaged. After some months we moved to whether the mother (Tanya) wanted the infant himself, as a separate person in whose individual capacities she took delight, or whether he was somehow an extension of her, the only man she needed, and thus not really a little boy in his own right.

In relation to this theme, I have found myself drawing greatly on my experience of parent-infant observation, but also on the ego structuring, developmental work long undertaken at the Anna Freud Centre, London, and described by Hurry (1998). This entailed asking what each was thinking of the other, what was in Luke's mind when he smiled or seemed apprehensive (as he increasingly did at nappy changing time), how he knew his mother was thinking about him – as if we were jointly the observers of the developing Luke. Stanley watched a television series on child development and read old books on infancy that he found in charity shops. He began to include aspects of attunement, gaze, Tanya reassuring Luke with her voice, as the central importance of Luke as a person was slowly allowed to appear. It felt as if there were times when a boy baby could begin to be safe and even enjoyed.

Interspersed with this was Stanley's liking for Thomas the Tank Engine, a series of children's books written by a Church of England vicar in the 1950s about steam engines operating on a railway line and their tasks and relationships. He occasionally brought a model of Thomas with him in his backpack and was passionate about a female engine, Lady. It emerged much later that he thought he had been given a Thomas the Tank Engine toy by his Grandfather Bert, his mother's father, when he was small. Grandfather Bert had been a nice man, and artistic, and when I wondered during the assessment if this could be where his drawing talent came from, Stanley beamed with pleased recognition. He died when Stanley was little. As we continued to meet, Stanley also declared a passion for Britt Allcroft who produced for children's television programmes based on Thomas. Ms Allcroft now possesses all the legal rights and has produced a film – another phallic lady! It has been easier for Stanley to fantasise being Britt Allcroft's stepson than to hold the male connection to Grandfather Bert in mind.

Stanley insisted that Thomas was, as the books call him, a Really Useful Engine; it was Stanley's ambition to be really useful. As a colleague has pointed out to me, the age of steam trains has passed, as has Thomas's real usefulness. This felt a moving comment on Stanley's anxiety about his own future and usefulness.

Some sixteen months ago – in the second month of treatment – Stanley let me see a page printed from the internet. It was for the 'Hubbies' web site, for hubbies (husbands) and naughty babies – patently a site for adult nappy wearers and seeming also to have something of the dominatrix about it – phallic women and men as babies. I offered rather obviously that this print out was very different from the adverts for Pampers and Milton that he had often brought or drawn. He nodded. I said that he found this exciting and he agreed. Stanley said he has a 'Big Babies' Kit' that he sometimes wears in bed at night under his pyjamas. I wondered about the sensations this gave – 'I don't really know'. I was thinking of skin and the kind of memories his traumatised body might have, plus the hidden sexual excitement in the nappy. 'I don't really know' means 'I am not yet ready to think about this – do not at this point pursue this topic.' He did, however, accept a comment about the importance of grown up baby men and strong women in his mind.

The drawings of a pregnant Tanya became less about Tanya and more about Luke – a large arrow labelled 'ME' pointed to the inside of the womb when she was drawn pregnant. I began to feel we were skirting around what had gone wrong, via looking at what was necessary for things to go right for the baby and, by displacement, Stanley. Luke's toys came alive when Tanya and Luke were not there – a sense that Stanley could be potent and mischievous when on his own.

Ambivalence towards Jim emerged from time to time. There was the beginning of enjoyment of conversations with him, and an appreciation of things Jim does for him. 'I don't really like Jim' came almost in the same breath and Stanley was able to talk about the disruption to him, alone with mother, when Jim arrived but that some things about Jim were also very interesting. Developmentally, this certainly offered possibilities.

Stanley moved into the outside world eight months into therapy. He was given a specialist placement at a Day Centre, a unit that helped young adults with learning difficulties to prepare for work. He went there every day except his therapy day. There he aligned himself, in a Really Useful kind of way, with the staff, finding the indiscipline and rebelliousness of another group member very hard to take and reacting like a 7-year-old who struggles with superego issues: 'He did it and he shouldn't!'

His drawings began to contain little bug-like figures (microbes) who were harmless to Luke and lived on the contents of the dirty nappies. His soiling until 5 and bedwetting until 9 or 10 meant his being in a nappy at night and must have given rise to a confusion of anal, phallic and sexual development. His anality is accessible in the microbes and additionally they perform the function he needs a non-narcissistic mother to perform – unlike the original 'out to camera' mother of his drawings, or the depressed mother of his reality, they can tolerate and appreciate his mess and the sense of agency and aggression that is bound up in anal interests.

After nine months of therapy, there was a brief glimpse of heterosexual masculinity in Stanley's choice of *Titanic* as his favourite film, although there followed a swift retreat from this in his two next favourites, *Harry Potter and the Philosopher's Stone* and *Thomas and the Magic Railway*. I was ill at the first session after Christmas: Stanley did not get the message and made the long journey to the clinic to find me absent. He could not access his anger or disappointment at this. Later that term, in March, I succumbed once more to 'flu. This time the message cancelling got through. Stanley came to his next session complaining of overwork and tiredness, and the demands of his week including his therapy. The Easter break loomed, as did Stanley's 21st birthday. He announced that he and his mother were having a holiday at his birthday (the last session before the Easter break) and he would not be attending.

On his return he had drawn his usual pregnant mother but suddenly she was in a nurse's uniform – a nursery nurse, he said. I wondered if this was a screen memory of hospital when he was born, or an acknowledgement of his painful year there at 12/13. There was also great potential in straightforward male fantasy about nurses! She was, however, clearly wearing my shoes. I did not know how to take this up but there they were, different from his usual, black with a heel. I felt guilty I might be producing a foot fetish in Stanley . . . Part of me felt amused (the dangerous collusive reaction), part felt assaulted (he has stolen my shoes – he doesn't want my thoughts but will take over my shoes). I reflected on his need, faced with a longer break than expected, to retreat to female identification and part-objects. In thinking about this development, the desperation and aggression within it, and the beaming idealisation Stanley shows when I come to collect him to start his session, I was greatly helped by Renik's article on the patient's use of the analyst as a fetish (Renik 1992).

Some 14 months into therapy Stanley brought a dream of a woman with one breast covered and one exposed. There followed drawings over two sessions and, for the first time, he drew in the session what he had dreamed. There is nothing infantile about his drawing of breasts and it was possible to interpret that the breasts were of importance both to babies (breast = food) and to young men of Stanley's age who would see them as very sexual. He nodded. I commented on how appropriate it was for, say, a 21-year-old Luke to find this a sexy and exciting drawing. He stared at it. He agreed it was exciting but covered it over with baby drawings. I thought that sometimes it felt safer to think of 'baby Luke' rather than 'young man Luke with exciting thoughts'. He began to put the papers away: it was, unfortunately the end of the session and I awaited the return of his sexy lady for several months.

Session

The following material, after a year's work, simply demonstrates how finely balanced the defences are, and how readily Stanley feels the phallic anxiety that summons them.

Stanley arrived, as usual 10 minutes early. I found him in the waiting room with a pad of paper. He gazed, beaming, then hastily collected his things. I noticed he did not have his backpack with him and found myself looking round for it, as if to tell him where it was like a nursery school teacher. I thought he looked significantly unburdened and thought of the turtle without its shell: was this a lightening of his defensive load or the evidence of vulnerability? He hastened along the hallway and down the stairs to the therapy room. Settling into his seat, he organised his sheaves of papers, his pad and a Simpsons' comic book. I observed this – both childish and adult, but certainly not compliant, the dysfunctional Simpson family of the comic book possibly contained a sense of hope of being different.

Stanley produced a small bundle of drawings interspersed with a few pages of text. These were all hand done. The themes were those of the previous months but, again, there were subtle shifts in the drawings. This time 'Luke', the baby, was not having his nappy changed. He was often on the floor, with a sidelong smiling look at his smiling mother. Good eye contact and mutual appreciation appeared to be important. The anxiety of earlier drawings appeared to have gone. I wondered if expressing the age-appropriate sexuality of the woman with the exposed breast had given permission for the appearance of a baby whose castration anxiety did not dominate his mind.

There were still, however, one or two of the little microbes, sometimes following the mother and inadvertently being stood on by her. I wondered about these. He shook his head: 'I'm still working out what they are.' I said that I had been thinking about how they do a very important task for Luke – they clean him up – and their function is one that the mother might do. Perhaps they do not quite believe that the mother can care for her little boy baby properly? Or perhaps, now that Tanya is much more in tune with what Luke needs, they are not needed?

Stanley told me he was working at a Garden Centre four days a week at the moment. He was feeling tired and could not understand why the others in his group were only doing two days a week. I (wrongly) wondered if he had thought this might be a compliment, that his competence was recognised. He looked puzzled. I should have waited for the affect rather than try to guess it. I had enacted a not-in-tune mother.

Suddenly he turned to face me and said, 'I had a dream last night. You were in it!' He was not sure what it meant but told me that I had talked to him in the dream. He smiled with great pleasure. I had never had a patient who had dreamed about me and was momentarily quite disconcerted. I wondered what had happened in the dream. 'You asked me if I wanted to be a woman.' He could not say what he had understood by this question. After a bit of thinking about what feelings went with the dream, and getting nowhere, I wondered to him if in the dream he was very unsure whether I was a therapist who wanted him to be a man and appreciated him as such, or did I want to steal away all the male bits – a little like baby Luke in his drawings when he is apprehensive about his mother changing his nappy. It was interesting that the memory of the dream, with its collusion with not being male and hiding the penis, came after my failure of attunement. He sat thinking with his brow furrowed, then added that he sometimes dreamed things that then happened. When he had been asked to take part in a focus group as a user of services for clients with learning difficulties, he found it was what he had dreamed of the night before. I thought that sounded rather magical and that his dream had been working for him, preparing for the next day's uncertainties. This made him connect to the dream that, he said, had made him go out to the theatrical costumier in a local town and buy the 'Big Baby Kit' in the first place. He had dreamed he was wearing a nappy. The next day he had gone to the shop and bought the kit.

I found myself struggling with this material. Stanley began to put his drawings in their file and this gave me space to wonder about the sequence of this conversation. There are often pauses – long pauses – in our sessions but today he had talked most of the time. My misunderstanding something about the work at the Garden Centre had led to his hiding his anger and disillusionment with me by diverting into my wishing him to be female. He colluded, moreover, in hiding the phallus by then bringing the dream that directed him to wear a nappy. A not-in-tune therapist turns so swiftly into a potentially rapacious therapist, whom one needs to defend against.

He returned to the theme of the Garden Centre. Four days a week he goes there from the Day Centre after lunch and he is finding it tiring. He is the only one doing four days: the others are doing two. After a lot of returning to this, it emerged that he was annoyed about it. He did not like working in this kind of job. The people who run it are nice and the public is nice when coming in to buy plants and gardening requirements, but he has worked in a shop before (a pet shop) and simply does not like it. He had told this very clearly to the staff at the Day Centre– and they placed him there despite this and for twice the time the others do. I commented on the need to be heard. He became lively – yes, he hadn't been heard. I said that he felt justifiably angry about this as he had done this work before and not been heard. YES! I wondered aloud whether he sometimes wondered if I would be a therapist who would be in tune and really understand him – that he had told me of the Garden Centre but I had not understood properly the first time about not being heard, but he had been brave and brought it back for us to think about. 'I'm not really sure.'

Leaving the room, still in the basement, he said, 'See you next week'. At the beginning of his therapy, he never said goodbyes and, indeed, he did not say hello but arrived and began, as if to deny any breaks and abandonments. For the previous six months he had said, 'See you next week' upstairs as he exited the clinic and the words were usually addressed straight ahead of him to the main door.

The next week we were back to the backpack and the safety of many drawings. He told me carefully that most were done on the two days prior to his session and I wondered if this could be connected – he needed the drawings less after our meeting but, when he was thinking about coming, he found the urge to draw. He looked at me silently, his brow wrinkled in puzzlement. The drawings were of nappy changing. The far more in-tune mothering was still very evident and I was able to make two interpretations – one about what might be in Luke's mind as the red fingernails approached him: 'It's my penis, don't hurt it and don't steal it.' This resonated with him and got a lively nod and smile. The second was to connect his frustration of the previous week about the Garden Centre (he had a further two weeks to do there) and the adults not hearing or being in tune with what he had said he needed, unlike Tanya who now knew how to be in tune with Luke.

Issues in technique

Monitoring the counter-transference, using colleagues for thought, avoiding counter-transference acting-out (Baker 1994) – all have been important in work with Stanley. To this Chasseguet-Smirgel (1981, 1985) adds the difficulty in establishing a therapeutic alliance, and the avoidance of insight and of the achievement of reality. This I have found with Stanley as I suddenly experience anxiety about being treated as an idealised but part-object – e.g. in the emergence of my shoes in his drawings – I wondered if his control over my difference, our individuality and his aggression takes the form of incorporating me. The pressure is thus to collude with the deception. I find something similar happens when my mind drifts, as it sometimes does. Usually, when this occurs with other young people, I find I am actually thinking of something that illuminates the therapy. With Stanley, I drift, and my mind is unconnected to the material. In this, colleagues have been helpful in pointing out that it is the phallic self being hidden again, a process of blocking me out from seeing his potency, and I can now use this as a cue for thought. Interpretations are often met with blankness, 'I don't really know', and rarely the sense I have offered something of meaning. At a later date I might have one fed back to me, as we all experience from patients when an interpretation has been meaningful and assimilated. With Stanley, it is hard to know at times if this has real internal meaning or if it is another rather adhesive identification with me. As the ego structuring work (e.g. affect recognition and legitimisation) continues, however, I think that there *is* a slow, gradual pace of genuine internalisation.

Much of the work has been done in the displacement of Luke and Tanya, or Thomas and Lady. I have had some weird conversations. Yet I think it has been important to set out some of the themes and anxieties in the manageable arena of the displacement, and slowly bring them into the real world. With such a concrete approach and such perilously sensitive anxiety about castration and potency, Stanley has needed great care about pace and timing.

Several commentators mention the pressure to collude, to be a voyeur (McDougall 1978), with 'the focus on the activation or enactment of the underlying unconscious fantasies in the transference' (Kernberg 1997: 30). This is very hard in the counter-transference and seems connected, too, to my moments of absence and the pressure to ignore his age-appropriate phallic potency. In the session material, it can be seen how swiftly, when I am not quite in touch, he initiates the female or infantile defence, and how long it can take for me to feel back in a comprehending mode.

Carignan has written that the passivity of analytic neutrality can be misconstrued as 'a repetition of early parental permissiveness and tacit encouragement of perverse behaviour' (Carignan 1999: 911). This represents the internal parents who prohibit genital sexuality but treat pregenitality or perverse activity with leniency, mirroring the external parents described by Gillespie (1964). Stanley's mother 'did not notice' Stanley's flight from genital sexuality – and may well have colluded with it – until the arrival of Jim whose concern (as a male) activated help. I find I constantly struggle as to how active to be – when to leave silences, when these become collusive with a fantasy of being merged, and when to intervene. There are times when, to Stanley, people are merely impingements – and often ego-threatening ones. The issue of how the ego protects itself from intrusion and abandonment at the same time (Stanley's early and lengthy hospital experience) is a crucial one in the therapy and one that also affects my thinking about silences.

In the first nine months of work there were very few indications of anger and aggression; I would be greeted with a beaming smile. I wondered if we would ever be able to access aggression and a sense of agency. My illnesses by chance helped open up the possibility of anger and demonstrated the threat that this presented to the immature self. Stanley wished to stop but could not quite put it in such aggressive terms! He was tired with being at the Day Centre, signing on at the Job Centre every fortnight, and then coming here. It was all too much for him and – exhaustedly – was making him ill. I sympathised with this, and commented on the great number of women who made demands of him – the staff at the Day Centre, his mother who found the place there for him, his experience at an earlier placement in a residential home for the elderly, and, of course, me who seemed to take for granted his coming here but who had let him down very badly by being off ill. I interpreted his great disappointment in me and the rightness of his annoyance.

When one thinks of the fetish as a response to trauma (Khan 1979; Hopkins 1984) one recalls Stanley's early experience of traumatic birth, unavailable mother (he was in an incubator, she was very depressed), his not being the son his mother must have anticipated, his painful months in hospital, especially those when he was entering puberty, abandonment by father, and failure to grow. He has had multiple traumas. Additionally, one wonders about the mother of any child who stays in nappies at night until the age of 9 or 10, and what the child might mean for her in his maleness that has to be so hidden. The role of mother as narcissistic predator appears in his drawings – the hands with long red varnished nails reaching anonymously into the cot where baby Luke looks growingly apprehensive. It is not surprising that allowing the memory of such a traumatic childhood into his mind is as yet barely possible for Stanley. As we develop a kind of treatment alliance, and if in the transference I can gain stability as a reliable, non-threatening, valuing object, we may be able to get to the traumas. For the moment, I carry them in my mind and merely elucidate manageable aspects of them.

Stanley had adopted an omnipotent, barren position of not needing people and of not being separate – or mourning the developmental achievements of individuation and separation. He could not entertain a sense of 'going-on-being' (in himself or his object) but appeared to insist on existing in the moment, denying separation or our week apart between sessions. This precluded both development (necessitating the fetish as the only route for sexuality) and reflection (the idea of the 'third' so well outlined by Britton (1989)). I have had to think carefully about intimacy and distance, taking care to engage him in the waiting room, where I greet him; and in the therapy room, when he instantly rushes for his papers as we sit down, I ask how he is. This makes him pause, reminding him of our separateness. Sometimes he brushes it aside as if unheard, but more often now he will respond in kind. At times, increasingly, he can manage not to reach for his drawings. I see this as progress – I hope it means that, although he anticipates a predatory narcissistic object, he can be brought back in touch with a potentially benign yet separate one. He can now spontaneously tell me of aspects of his week – we *have*, then been apart – and how he felt. Moreover, his 'sexy lady' has returned, allowing a sense of phallic potency into the therapy room, with an apparent diminution in castration anxiety. Two weeks ago, after a long gap, he brought a further drawing of Luke. He was grinning, crawling on the floor, and his mother was in an armchair, reading, at an appropriate distance from him. 'I thought I would draw it for old times' sake,' said Stanley. We thought together about the boy child, growing up knowing it was all right to be a boy. Stanley smiled and put Luke away in his folder.

Conclusion

We have a long way to go: the work is slow, not easy, and relies greatly on monitoring the counter-transference. Stanley, fortunately, seems glad to continue. I am often puzzled as to why and hope it is not all just one gross collusion. His mother and Jim have noticed significant change – Stanley is now willing to engage more with the external world (he has recently gone back to college to do a morning's Art course) and he is much more communicative at home. He and Jim have more of a sense of 'chaps facing the world together' – it was Jim who dropped him off for his first day back at college two weeks ago and who ensured that he had enjoyed his time there. Having an external male who values him and lets him know this – a father who claims him as male – is an important asset, however ambivalent Stanley might at times be, although I note the ambivalence is receding. In the therapy room, over the last two months, there has been very little mention of his drawings. Thomas has also taken a back seat. His interests are more latency ones – football, and the television soap drama, *Eastenders*, where Stanley's initial identification with a female character has been replaced by a range of personalities, all with their own potential, men as well as women. The 'real world' advent of a benign, interested man, directing Stanley's interests outward and away from the terrifying and seductive need for merging, has complemented the therapy. Oedipus conquered, or at least able to be contemplated, the tasks of latency and adolescence perhaps become possible.

Note

1 This paper appeared in the *Journal of Child Psychotherapy* 2003 29(1).

References

Baker, R (1994) Psychoanalysis as a lifeline: a clinical study of a transference perversion *International Journal of Psycho-Analysis* 75(4): 743–753

Britton, R (1989) The missing link: parental sexuality in the Oedipus complex. In R Britton, M Feldman & E O'Shaughnessy (eds.) *The Oedipus Complex Today: Clinical Implications* London: Karnac

Campbell, D (1989) Charles: a fetishistic solution. In M Laufer & ME Laufer (eds.) *Developmental Breakdown and Psychoanalytic Treatment in Adolescence* New Haven & London: Yale University Press

Carignan, L (1999) The secret: study of a perverse transference *International Journal of Psychoanalysis* 80: 909–928

Chasseguet-Smirgel, J (1981) Loss of reality in perversions – with special reference to Fetishism *Journal of the American Psychoanalytic Association* 29(3): 511–534

Chasseguet-Smirgel, J (1985) *Creativity and Perversion* London: Free Association Books

Colarusso, CA (1992) *Child and Adult Development: A Psychoanalytic Introduction for Clinicians* New York/London: Plenum Press

Coltart, N (1996) The man with two mothers. In *The Baby and the Bathwater* London: Karnac Books

Cooper, AM (1991) The unconscious core of perversion. In G Fogel & W Myers (eds.) *Perversions and Near-Perversions in Clinical practice – New Psychoanalytic Perspectives* New Haven & London: Yale University Press

Coopersmith, SE (1981) Object-instinctual and developmental aspects of aggression *Psychoanalytic Review* 68(3): 371–383

Freud, A (1965) *Normality and Pathology in Childhood: Assessments of Development* New York: International Universities Press

Freud, A (1966) *The Ego and the Mechanisms of Defence* London: Hogarth Press

Freud, A (1972) Comments on aggression *International Journal of Psycho-Analysis* 53: 163–72 Reprinted in *Psychoanalytic Psychology of Normal Development* London: Hogarth Press 1982

Freud, S (1905) Three Essays on the theory of sexuality *SE* 7 123–245 London: Hogarth Press

Freud, S (1915) Repression *SE* 14: 141–158 London: Hogarth Press

Freud, S (1919) A child is being beaten – a contribution to the study of the origin of sexual perversions *SE* 17: 175–204 London: Hogarth Press

Freud, S (1927) Fetishism *SE* 21: 147–157 London: Hogarth Press

Freud, S (1940/1938a) An outline of psycho-analysis: Chapter VIII – The psychical apparatus and the external world *SE* 23: 195–204 London: Hogarth Press

Freud, S (1940/1938b) Splitting of the ego in the process of defence *SE* 23: 271–278 London: Hogarth Press

Gillespie, WH (1940) A contribution to the study of fetishism *International Journal of Psycho-analysis* 21: 401–415. Reprinted in MDA Sinason (ed.) *Life, Sex and Death – Selected Writings of William H Gillespie* London: Routledge 1995

Gillespie, WH (1964) The psychoanalytic theory of sexual deviation with special reference to fetishism. In I Rosen (ed.) *The Pathology and Treatment of Sexual Deviation* London: Oxford University Press

Glover, E (1933) The relation of perversion formation to the development of a reality sense *International Journal of Psycho-Analysis* 14: 486–504

Hopkins, J (1984) The probable role of trauma in a case of foot and shoe fetishism: aspects of the psychotherapy of a six-year-old girl *International Review of Psycho-Analysis* 11(1): 79–91

Horne, A (1999) Thinking about gender in theory and practice with children and adolescents *Journal of the British Association of Psychotherapists* 37: 35–49

Horne, A (2001) Of bodies and babies: sexuality and sexual theories in childhood and Adolescence. In Harding, C (ed.) *Sexuality: Psychoanalytic Perspectives* London: Brunner Routledge

Hurry, A (1998) *Psychoanalysis and Developmental Therapy* London: Karnac

Kernberg, OF (1997) Perversion, perversity and normality: diagnostic and therapeutic considerations *Psychoanalysis and Psychotherapy* 14(1): 19–40

Khan, MMR (1979) *Alienation in the Perversions* New York: International Universities Press

Kohon, G (1999) Fetishism. In *No Lost Certainties to be Recovered* London: Karnac

McDougall, J (1978) *Plea for a Measure of Abnormality* New York: International Universities Press

McDougall, J (1995) *The Many Faces of Eros* London: Free Association Books

Mancia, M (1993) The absent father: his role in sexual deviations and in transference *International Journal of Psycho-Analysis* 74(5): 941–950

Parens, H (1989) Towards a reformulation of the psychoanalytic theory of aggression. In SI Greenspan & GH Pollock (eds.) *The Course of Life* Vol. 2: *Early Childhood* New York: International Universities Press

Rabain, J-F (2001) Angoisse d'engloutissement et scenario fetichique. [The anxiety of being engulfed and the fetishistic scenario] *Revue Francaise de Psychanalyse* 65(5): 1625–1639

Renik, O (1992) The use of the analyst as a fetish *Psychoanalytic Quarterly* 61(4): 542–563

Siskind, D (1994) Max and his diaper: an example of the interplay of arrests in psychosexual development and the separation-individuation process *Psychoanalytic Inquiry* 14(1): 58–82

Sperling, M (1963) Fetishism in children *Psychoanalytic Quarterly* 32(3): 374–392

Winnicott, DW (1950–55) Aggression in relation to emotional development. In *Collected Papers: Through Paediatrics to Psychoanalysis* London: Hogarth Press 1975

Winnicott, DW (1951) Transitional objects and transitional phenomena. In *Playing and Reality* New York: Basic Books 1971

Winnicott, DW (1962) The aims of psycho-analytical treatment. In *The Maturational Processes and the Facilitating Environment: Studies in the Theory of Emotional Development* London: Hogarth Press 1965

Wulff, M (1946) Fetishism and object choice in early childhood *Psychoanalytic Quarterly* 15: 450–471

9 Thinking about gender in theory and practice with children and adolescents[1]

Prologue: George, Sam and Orlando

George had enjoyed dressing in his mother's clothes and jewellery since he was 3 years old. Now 8, he disliked boys' games, hated football (the main boys' occupation at break time in his school) and preferred to chat with the girls. He was a gifted young actor, a member of a local children's dramatic society, took tap dancing lessons and was a choir member. He knew the words and music of all the Spice Girls' songs and the scores of many musicals – *Annie* and *The Sound of Music* were favourites, as was *Oliver* in which he had appeared on stage. George had confessed to his parents that he wished to be a girl.

Sam had also cross-dressed since he was 3 years old. He recalled the silky feel of his mother's underwear and the sensation against his skin. He had good male friends, experienced no difficulties in friendships and followed stereotypical male pursuits with his friends. At 17, he continued to experience a compulsion to cross-dress, got into debt buying girls' clothes and, while quite clear that he was male and had no wish to be female, had a persistent fantasy of an encounter with another male transvestite where they had a sexual relationship. 'I think I'm heterosexual but I can imagine a relationship with another trannie.' Sam has had one girlfriend and noted that his transvestism abated during the relationship.

Orlando recalls being dressed in girls' clothes by his mother, aged 3, but says his mother now lies to him about this, saying she did not do so. He knew he was really a girl from as early as he could recall until 8 years old, then he was content to be male. At 15½, however, he once more felt that he was really female – or, at least, being both male and female, the female side was now striving to become dominant. He thought that his life of being defined by others as a 'divv' or a 'retard' would change if he changed physically. He experienced difficulties in peer relations and in academic work. Orlando, now 20, expresses himself in very concrete terms: there is no 'as if' quality to his conversation.

Introduction

One is accustomed, in work with children and adolescents, to engage with a fluidity of psychological structure and possibilities, or to work towards the recovery of such fluidity. There is a process of development and a developmental 'track' with which, as therapists, we seek to re-engage the child, as the defences become less inappropriate and the ego strengthens. When faced with issues of gender dissonance and dysphoria in children and young people, however, one encounters not only a most painful disjunction between psyche and soma but at times a rigidity of defence that can be both shocking and challenging. The task, therefore, becomes one of keeping the developmental processes in mind and, if possible, open, precluding the foreclosure of a transsexual defence and the finality of surgery.

In this paper I hope simply to explore a little of the theoretical understanding reached by those who work with children where gender is an issue, and perhaps to stimulate others to think about theory and the implications for practice. The force to write it has come from my clinical experience and the need to struggle with making sense when there appears to be a drive towards madness – how to find space for thought and reflection in the face of a desperate insistence on action.

The children in the Prologue to this paper all present with familiar constellations of symptomatology and behaviour. It has been said that it is often in the most rigidly defended children that one hears a story of gender dysphoria from around 3 years of age or from 'as early as I can remember': 'Atypical organisations that develop very early in the child's life may be more likely to become rigidly structured than organisations that develop later in response to some traumatic experience' (Di Ceglie 1998).

For George, Sam and Orlando an early realisation of something not right between perceptions of body and psychological sense of self was an experience they had in common. Their pathways since then, however, have been diverse. I would hope, therefore, to stress that atypical positions adopted by children in relation to gender may not fit cleanly into our theoretical assumptions and expectations (or our theoretical disputes), and suggest that we retain an openness to the individuality of the young person's experience and psychological stance. Yet such a position of open-mindedness is not easy to sustain in this work, so rigid is the defence and so strong the rush to foreclosure when it involves something as fundamental to the sense of self as gender identity.

Context

The explosion of gender studies in the last 30 years has been paralleled by an equal acceleration of interest in gender in the psychoanalytic world. The influence of the feminist movement, the rediscovered writings of early theorists (e.g. Karen Horney and Ernest Jones) and the re-assessment of Freud's theory of female sexuality from a clinical base (Chasseguet-Smirgel 1964/1970), paralleled the work done by Money (1955, 1994) and Stoller (1968, 1996) on the concepts of gender identity and gender role. A healthy dialogue with Anthropology, Philosophy, Biology and Sociology has ensued, allowing evidence of cultural and biological influence to be tested and to inform hypotheses about the development of internal self-constructs (Brain 1998; Imperato-McGinley et al 1979; James 1998). For a more detailed overview of this progression the reader is directed to Person and Ovesey (1983), Young-Bruehl (1996) and to Gaffney & Reyes (1999). From the latter studies, and from the work of Money on intersex disorders, we can assert fairly firmly that there is not a proven biological cause of gender dysphoria in childhood (Brain 1998). On the issue of biological pre-disposition, the jury, according to Brain, is still out:

> It is not clear, however, whether any of the specified cultural differences so far demonstrated are predisposing factors in their own right, or whether they are the result of some environmental factor or independent external event which itself is the main source of the gender identity disorder.
>
> (Brain 1998: 78)

The psychoanalytic debate today has become preoccupied with the deconstruction of gender (e.g. Dimen 1991) and is notably influenced by the American relational school of psychoanalysis, in debate with contemporary feminism. For the psycho-therapist engaged in work with children and young people where biological sex has become a denied part of the self or where there is ambivalence experienced, there are several theorists who offer their own direct experience of work with children as well as those who write from a reconstruction of the experiences of adult transsexuals.

Thoughts on theory

Several themes as to causation emerge when one explores the theory in this area. Contemporary Freudians, following Anna Freud's developmental lines, have pos-ited a developmental line for the establishment of gender identity, with much work on delineating points on that line (Tyson 1982; Bernstein 1993; Fast 1990). This approach, in tune with others, locates the achievement of 'core gender iden-tity' by the end of the anal stage, around 18 months of age, 'core gender identity' being: 'the most primitive, conscious and unconscious, sense of belonging to one sex and not the other' (Tyson 1982, referring to Stoller).

The classical position of castration anxiety in boys is taken as indicative of a core gender identity. In girls, the discovery of anatomical difference, as in Freud's (1905) 'Three Essays on the Theory of Sexuality', is a major factor in feminine identification and the development of the maternal ego ideal, immediate precur-sors to core gender identity consolidation. One can thus see the move from anal to phallic phases, with the dependence on the environment that this entails, as critical classically in the establishment of gender dysphoria.

Amongst other writers, several themes emerge. Issues in identification and/or dis-identification (e.g. Winnicott 1968; Greenson 1968; Benjamin 1991; Diamond 1997), and the process by which one becomes the same but different, have a role. Wilson proposes the interesting idea that, in adopting a position of alienation from his/her gender and body of origin, the child is making a statement of difference (Wilson 1998). Where similarity is overwhelming, or merging a threat, this would make sense. Indeed, problems of the individuation-separation phase, including the wish to merge with the object, feature in Stoller's understanding of gender confusion (Stoller 1975).

> Sam's parents had a volatile relationship. Married young, they fought throughout their marriage and at one point separated. Sam was the first child, followed by three girls. He has painful memories of his father's violence towards his mother – although it took longer to recall his mother's provocation of this and his father weeping with Sam in the kitchen when Sam was a toddler. Identification with a father whose aggression was fearful or who was perceived as weak seemed an impossible and unwanted task. Sam, moreover, recalled in therapy his sense that his father was jealous of him, and even when he was a small child he would experience his father's rage at his mother's preoccupation with him. He could not understand why his father did not like him. Later in therapy he managed to stand up to the aggressive father who, with some relief, began to enjoy a relationship with his son.
>
> In addition, Sam appeared to be negotiating his intimacy and distance from his mother – his use of her clothing as a toddler was, he thought, known to her and he described the touch of it like skin. As his fetish developed, it became more apparent that there was a narcissistic delight for him in being cross-dressed: he would let loose his long hair, dress up and delight in looking at himself in the mirror from the neck down, avoiding seeing his face. His individuation and identification problems were solved: he sustained both sexes in one and had no need of any object. Sam's excitement lay in the preparation for this: afterwards he would be disgusted and often gave away his female clothes.

More frequently in the literature, separation anxiety, object loss, abandonment and early trauma (Coates & Person 1985: Coates, Friedman & Wolfe 1991; Coates & Moore 1998; Bleiberg, Jackson & Ross 1986; Roiphe & Galenson, 1973) feature, and a general agreement that the locus of conflict is pre-oedipal. A cross-gender fantasy may enable the child to cope with unmanageable levels of anxiety. Many of the children who present with gender dissonance have histories that bear this out:

> George was born 15 months after the death of his sister, Jeannie, from sudden infant death syndrome. Jeannie had been the second child, a much wished-for girl after the first-born boy. George's parents had been devastated: in their grief, they had also found areas for disillusionment in each other and it was in an atmosphere of depression and antipathy that they decided to try immediately for a replacement child. George, as a boy who lived, was both pleasure and disappointment. His parents' depression continued into his toddlerhood. By the time they noticed George's gender confusion, their marriage was back on track and the depression gone. A sister was born when George was 3 years old. His dressing up and play with girls was looked on as mild eccentricity, it being too painful to think otherwise.

One would wish to add to this list of factors the importance of the body ego as the first 'self' – cross-gender identification, after all, is one of many childhood and adolescent symptoms indicative of the despair with which the arrival of an adult, sexual body may be met. It has at times seemed unfashionable to write of bodies, yet it appears to me highly important that we do so. Gaddini's reminder of the entwinement of mind and body seems timely (Gaddini 1992). If, as seems likely, the location of gender difficulties lies in the first 18 months of life, we are dealing with children when they are pre-verbal or 'beginner practitioners' at being verbal. There is not yet, therefore, an arena for symbolisation – or for other than physical expression of the deficit, trauma or absence that influences the later choice of a cross-gender identified position as the only perceivable position for the child to adopt. The affirmation of the body – the physical boundariedness of the baby and delight in its being – would then emerge as critical in the process of the development of a sense of 'male' or 'female' as wished for and desired by the object.

> Orlando recalled his mother dressing him as a girl. He disparaged his father, an Italian whose wish for him to learn Italian was construed by Orlando as not seeing him but simply wanting 'a son like himself, not me as me'. After more than a year's therapy, Orlando confessed that his Dad was 'not such an arsehole,' that he had some recent interesting conversations with him. His wish for a benign father seemed hopeful. He thought that his mother had excluded his father from him, and began to be able to tolerate thinking that this might have been experienced by his father as a loss. An early oedipal dream demonstrated the power of his rivalry and feared oedipal revenge as he recounted that he had often dreamed that he got up in the night and wanted to go to his mother's bedroom. [This was both parents' bedroom, but he had obliterated his father from it in the dream.] As he opened his bedroom door, he was almost flattened by a large express train thundering down the hall-way. Over many months he was able to think about the role of his father in affirming masculinity – a theme paralleled by his love of Astronomy and his spending nights in the garden 'with my telescope. I wish I had a bigger, more powerful one, though – it's only little – well, not that little but I could do much more if it was bigger.'

Part of the oedipal resolution should involve not only the renunciation of the opposite-sex parent but also lead to the child's experiencing an affirmation of gender and gender role by that parent. McDougall (1995) quotes an unpublished thesis by Seccarelli who found that girls seeking sex reassignment have fathers who play a predominant role, treating these girls as sons, encouraging them in boys' games. In the Gender Identity Development Service, we have found the absence of fathers in psychological terms (and hence of any affirmation of femininity by the father) also to be significant in the experience of girls who present with gender dysphoria in latency and pre-puberty. In both cases, the affirmation by the opposite-sex parent is missing.

Stoller (1996) describes one scenario as follows:

> The reverse [of son-mother symbiosis] dominates the situation with extremely masculine girls, where mother was unable (e.g. because sorely depressed) to function adequately as a mother during this daughter's infancy, the baby having, been perceived by mother as not pretty, not feminine, not cuddly. And in each case, the child's father moves into the vacuum . . . Unfortunately, father and daughter join not in a heterosexual style but with father encouraging his daughter to be like him.

One can understand this in terms of negotiating the incest taboo. However, the unavailability of a depressed mother who cannot enjoy the baby girl's body appears to me more important as the first step, and the impossibility of identification with a depressed object follows before identification with the father becomes possible. There is an important recognition, in the psychological development of girls, of an internal space (for intercourse, babies) that has to be adopted into the construct of 'body' and 'self'. I wonder if the inability to tolerate this does not also arise from the sense of gap and absence that it entails – the internal space is empty and needs an object in adulthood if it is to become filled. For some girls, penetration, intercourse and pregnancy may be impossible because they remind one of the absent object, the unavailable mother of infancy and childhood, and an asexual transsexual position is sought as a defence against this pain.

It is also important to keep in mind McDougall's caveat, quoted at the start of this paper, that the bisexual nature of the human psyche makes imperative a process of mourning if one is to establish a singular sexuality in adulthood. Indeed, Freud's explication of the fundamental bisexual nature of our psychological constructs of self was later developed by Kubie into a comment on 'the drive to become both sexes' which he saw in many patients as a further 'source of conflict, namely that which arises out of man's frequent struggles to achieve mutually irreconcilable and consequently unattainable identities' (1974: 352).

For those of us working with children, an awareness that any developmental gain contains within it a parallel loss is essential; hence the loss of bisexuality and the potential to be and to have both sexual objects is painful. Denial – an early defence mechanism – is a feature in work with gender-confused children and young people. Indeed, with many an overtly asexual position seems to be sought, denying not only bisexuality but also the existence of two sexes.

McDougall (1995), from her work with adult patients, brings together three issues with great compassion and insight:

a)   the wish to have and to be both sexes;
b)   the ambivalence of unfulfilled longings with the corollary of the reluctance to relinquish, to perceive loss and mourn;
c)   the importance of the primal scene (pp.xi–xvi).

The last is also found important by Aron (1995) who develops a relational approach to the internalised primal scene. In work with Orlando, all three have featured, the earlier dream of the train perhaps expressing some fears about the primal scene.

Orlando described himself as being like a computer with two hard drives – one male, one female. When the male drive felt depleted, the female side would 'kick in'. In an attempt to preserve his maleness, or so it seemed, when he was sexually aroused by watching videos or reading magazines, Orlando's female side would urge, 'You really want to *be* her, don't you!' denying the sexual desire.

After almost two years of once weekly therapy, Orlando had reached a state of tentative object-relatedness, both in the transference and in the external world. He lurched into an adolescent passion for a female tutor at college who, following an overture by him (it seemed to him), left the college. This abandonment led to a denial of affect or relationships and a flight into a female identity: better the narcissistic defence of being the object than the depression of loss and mourning.

More recently, Orlando has announced: 'I don't think I'm male and I don't think I'm female. I'm a machine.'

In thinking about this aspect of Orlando, and in my work with Sam, I have found Arnold Cooper's re-assessment of the narcissistic base of perverse development to be very helpful:

> . . . the core trauma in many if not all perversions is the experience of terrifying passivity in relation to the pre-oedipal mother perceived as dangerously malignant . . . The development of a perversion is a miscarried repair of this injury, basically through dehumanisation of the body and the construction of three core fantasies designed to undo the intolerable sense of helpless passivity
>
> (1991: 23)

Cooper defines this dehumanisation as a strategy to protect against human qualities – loving, vulnerability, unpredictability – and continues: 'All attempts to abolish difference . . . have dehumanisation, the absence of individuation, as one of their goals and consequences' (*ibid.*: 24).

The three core fantasies are that the mother is non-existent and I am in control; I cannot be controlled as I am non-human or subhuman; I control because I take pleasure from the 'monster mother'. As a consequence of each of these, I need not fear the object. For Orlando, the second is clearly operant.

It would also, finally, seem important when thinking about children that we keep in mind the fluidity of positions open to them. There can be a danger in taking a 'snapshot' rather than 'film' view. Dahl (1993), commenting on oedipal children, theorises that, in their play, they show a 'multi-dimensional gender identity' built on an accurate core but nevertheless exploratory of 'masculine' and feminine' aspects. The process is encapsulated in the query of one lad: 'Can I be a boy who likes Vivaldi?' Coates also underlines the fluidity of positions taken up by children, asking 'How important is gender to the child in the scheme of things?

How does it vary from one individual to the next? When can children treat gender as a performance that can be played with?' (Coates: 1997: 49).

Perhaps one end of the spectrum is evident in a delightful note by Winnicott (1996), entitled 'The Niffle' by his editors, wherein he describes the trauma of a 5-year-old boy who, having had an accident on holiday, is flown alone by air-ambulance to a hospital in a strange city. His mother cannot be with him; his transitional object 'his precious wool object, a special piece' – the niffle of the title – is posted to him by his mother but does not arrive. Safely home once more, Tom reacts not to the hospitalisation and accident but to the traumatic loss of the niffle. He regresses, resists being dressed, puts on a girlish voice (Winnicott reflects, possibly a baby voice) and offers at one point: 'Some boys think they will turn into girls if they lose something like that' (the niffle). Such a description of anxiety caused by the trauma of separation fits well with those theorists who perceive, in unmanageable, overwhelming anxiety and early trauma, threats to the ego and to a consolidated gender position.

Thoughts on practice

In work with children it is always vital to be part of a team. Where gender issues arise, the importance of colleagues who work with the family and with the network surrounding the child cannot be too highly stressed. Such children can present with learning and behavioural difficulties, depression, suicide attempts (often the way in which adolescent gender conflicts come to light) and social rejection and bullying. While the therapist struggles to engender a sense of curiosity in the child, parents and network need support. Parents, in addition, have great need of help in not replicating in the present the internalised parents of the patient, a position sought unconsciously by the child. It is also vital to keep in mind the tendency of any network to re-enact the internal world of the disturbed patient (Davies, 1996); hence colleagues who understand the mechanisms at work and who can verbalise these helpfully are essential.

In many of these child patients one encounters an absence of any capacity for symbolisation and a reliance on concrete thinking. This can mean that the process is long and slow, building up the psychological structure and working on developmental deficits (Hurry, 1998). That the capacity for symbolisation depends on the sense of separateness from a perceived (and perceivable) 'other' means that reaching this stage is a marked achievement. Although he retreated from this position, I can recall my sense of hope when, in response to my use of the word 'startling', Orlando looked me in the eye and said, 'Startling – that's a good word! A very good word!' It seemed as if it was possible to recognise a benign object whose words might feed and nourish. The absence of an 'as if' quality, however, means an especial care in interpretation as words take on concrete reality.

Within this 'structuring', one can feel enormous pressure in the countertransference, especially with adolescents for whom the pain of object-relatedness can all too easily be dealt with by the foreclosure of flight to surgical intervention. It is, in many ways, an asset that in this country irreversible interventions are not permitted prior to age 18. There is a view elsewhere in the EU that pre-pubertal sex reassignment is successful as it results in an absence of conflict at adolescence. There is a 'transsexual imperative', a thrust to escape or deny psychic conflict and a clustering of identity and sense of self around the certainty of being of the wrong gender. Technically, it is extremely important to respect this defence while struggling to engage a sense of curiosity about this self. This, too, entails not only experiencing the most profound despair in the counter-transference but also getting in touch with rage and sadism – 'being the object' is not simply a denial of difference but also an attack on that object. One can feel attacked and obliterated in the transference, and be put in touch with the most profound rage against the child's internal parents, rage that takes the child himself some time to reach. The area of curiosity is, moreover, not without its problems. Fantasies of cross-genderedness have often been secret, fantasies of primal scene have surely been so, and a suppression of curiosity is a feature of these children (Di Ceglie, 1995). The therapist's curiosity can feel unbearably penetrating or be experienced as forbidden or dangerous.

Keeping a strict analytic frame is imperative. I have found with Orlando an invitation to collude with – no, join in – the defence. He attempts to engage on a level of 'woman to woman' with diversions into make-up, shoes, dress. In this I have felt both a merged object (the 'sameness' can be addressed) and a part object made merely of different female attributes and clothing – close to the dehumanised mother of Cooper's core fantasies (Cooper, 1991). Keeping my separateness and integrity in mind has been vital. The omnipotent defence against loss and mourning means that one has to expect depression and ensure a structure that will contain and support the child/adolescent. The suicidal risk, described by Limentani (1979) as 'blackmail', is a real one. Sadowski and Gaffney (1998) locate this within the constellation of factors increasing risk in adolescence but add that the impact is greater where a stable sexual orientation has not been achieved or difference in gender identity is perceived.

At times, one of my major questions has been, 'Who holds the madness?' Classically transsexuality has been viewed as a defence against psychosis or a defence against homosexuality. In the therapy room one is faced, as with many borderline patients, with a child who appears to have direct access to one's unconscious and for whom the realities of the animal kingdom (male – female – procreation) are turned upside down. In the counter-transference one is put directly in touch with this distortion of reality. After sessions with Orlando, I have often emerged, seeking a colleague to talk with, wondering just which one of us is mad. Recovery time after such encounters is essential, and a rediscoverable sense of one's own 'groundedness'.

Finally, when one considers the defence against homosexuality, it is important to say that the research in this area shows that most children presenting with gender confusion go on to become homosexual in adult life. The next largest group becomes heterosexual or bisexual. Only a very small number find a transsexual 'solution' (Zucker & Bradley, 1995). How we engage with and support all sexualities is a matter of urgency.

Conclusion

The three case examples at the start of this paper have much in common: yet therapy has enabled different stories and different prospects to emerge. All show early, pre-verbal disruption of attachments, experienced as overwhelming by the immature ego. All contain elements of an internalised mother who is at best ambivalent and at worst hostile to her male child. All have fathers with whom identification has been problematic – through aggression, depression or exclusion.

Sam is working hard on his transvestic fetishism and is clear that his core gender identity is male. He has cut his long hair, established a relationship with his father and can think about career and life prospects. He can connect his cross-dressing to internalised parental ambivalence and hatred but remains vulnerable to provoking parental reaction – sometimes in an appropriate adolescent way, but occasionally in more perverse directions. He remains in therapy.

George's issues centre around depression, the capacity to recognise and use his objects and the development of an ego ideal and self that is not burdened by assumed parental introjects, and his gender dysphoria has receded in the face of this work.

Orlando's gender confusion remains intensely worrying, his flight into female identification representing a response to a profound narcissistic hurt in his abandonment, latterly by his tutor but initially psychologically by both parents. He more clearly demonstrates gender issues as defensive against psychosis and suicide, and is protective of his objects by turning his rage on his maleness. Just as sexually abusing adolescents often turn out to have mothers who, themselves abused, unconsciously project an expectation of abusing men onto their male children (a discovery of the research team at Great Ormond Street Hospital, London (Lanyado, 1998)), so he demonstrates the impact of an object who, he feels, does not wish his male self to survive. His current position is, at least, one of survival of a kind: he can moreover bear to stay in touch and he has managed not to proceed to a surgical 'solution'.

Note

1 First published in the *Journal of the British Association of Psychotherapists* 1999 37.

References

Aron, L (1995) The internalised primal scene *Psychoanalytic Dialogues* 5(2): 195–237
Benjamin, J (1991) Father and Daughter: Identification with Difference – a Contribution to Gender Heterodoxy *Psychoanalytic Dialogues* 1(3): 277–299
Bernstein, D (1993) *Female Identity Conflict in Clinical Practice* Northvale NJ: Jacob Aronson
Bleiberg, E, Jackson, L & Ross, JL (1986) Gender identity disorder and object loss *Journal of the American Academy of Child and Adolescent Psychiatry* 25(1): 58–67

Brain, C (1998) Biological contributions to atypical gender identity development. In D Di Ceglie (ed.) *A Stranger in my own Body: Atypical Gender Identity Development and Mental Health* London: Karnac

Chasseguet-Smirgel, J (ed.) (1970) *Female Sexuality* Ann Arbour: University of Michigan. Originally published in Paris as *Recherches Psychoanalytiques Nouvelles sur la Sexualite Feminine* 1964

Coates, SW (1997) Is it time to jettison the concept of developmental lines? *Gender and Psychoanalysis* 2(1): 35–53

Coates, S & Moore, MS (1998) The complexity of early trauma: representation and transformation. In D Di Ceglie (ed.) *A Stranger in my own Body: Atypical Gender Identity Development and Mental Health* London: Karnac

Coates, S & Person, ES (1985) Extreme boyhood femininity: isolated behaviour or pervasive disorder? *Journal of the American Academy of Child Psychiatry* 24: 702–709

Coates, S, Friedman, R & Wolfe, S (1991) The aetiology of boyhood gender identity disorder: a model for integrating temperament, development and psychodynamics *Psychoanalytic Dialogues* 1(4): 481–523

Cooper, AM (1991) The unconscious core of perversion. In G Fogel & W Myers *Perversions and Near-Perversions in Clinical Practice – New Psychoanalytic Perspectives* New Haven & London: Yale University Press

Dahl, EK (1993) Play and the construction of gender in the oedipal child. In A Solnit, D Cohen & P Neubauer (eds.) *The Many Meanings of Play: A Psychoanalytic Perspective* New Haven, CT: Yale University Press

Davies, R (1996) The inter-disciplinary network and the internal world of the offender. In C Cordess & M Cox (eds.) *Forensic Psychotherapy: Crime, Psychodynamics and the Offender Patient* Vol. II: *Mainly Practice* London: Jessica Kingsley

Diamond, M (1997) Boys to men: the maturing of masculine gender identity through paternal watchful protectiveness *Gender and Psychoanalysis* 2: 443–468

Di Ceglie, D (1995) Gender identity disorder in children and adolescents *British Journal of Hospital Medicine* 53(6): 251–256

Di Ceglie, D (1998) Reflections on the nature of the atypical gender identity organization In *A Stranger in my own Body: Atypical Gender Identity Development and Mental Health* London: Karnac

Dimen, M (1991) Deconstructing difference: gender, splitting and transitional space *Psychoanalytic Dialogues* 1(3): 335–352

Fast, I (1990) Aspects of early gender development: towards a reformulation *Psychoanalytic Psychology* 7(suppl.): 105–117

Freud, S (1905) Three essays on the theory of sexuality *SE* 7: 125–243

Gaddini, E (1992) Notes on the mind-body question In E Gaddini (ed. A Limentani) *A Psychoanalytic Theory of Infantile Experience* London: Routledge. Paper originally given in Bologna 1980

Gaffney, B & Reyes, P (1999) Gender identity dysphoria. In M Lanyado, & A Horne (eds.) *The Handbook of Child and Adolescent Psychotherapy: Psychoanalytic Approaches* London: Routledge

Greenson, RR (1968) Dis-identifying from the mother: its special importance for the boy *International Journal of Psychoanalysis* 49: 370–374

Hurry, A (ed.) (1998) *Psychoanalysis and Developmental Therapy* London: Karnac

Imperato-McGinley, J, Peterson, RE, Gautier, T & Sturla, E (1979) Androgens and the evolution of male gender identity among male pseudohermaphrodites with 5-alpha-reductase deficiency *New England Journal of Medicine* 300: 1233–1237

James, A (1998) The contribution of Social Anthropology to the understanding of atypical gender identity in childhood. In D Di Ceglie (ed.) *A Stranger in my own Body: Atypical Gender Identity and Mental Health* London: Karnac

Kubie, L (1974) The drive to become both sexes *Psychoanalytic Quarterly* 43: 349–426

Lanyado, M (1998) Personal communication

Limentani, A (1979) The significance of transsexualism in relation to some basic psycho-analytic concepts *International Review of Psycho-Analysis* 62: 379–99

McDougall, J (1995) *The Many Faces of Eros* London: Free Association Books

Money, J (1955) Hermaphroditism, gender and precocity in hyperadrenocorticism: psychological findings *Bulletin of the Johns Hopkins Hospital* 96: 253–264

Money, J (1994) The concept of gender identity disorder in childhood and adolescence after 39 years *Journal of Sex and Marital Therapy*, 20: 3

Person, E & Ovesey, L (1983) Psychoanalytic theories of gender identity *Journal of the American Academy of Psychoanalysis* 11(2): 203–226

Roiphe, H & Galenson, E (1973) Object loss and early sexual development *Psychoanalytic Quarterly* 42: 73–90

Sadowski, H & Gaffney, B (1998) Gender identity disorder, depression and suicidal risk. In D Di Ceglie (ed.) *A Stranger in my own Body: Atypical Gender Identity Development and Mental Health* London: Karnac

Stoller, R (1968) Male childhood transsexualism *Journal of the American Academy of Child Psychiatry* 7: 193–201

Stoller, R (1975) *Sex and Gender* Vol. 1 *Splitting: A Case of Female Masculinity* London: Hogarth Press

Stoller, R (1992) Gender identity development and prognosis: a summary. In C Chiland & JG Young *New Approaches to Mental Health from Birth to Adolescence* New Haven & London: Yale University Press

Stoller, R (1996) Gender disorders. In I Rosen (ed.) *Sexual Deviation* 3rd edition London: Oxford University Press

Tyson, P (1982) A developmental line of gender identity, gender role and choice of love object *Journal of the American Psychoanalytic Association* 30: 61–86

Wilson, P (1998) Development and mental health: the issue of difference in atypical gender identity development. In D Di Ceglie (ed.) *A Stranger In My Own Body: Atypical Gender Identity Development and Mental Health* London: Karnac

Winnicott, DW (1968) The use of an object and relating through identifications. Reprinted in DW Winnicott *Playing and Reality* Harmondsworth: Penguin 1980

Winnicott, DW (1996) The Niffle. In DW Winnicott *Thinking about Children*, eds. R Shepherd, J Johns, H Taylor Robinson London: Karnac

Young-Bruehl, E (1996) Gender and psychoanalysis: an introductory essay *Gender and Psychoanalysis* 1(1): 7–18

Zucker, KJ & Bradley, SJ (1995) *Gender Identity Disorder and Psychosexual Problems in Children and Adolescents* New York & London: Guilford

Part III
An Independent upbringing

10 Interesting things to say to children – and why[1]

Prologue

James's father was waiting in the hallway of the clinic. 'James is in the car but he won't come in. I wondered if *you* could get him to come in – I can't. He has been bullied at school but the bullies are all taking their national exams (i.e. they are 4 years older than James) so James has been asked to stay off until they are punished after their exams. I think it's affecting him. I think it's very unfair – as if he is the one to be punished. Oh, and he's wearing a skirt.'

I said that I would not go out to persuade him to come in but I would say hello to him as he had made the very long journey (1½ hours by car) to get here. As I approached, James (age 12) shuffled his belongings across the back seat to make space and I asked if he were inviting me in. He nodded. His father sat a little distance away on a low wall. Inside, I said that it seemed a shame to have come so far and for us not to say hello. He nodded and smiled. I wondered if he found it hard to talk of what was so much on his mind? 'I'll come in!' – firmly and clearly. He pulled his trainers on to his bare feet: they were quite large and black and seemed very incongruous with the brief denim skirt he sported and which he tugged modestly down. Then he rummaged behind him, found a pair of sports shorts, and pulled these on under his skirt. I looked at this. 'Having things both ways today?' James grinned and nodded. 'Ready?' Nod. I tried to open the back door. The child safety locks were on . . . . We were trapped like two children together. James found this hilarious.

Was it 'right' to go out to the car to see James?

Was it 'right' to go into the car?

Was it 'right' to laugh with him about our predicament?

Is psychotherapy sometimes allowed to be playful?

Introduction

It takes time in work with young people to gain confidence not only in making interpretations to them but in making decisions about what one should or should not do as a therapist. Over one's shoulder there lurks a superego figure of a kind, 'The Great Child Psychotherapist in the Sky' as I call it, whom one assumes would do it all

a)   correctly (an interesting concept);
b)   calmly; and
c)   in a brief sentence, gathering all aspects of the child's problems and behaviour into one succinct mutative interpretation – the all-encompassing comment that changes the way the child makes sense of himself.

Moreover, it would all probably be done from the therapist's seat in the therapy room, obviating the need occasionally to be under tables, or running downstairs after agile latency-aged boys, to be jumping to save goals – or to find oneself in the back seat of a Ford estate car, locked in, with a 12-year-old boy wearing a skirt.

Aspects of such a harsh professional superego are clearly destined to be taken to one's own analyst or therapist where one hopes a slightly less punitive conscience can be fostered. However, there does remain the central technical issue of *how* one addresses children and young people and the troubled parts they bring with them, and how one simply *is* with them. This emerges constantly in supervision. It is remarkably easy, when one is working as a supervisor, to think of what might have been said: it is the time of calm reflection after the event, after all, and time to think is something that many children do not grant us in the passion of the therapeutic encounter. This chapter, therefore, is offered as one way of thinking *before* the event – and it may enable trainees to see their wise old bats of supervisors as less than magical, as occasionally flummoxed themselves and as just having more experiences from which to have worked things out! It also keeps a promise to my supervisees that *someone* has to write the paper on 'Interesting things to say to children'. . .

The experience of supervising, of being a supervisor, involves in itself the creation of a 'transitional space', an 'intermediate area of experience' (Winnicott 1951/1971) in which the child *qua* child, the child as perceived and experienced by the trainee, and the child as perceived by the supervisor all come together. Casement describes the progress of supervision as leading to a dialogue between the external supervisor, the internalised supervisor and the 'internal supervisor' that becomes established in all of us and that, with time and experience, is available to be called upon when we need space for thought in a session (Casement 1985: 32). This 'internal supervisor', however, needs to be able to operate with playfulness if it is not to re-enact harsher aspects of our own or our patients' superegos. I would also argue for playfulness between supervisor and supervisee. If, as Strachey first outlined (later developed by Loewald 1960), during an analysis the analyst as 'new object' is introjected into the patient's superego, modifying its harshness (Strachey 1934), so the process is parallel with the supervisor in supervision.

We fear 'acting in' – normally an expression used when the patient acts out part of their psychopathology within the session, but I would also like to think about it in relation to psychotherapists who fear they may act (rather than reflect) when in the presence of a particular child and the material that the child brings. This can be true especially when we feel the force of our counter-transference, when our own feelings become hard to manage – feelings of being overwhelmed and paralysed, of great sympathy and compassion, or of rage and an internal urge to be angry with the patient or to retaliate sadistically. Space for thinking is vital. It is also equally vital when we think of challenging our professional superegos and doing something different with a child. It is always in the unexpected place in therapy (unexpected to the child) that we consciously do not act in accordance with the child's internal objects and psychic structure – e.g. we are careful not to give interpretations that mirror the child's superego if this superego is punitive. Indeed, 'tempering . . . (the) superego' is part of the patient-therapist relationship whereby 'the patient internalises affective attitudes from the therapist' (Gabbard & Westen 2003). Such care is usual and can have a huge impact on child or adult. It is also in the unexpected place in the therapy that we may consciously do something more playful. Such interventions must arise from a clear understanding of the child's psychopathology, the nature of the treatment alliance and our clinical knowledge and framework. To say to James, 'Having it both ways today?' was fine but may well have been contra-indicated with another child.

Defences: respecting and engaging with curiosity

We were approaching a holiday break. Pamela had been a hard child to work with, resistant even to the articulation of feelings, never mind being miles away from gaining insight. When I told her of the approaching break she shouted, 'Good!' I smiled at her (she had expected something punitive from this outburst). 'Well, you wouldn't want to miss therapy too much!' She roared with laughter – it somehow spoke to the bizarre in assuming she might miss me when in sessions she constantly muttered darkly how she would like to stop coming, but it also addressed her attachment and wish for the therapy to continue. We had captured something, and she felt recognised in her ambivalence and in her reversal – if I were discarding her for the summer she would most certainly discard me verbally. I wished that I had been more playful with her earlier. Anne Alvarez has talked of a similar approach: to the child who hurls, 'I hate you!' at her, she may well say, 'Well, you wouldn't want to like me *too* much,' similarly reaching the defence and ambivalence but in a non-persecuting way.

Timothy was 13 and invariably late for sessions. The Child Guidance Unit in which I then worked had closed by the time he was due for his appointment; there was no one in the reception area, and I would go to the waiting area at the time of his session. If he was not there, I returned to my room, leaving the door open for him to enter. About 15 minutes into his session time, I would hear in the distance a faint tuneful whistling – the *Monty Python's Life of Brian* song 'Always look on the bright side of life'. It grew gradually louder and behind it arrived a defensively smiling Tim. Looking on the bright side of life was not easy for him, trapped in a sado-masochistic relationship with a single parent mother who beat him and intruded into his sexuality. He felt compelled to exclude major adults in his life (he spent his Maths lessons reading novels, silently winding-up his Maths teacher) as contact so easily felt like impingement and intrusion to him. It was hard to hope that a therapist would not also be sadistic.

I struggled for several weeks with how to address this (this was a three times weekly therapy, an important post-qualification experience for me of more intense work, so it meant a *lot* of sessions where Tim missed time). Eventually I said that I thought he really needed to be in control of when our sessions began – so many things felt out of his control and it was essential to take charge of what he could. It was a pity, however, that taking control in *this* way also cost him 15 minutes of *his* time. I sympathised with his dilemma and wondered if he might reflect on it himself. Tim began to come on time. It fitted into a general theme in the therapy about control and what I called his tendency to shoot himself in the foot – by his need for one particular defence (e.g. to keep any intrusion out), or by repeating the anxieties of his childhood as he did in Maths, silently goading his teacher into retribution and so setting himself up masochistically for punishment, he would often end up in trouble in school. It was a good day when he reported that he had met with the Deputy Head (a benign man, confused by Tim but willing to help him) and in this meeting told him, 'Ann says I shoot myself in the foot.' Now Tim was being proactive in enabling the environment to respond appropriately – and the phrase seemed to have developed real resonance for him. Such phrasing allows one to ally oneself with the child – not with the defence – and to return the projections for thought.

During my own training I was fortunate – very fortunate – in my teachers. It seems invidious to single out one when I learned from so many. However, Anne Alvarez in clinical seminars introduced me to the phrase 'It seems difficult to hope that. . . ' This phrase draws heavily upon Anna Freud's understanding of the defences as necessary – possibly inappropriate, but the only solution to be found by the child at that point – and so to be respected (Freud 1936). It does not deny, collude with or attack the defence as it is being used; rather, it addresses the issues underlying the need for that defence and also includes the possibility of change, of things being differently perceived or experienced. It remains one of the most helpful 'interesting things' to say to a child when one is being creative about the defensive structure. George gives a good example of when this phrase can be used:

> George (see Chapter 9) had expressed a strong wish to be a girl, leading to his referral at the age of 9. A 'replacement child', conceived after the death, at birth, of a much-wanted girl, and ill at his own birth, he was for his parents both blessing and bane – his survival was celebrated, his masculinity not. He attended for once weekly therapy for two years. A talented child, he gained a sense of self from his singing, acting and dancing skills and performances. During his therapy he would from time to time use the couch – spread out on it in seeming relief – and was able to talk or be quiet, as he felt the need. One day he managed to talk of how angry he was at his sister's death. Angry with

the hospital and also just angry. There was a painful pause. I commented quietly that he was rightly very angry with all the grown-ups and sometimes he found it very hard to hope that they wanted him just to be George. After a few moments he swung his feet off the couch and stood up. 'I wondered what kind of singing voice I'll have when my voice breaks?' 'Can we hope for a George voice?' I offered. 'A George voice!' – he smiled.

Anxiety

It has long been a feature in psychoanalytic work with children to take issues up in the displacement, especially when the child's anxiety is too great to enable a transference interpretation to be made or when words have for the child a concrete reality. Talking of murderous rage can be heard as accusing the child of actually killing the objects. Displacement is especially effective with younger children where anthropomorphism – of animals and even bricks – allows high emotion to be explored in a safe, removed arena. It can lead to some extremely bizarre conversations, as it did for me with a 20-year-old who sidled up to relationships via his love of Thomas the Tank Engine. 'How would Thomas feel about. . . ' was useful and could open up fantasy in the displacement of Thomas and his favourite female engine, Lady. But one had to concentrate on not feeling foolish – possible if one is absolutely certain as to the value of such displaced, parallel conversations (see Chapter 8).

> Anna Freud has pointed out that the procedure of giving interpretations about a person or figure onto whom the child has externalised aspects of his own self, thus accepting the externalisation for the time being, is not necessarily collusion but, rather, a way of approaching threatening mental content gradually
>
> (Sandler, Kennedy & Tyson 1980: 165)

For the abused child, indeed, it is often through such displacements that affects can begin to be recognised and given the symbolism of words for the first time:

> Maria had suffered extreme sexual abuse at the hands of her drug addict mother's partner, and severe emotional and physical neglect. She tended to deal with her world by dissociation, inhabiting a realm of wild animals, which seemed to her to be more honourable in their interactions with each other than untrustworthy humans. For several months, conversation between therapist and child concerned these animals – rapacious only when necessary, at the mercy of humans, strong yet vulnerable. Only once extremes of affect could gradually be recognised and named in the animals could Maria begin to tolerate their resonance with parts of herself and their relevance to the transference relationship.

In this way she slowly, in Miss Freud's words, 'came near the defended content' (*ibid*: 169). We may be more inclined to think of such a technique when we have the child's shame in mind – e.g. shame about murderous feelings towards siblings – or narcissistic pain, where too direct an approach may reinforce and strengthen inappropriate defences (Parsons 2003). We also need to be able to use it when affect, if reawakened too quickly, may overwhelm and drive the child to more desperate defences.

'Me-to-choose time' arose in work with an abused and abusing adolescent boy:

> For the first few months Wayne found the process of attending for fifty-minute sessions desperately persecutory. Arriving felt like being locked away by his father, when anything could happen; leaving – no matter how carefully the therapist tried to prepare and warn him – was a repetition of abandonment. After much thought, his therapist gave him control of the last ten minutes of the session: he could choose at what point he left within this ten-minute space, although she would always remain in the room for his full time and he would wait in the waiting room with his escort until she emerged to say goodbye. He rarely used this control, although he occasionally drew attention to the fact that it was now 'me-to-choose time'. Much later in his therapy he reflected on this and on the impotence he had felt as a child. He could now recognise states of anxiety and think rather than act.
>
> (Horne 1999)

Anne Hurry in a lovely paper describes the work of assessing troubled adolescents (Hurry 1986). Following a helpful passage in which she describes the use of neutral words – 'strange' feelings rather than fearful or shameful ones – she has pertinent comments to make on hope and despair, recognising this axis and the capacity of the adolescent to cling to one, denying the other:

> ... it is necessary to bear in mind the adolescent's potential ambivalence towards change, and to bear in mind that for many young people despair can be less painful than hope which places them in what is felt as a much more vulnerable position. ... Technically then, it is important to be prepared to take up whichever aspect of his ambivalence the adolescent is least conscious of. When the adolescent despairs it is possible to interpret the hope which he is inviting the interviewer to carry for him, and to note the evidence for this hope in the very fact that he has come. When the adolescent is only enthusiastic about treatment, it may be necessary to take up his need to deny his doubts and fears, or even the way in which he is seeking in his choice of therapy to perpetuate the childhood state wherein he does not bear responsibility for himself.
>
> (Hurry 1986: 41–42)

Public situations and therapist humiliation

I have lastingly embarrassing memories of trying, not long after I had qualified, to assess a seriously abused and emotionally neglected child who stormed and raged, kept the therapy room door open, and made noisy excursions to the waiting room where her mother sat, glad of the break from her daughter and patently enjoying my only too evident struggles. The Great Child Psychotherapist in the Sky loomed large in my mind at this time. At one point, Kelly attacked me viciously, kicking, punching and spitting. I told her that if she continued, I would have to hold her flailing arms, thinking that the usual tack of having to end the session would probably not work as the boundaries of the session had become so permeable anyway. I tried to grapple in my mind with her seeming sadism and my humiliation. She attacked again. Telling her what I was doing, I held her arms. At the top of her voice she yelled, 'She's sexually abusing me! Help!' I let her go with a sense of despair; she ran out to the waiting room in triumph.

The work continued with Kelly, her mother and her baby sister together. I think this was right but have often wondered what a comment on the lines of 'It seems difficult to hope that I will not be a grown-up who abuses you' might have done. At that point, I was too caught up with my superego and my counter-transference to be able to think. It was a useful, if salutary, lesson. Now, I think, I would not continue the individual assessment sessions as they were too fearful for Kelly (yes, fearful – this was anxiety leading to attack to protect the self), and be explicit about this, but move speedily to seeing the three together – but I have had a very long number of years to reflect on it!

The vignette of James, stuck in the back of the car despite having made a very long journey to the clinic, shows how one can begin to think about the private and public boundaries of therapy and the therapeutic relationship. His history is important.

James is the second of his parents' three children. He has a brother who is two years older than he is and a sister who is three years younger. Referred by his doctor for gender dysphoria – it was said in the referral letter that he dressed often as a girl, his close friends were girls and that he displayed effeminacy, but it was uncertain whether he was aware of this – he had been referred on to me by a specialist Gender Identity Development Service to see if he might be engaged in psychotherapy, while my Gender Service colleagues continued to work with his parents and school. Despite his not being around to be brought to the first appointment – he was eventually found hiding in the boot of his father's car – at the next appointment when he and his father met me with the specialist child psychiatrist, he separated surprisingly easily to spend time on his own with me. The child psychiatrist had judged the timing of this meeting and separation exceptionally well.

At our first encounter, James ignored all the toys in the room and curled up in an easy chair, his thumb in his mouth. He spoke so softly I could barely hear him. He kept his eyes on my face – unusually not exploring, even visually, the room in which he now found himself. I did not feel an object of curiosity in this, however, rather an object to be kept in sight in case it did something unpredictable. The regressive pose said a lot about what felt safe for him in relation to a new object – being a regressed baby was preferable to risking being a pre-pubertal boy. James smiled a lot – especially when I could not hear him and had to ask him to repeat things. There was control here, too.

I did not make this a long meeting. James surprisingly asked to return to meet again at the earliest time I could give him. In subsequent sessions he often played an aggressive and violent mother. At one point he stated, 'Mums like girls, Dads like boys. So, girls get off with everything with their Mums.' A less evident theme was the equation of any sense of male potency and agency as delinquent and to be discouraged. I heard that his mother helped him choose which of her old clothes – including her underwear – he might play with and be given by her to wear. James also told me clearly that he was a boy, not a girl, and had no wish to be a girl. We came to a form of words about 'playing with ideas of boy and girl' that he agreed with. I had thought that fortnightly sessions might be all the intimacy he could manage but both he and his father, after a term of fortnightly therapy, agreed to weekly work.

James is brought by his father, a large, obese man who suffers from diabetes and a heart condition. His work is sedentary. His vulnerability is not put into words but is, I think, in his son's mind. James's mother has an Asperger-ish quality about her and finds it too easy to be cruelly castrating of James: their times of intimacy seem to centre round his fetish.

What I feel I can say to James is underpinned by my understanding of him: a boy whose development verges on puberty and the questions of sexuality and identity that raises, whose masculinity is attacked by a mother who supports his cross-dressing, who cannot bear any energy, dissension, or sense of masculine potency from him, and who complains bitterly about such behaviour. Misbehaviour in James's case is developmentally very appropriate – the only way to separate physically and sexually from such an ambivalent object. Yet identifications with a fragile-seeming father are also difficult and James has not yet been able to engage with any male influences in school.

It was important not to fall into the trap of becoming 'the expert' who would winkle James out of the car – this would have been doomed to failure and is a situation that we are often put into by families. It would also have undermined his father's role. It was, however, important not to replicate the castrating or distant mother, hence my trip out to the car, beyond the boundary of waiting room and therapy room, and my engagement with James. His pulling on his shorts *under* his skirt was fascinating as it enabled him to maintain the feminine outside but with a male covering (boy's shorts) of the male organs: thus, I commented on the need for both. Playfulness is really quite a serious and informed business!

Acting out

The 'nice neurotic child' of the early days of psychoanalysis may have been a little bit of a myth – or a feature of private practice. Today in public service work, we are more likely to have referred to us children whom others struggle to understand and contain. Where thought is generally absent, it becomes important to create an arena where it might become a possibility. In doing this, we have to wonder constantly about the nature of the anxiety that the child struggles with, that necessitates the only discoverable response of mindless activity. Being able as therapists to seek a space for thinking is essential.

There is an interesting piece of 'Portman lore' – ideas refined over the years by the psychotherapists and psychoanalysts who work at the Portman Clinic in London with a patient group who are always difficult and often dangerous – that helps us think about the concepts of 'activity' and 'danger'. If a therapist is working with a violent patient, the tendency in many therapeutic settings is for the therapist to sit in the chair nearest to the door: if the situation feels unsafe, there is a quick exit for the therapist. Seemingly paradoxically, but actually constant in psychoanalytic terms, Portman lore says that the psychotherapist should allow the patient the seat nearest to the exit. For most violent patients, the anxiety aroused by a suddenly perceived threat to the ego leads to a violent reaction in the service of protecting the ego (Glasser 1998). Having an exit available thus frees the patient *not* to have to attack, but to preserve the ego (self) by escape.

In such a brief description one can see how the therapist has to do three things:

a) there has to be awareness of the risk of danger – after all, that is probably why the patient was referred;
b) there has to be a clear understanding of the meaning of the violent act and why violence might occur;
c) there has to be considerable trust in the psychoanalytic knowledge base and the therapeutic process.

It is also important that we think about the context of the therapy – in terms of the clinical space but also with young people in terms of the supportive network that allows therapy to become a treatment of choice. Too often I have heard of therapists who engage with children when the environment is neither supportive nor able to withstand the impact of the therapy, and the therapy is stopped when the children act out. This is abusive and thoughtless.

With adolescents, in particular, one has to be careful to avoid humiliating them with one's interpretations – or using the interpretation as a weapon with which to hit back. Splitting off the adolescent's more infantile part from the adult, thinking part can help the young person and engage them with the mature part of the self that can then reflect on the activity-based defences of the infantile part. Addressing this with curiosity – joining with the thinking part – is also useful: with the risk-taking delinquent one can comment on the little part of them that wished it could run or escape the past traumatic experiences, and how this part still repeats the feelings of risk, fear and high adrenalin surge, hoping this time to be in control of them. One can then be curious about why this still happens – and space for thought is created.

In a similar way, for the child or young person who acts out with the body, who might be viewed as functioning at a level of what I think of as 'body-based defensive manoeuvres', one can address the body itself as a separate entity that cannot itself think but which does operate as a source of memories and at times acts on these. Katiebelle (Chapter 6) had been abused from the age of 3 by her half-brother who had himself been abused sexually by his mother (who still cared for Katiebelle and her younger siblings). She had begun to act out sexually at the age of 6, with peers in school and with her little brother. This was impossible for her to talk of – indeed, when I met her at age 7, words for Katiebelle were concrete entities where to speak them made their content real. Eventually, after her mother had accosted me in the waiting room with a muffled, 'She's doin' it again – you know – these dirty things – with her brother', Katiebelle and I managed a fleeting conversation about her body and the interesting way it remembered things that had happened to it. When it felt compelled to do things to her brother, it was remembering what had happened to it. This was heard and made sense to her. Her eyes shone – she was overwhelmed that there might be a reason and that it did not mean that she was simply 'bad'.

It is not simply with bodily acting out, however, that one can use such a deliberately created split. Anna Freud describes how, in engaging with

> a seven-year-old neurotically naughty little girl. . . . I suddenly separated off all her naughtiness and personified it for her, giving it a name of its own and confronting her with it, and eventually succeeded in so far that she began to complain of the person thus newly created by me, and obtained an insight into the amount of suffering she had endured from it. The 'analysability' of the child came hand in hand with the insight into the malady established in this way.
>
> (Freud 1927: 12)

The word 'interesting' is one I tend to overwork . . . Partly, the phrase 'Now that's very interesting' gives one a tiny space for thinking, even while one is fleetingly wondering what the Great Child Psychotherapist in the Sky would do this time. More importantly, it gives one a form of words for engaging with the thinking part of the child in relation to the infantile part, and sets up a climate of curiosity. To the child who has acted in the session one can say, 'Now that was really interesting' – and the unexpected phrase challenges superego and defence, addresses the ego, and enables thought. I learned this from my own supervision: as I brought my intensely passionate but often Houdini-like adolescent training patient to Anne Hurry, she would say, 'Now why did you do that? That was interesting.' It opened up supervision as an exercise in curiosity and learning. I use this still.

The struggle for thought and thinking space

Lucy Alexander, at the time a BAP trainee, was working in three times weekly psychotherapy with a bright, passionate 5-year-old, dislocated from her native Italy and brought, together with her two brothers and half-brother, to a small English city by her Italian mother and English father. Ariadne would regularly become a whirlwind in sessions, both with her body and in her words and feelings. This prevented thought on the part of her therapist and on Ariadne's part, too. After some reflection in supervision, we decided that Lucy would introduce the concept of 'thinking time' towards the end of each session – a 10-minute period for thinking about that day's session. Sometimes this works, sometimes 'thinking' is too scary a concept for a child. Ariadne took to it with great delight. Occasionally, she would include the toy elephants who, she said, also needed to think – especially if they had been playing out difficulties in their elephant family, oedipal rivalries and sibling wars, and uncertainties about the place of girls. Always, in this 'thinking time', she bravely brought the theme back to her own anxieties. Between them, Lucy and Ariadne went on to create their own special containment during the session – 'the slowing down place', Ariadne's idea, a corner of the room where Ariadne went of her own accord when her feelings became tumultuous. This was such an imaginative invention and was possible because of the nature of their therapeutic relationship and because the therapist, Lucy, was available to meet the creativity of the child. It was a real Winnicottian creation. It did not arise from supervision: it occurred in the 'overlap of the two play areas' (Winnicott 1971), that of the therapist and that of the child.

It can be interesting (again a useful word!) in the early stages of trainees' work to see that they worry about enjoying sessions with children. Could this really be psychoanalytic psychotherapy when it is also, from time to time, fun? As they gain experience and near the end of training, they can allow themselves to enjoy the process of work and the progress made, and recognise that 'fun' accomplishes huge internal and developmental shifts. 'Play is work,' as a child once reputedly told Winnicott with great seriousness.

When play is not possible

First you have to build the house before you can throw anyone out of it.
(Anna Freud, quoted in Sandler, Kennedy and Tyson 1980)

I agree with Winnicott that, 'if the therapist cannot play, then he is not suitable for the work', absolute though the statement may seem (Winnicott 1971). For the *child* who cannot play or be playful, for whom Winnicott urges 'something needs to be done to enable the patient to become able to play, after which psychotherapy may begin,' there is still the psychoanalytic solution of 'developmental therapy' and the therapist as 'developmental object' (Hurry 1998). We do not often enough value Anna Freud's great contributions of the analysis of the ego and the superego, as well as the unconscious id (Edgcumbe 2000); Hurry's book also reminds us of the Hampstead Clinic's work on developmental deficit and help.

Failures in the early environment inhibit 'the evolving mental process itself, which is a more generalised, primitive defence' (Fonagy, Moran, Edgcumbe, Kennedy & Target 1993). The capacities for thought, curiosity, feeling and emotion may be stunted as in the case of Maria (above) and as in the cases of many of the children we see today when there has been early, especially pre-verbal, trauma. As Anne Hurry reminds us, whether this be due to conflict (and thus a primitive defence) or deficit, 'the analyst's task is to engage inhibited or undeveloped processes within the analytic encounter' (Hurry 1998: 67). Work on noting affect, naming it and giving it legitimacy is necessary before the child is able to gain mastery, predict emotional actions and reactions, and be able to regulate that affect.

Spontaneity is the key, as Hurry and her colleagues describe, but crucially the interventions arise from that transitional space, the play area that the therapist reminds the child lies between them.

This ego structuring matters if the child is to be able to come to use therapy. Moreover

> it is also important that the analyst be prepared to move between the developmental/relational stance and the interpretative, as Anna Freud described. . . . Both developmental relating and understanding are necessary; each can potentiate and reinforce the effects of the other.
>
> (Hurry 1998: 71–72)

Conclusion

Perhaps we can now see that ideas of 'right' or 'wrong' – my questions about James at the start of this paper – fit uneasily into a perspective that takes the relationship as primary and where curiosity and engendering curiosity (about child, about therapist, about the process between them) is a key tool in what we do in the analytic encounter.

It can be very helpful in work with children and young people to use the unexpected or surprising in our comments to them: it enables us to become 'subjective objects' and 'new objects' for their engagement and use. We need to be clear about the children we see, to have a flexible formulation as to their difficulties in mind. We need to be firm in our trust in the psychoanalytic method and its usefulness. Then we can begin to play – with perceptions, with ideas and above all with possibilities.

Note

1 First published in 2006 in M Lanyado & A Horne *A Question of Technique* London & New York: Routledge

References

Casement, P (1985) *On Learning from the Patient* London & New York: Tavistock Publications

Edgcumbe, R (2000) *Anna Freud: A View of Development, Disturbance and Therapeutic Techniques* London & Philadelphia: Routledge

Fonagy, P, Moran, G, Edgcumbe, R, Kennedy, H & Target, M (1993) The roles of mental representations and mental processes in therapeutic action *Psychoanalytic Study of the Child* 48: 9–48

Freud, A (1927) *The Psycho-Analytical Treatment of Children: Technical Lectures and Essays* London: Imago Publishing Co. Ltd.

Freud, A (1936/1968) *The Ego and the Mechanisms of Defence* London: Hogarth Press

Gabbard, GO & Westen, D (2003) Rethinking therapeutic action *International Journal of Psychoanalysis* 84: 823–841

Glasser, M (1998) On violence: a preliminary communication *International Journal of Psychoanalysis* 79(5): 887–902

Horne, A (1999) Sexual abuse and sexual abusing in childhood and adolescence. In M Lanyado & A Horne (eds.) *The Handbook of Child and Adolescent Psychotherapy: Psychoanalytic Approaches* London: Routledge

Hurry, A (1986) Walk-in work with adolescents *Journal of Child Psychotherapy* 12(1): 33–45

Hurry, A (ed.) (1998) *Psychoanalysis and Developmental Therapy* London: Karnac Books

Loewald, HW (1960) On the therapeutic action of psychoanalysis *International Journal of Psycho-Analysis* 41: 16–33

Parsons, M (2003) personal communication

Sandler, J, Kennedy, H & Tyson, R (1980) *The Technique of Child Psychoanalysis: Discussions with Anna Freud* London: Hogarth Press & Institute of Psycho-Analysis

Strachey, J (1934) The nature of the therapeutic action in psychoanalysis *International Journal of Psycho-Analysis* 15: 127–159

Winnicott, DW (1951/1971) Transitional objects and transitional phenomena. In *Playing and Reality* London: Tavistock. Reprinted 1980 Harmondsworth: Penguin Educational

Winnicott, DW (1971) Playing: creative activity and the search for the self. In *Playing and Reality* London: Tavistock. Reprinted 1980 Harmondsworth: Penguin Educational

11 Towards a voice of one's own
Reflections on technique, training and the trousers of time[1]

Charlie had been in three-times-weekly psychotherapy for two years and three months, starting at age 3 years and 3 months. His symptoms of clinging, demandingness, tantrums, acute separation anxiety, refusing to sleep alone and dominating his mother had become unbearable for her (although one suspects that earlier there might have been some consolation for a divorced and saddened mother in the physical closeness of her only child) and she had, at her own analyst's suggestion, approached the BAP for help. Somewhat surprised to find herself being offered an assessment for more intensive work in Peckham (south-east London) when she lived in north London – perhaps, too, *Only Fools and Horses* on television at the time made it an even more startling invitation – she gamely brought Charlie to the clinic to meet Peter Wilson. Charlie was to be my first training patient and was to allow me to begin to think, to trust the theory (I swear he was reading Freud and was several chapters ahead of me in it) and to learn to be observantly quiet. I shall return to this last when we reflect on technique.

I consider myself very fortunate to have seen a mildly neurotic and very bright under 5 as my induction to the weird world of infantile sexuality and grown-up interpretation. Today's trainees often have a baptism of fire with children who are driven to act, with histories of gross neglect, abuse and precious little mother-infant reverie, containment and holding. I did not meet such trauma head-on in individual work for some time and in the early 1980s child sexual abuse was an area where all clinic workers found themselves on a very steep theoretical and technical learning curve. With Charlie, I could learn about my counter-transference, question my feelings and what I thought I was seeing, and be a beginner child psychotherapist in considerable safety. That seemed particularly important as there were few trainee posts and two of us had to add all we were doing in training to the day job. Fortunately, I was working in a Child Guidance Unit in Peckham.

Therapy ended at the end of July. During that summer Charlie and his mother moved north to her home town. Our therapeutic work *was* finished but the coincidence of leaving London, having his father remain here and ending his therapy was not easy for a boy of 5½. I wondered frequently how he was managing.

In late January, six months later, his mother phoned the clinic. Charlie was coming to London in February for half term to see his father and had asked if he could also see me. Could he just! I did, however, have the sense to talk about it in the clinic with Adam Phillips. 'You must not seduce him back into being a patient – however much you both desire it!' I needed someone to say exactly that. The agenda was Charlie's – whatever that might actually prove to be. At his appointment time I went to fetch him from the waiting area. He was perched eagerly on the edge of his chair, looking towards the door leading to the therapy rooms. His mother smiled hello and retreated behind her book. He beamed – a great smile flooded his features. An equally great smile filled mine. I was never very good at this 'keeping po-faced' stuff.

I had put out his old box of mixed toys and stationery amidst the communal toys. He looked around the room, seeing and remembering, trying out the little chair as if his body were reminding itself of what that had been like, noticing and recognising the animals almost as if in greeting. He had just turned 6, was taller – a proper schoolboy. We each looked at the other, delighted to meet and wondering if we were, in the words of Adam, still desired. Charlie turned and flapped his arms exhaustedly against his sides. 'It's a long way,' he said – 'a very long way!' He picked up the pad of drawing paper and the packet of felt-tip pens. He drew a messy mark near the top of a page. 'That's Bolton.' Angry squiggly lines followed, across and round and down the page, eventually ending in a cross. It felt an enormous exasperating effort. 'That's London!' The motorway system in anyone's book . . . He looked at it. Rather sadly he repeated, 'a very long way.'

'And a long time,' I added. He stared at the page and nodded.

He took out some of his cars – the ones he hadn't taken with him in a final deliberation when he left – and there was play that recapped his old themes of cars getting close, parking together, and how could this intimacy stay safe. Then, looking at the wheeled chair at my desk, he asked if he could play on it 'again'. This was a known game. Charlie sat on the chair, holding on tightly, and requested to be spun. We enjoyed the repetition of old times and he enjoyed the excitement. 'Faster! Faster!' As he went a little too speedily, he called out 'Enough!' I slowed the chair down. He looked at me. 'I said "enough"; I didn't say "stop"!' We had reached his reason for returning. I nodded. It was important to have enough, like his therapy; and important who said stop.

Some modest play followed until time was up. He left in good spirits saying goodbye for the last time. I have not seen or heard from him since. 'Mothers,' as Erna Furman (1982) tells us Anna Freud used to say, 'have to *be there* to be left.' I wonder at times how Charlie, in his 30s, is doing.

Introductory context

When I was invited to prepare a talk for this evening, it was some 9 months ago and tonight seemed – like Bolton – a very long way away. The BAP about to turn 60 is a celebratory achievement and the Child Training is turning 29.

One theme of this paper is likely to be that things come full circle, that there is a force for integration at work in life, an energy that Winnicott described in children as 'the general inherited tendency that the child has towards integration'

(Winnicott 1945: 8) and which I find manifests itself again as the years pass. Plus ça change . . . The *danger*, as the years pass, is that it is accompanied in the ageing mind by an equal force for fragmentation . . . The invitation, however, was to think – mainly clinically if possible – about the passing of time and changes in one's work. The trousers of time. Do we, in our teaching and practice, still dart down the same leg of the trousers of time as we used to; do we scurry down the wrong leg (can there be such a thing?); should we all be equipped with more decorative trousers nowadays – bright checks perhaps – and is the answer to life, the universe and everything to wear the kilt? Those of you versed in the Discworld novels of Terry Pratchett will recognise the legs of the trousers of time as shorthand for parallel universes. Our historical differences over the years – classical Freudian, contemporary Freudian, Jungian, Kleinian, post-Kleinian, Lacanian, Relational, Independent – 'by schisms rent asunder, by heresies distressed' (Stone/Wesley 1866) – have made it often seem in our discussions as if we inhabit parallel universes of an extreme religious fundamentalist kind. By 1951 when the British Association of Psychotherapists was formed, there were already three child psychotherapy trainings in London – Margaret Lowenfeld's Institute of Child Psychology (1935), the Hampstead Clinic under Anna Freud (1947) and the Tavistock training with Esther Bick (1948), the last a part of the new NHS following John Bowlby's inspired direction. The overarching body, the Association of Child Psychotherapists, had also taken shape in 1949. As some of you are aware, *I* believe (there it goes again – matters of belief. . .) that the formation of the BAP Child Training in 1982 has been a prime force in our profession for, if not integration, certainly a greatly increased capacity to listen, debate and be interested in each other's position. This has been the direct consequence of having seminar leaders and supervisors from all airts of psychoanalytic thought. The forum was created here at the BAP – and the gyre has widened. The impetus from the 3rd BAP intake – Deirdre [Dowling], Julia [Mikardo], Mary [Walker], Niki [Parker] et al (they know who they are!) – to found with the other trainings the joint student body across training schools was also important, enabling a sharing of ideas and a demythologising that had a vital influence on a generation.

Other innovations in the organisation of the training of child psychotherapists have also begun here and gradually been recommended/adopted by the ACP as appropriate, then required, procedures: written shared feedback for trainees on their progress in training cases and on the course; feedback from trainees about all aspects of training; a personal tutor for each trainee; practice placement visits, liaison and co-ordination; meetings of supervisors. The past, if we survey it from an organisational position, was certainly a foreign country; it is only 15 years since we formalised feedback (a little longer for placement liaison) and there were some remarkably brisk discussions with our grandmothers, who saw this as unanalytic, before the changes could be made.

Equally, there were two important aspects of Rosalie Joffé's particular cut of the cloth of the trousers of time that were miles ahead of their generation (Rosalie chaired the Training Committee for many years). The BAP already had a Full (senior) Membership scheme and Post-Graduate structure. While the former has altered, tailored more appropriately to post-graduate experience and needs, it did emphasise the necessity for continuing professional development back in the late 1980s. The adolescent course – developed and run by Rosalie as a route to full membership – was one of the most stimulating available and encouraged members of Psychoanalytic, Child and Jungian sections to meet and think together with often inspiring seminar leaders. The second leg of Rosalie's trousers (can one have too much of a metaphor, I ask myself?) was the development in the mid-1990s of the first series of termly master-classes on supervision for those interested in becoming supervisors for the Child Training. This was a first essay: the External Courses committee now runs a very successful Supervision Course.

The task – has it changed?

I'd like to begin with a little reminder, courtesy of Alvarez who writes:

> When during the celebration of his seventieth birthday, one of his disciples hailed Freud as 'the discoverer of the unconscious,' he answered, 'The poets and philosophers before me discovered the unconscious. What I discovered was the scientific method by which the unconscious can be studied.'
>
> (Alvarez 2006: 17)

Al Alvarez is a poet, literary critic, writer, mountaineer, poker player. For one who found the publication of his volume *The New Poetry* in 1967 a radical introduction to poetry as it had not been revealed in either school or university, it was to be later astonishing that, in *our* field, Al Alvarez was simply husband of the more famous Anne.

In the lines I have quoted, two things stay in mind: that the unconscious is not new, and we do not need to inhabit any purely analytic world to encounter it. It has been expressed in art and literature for a very long time. Nor is it – as Strachey rather wearily wrote to Glover of what he perceived as Miss Freud's position on psychoanalysis – our personal game reserve (Strachey 1940 in Rayner 1991: 18). Yet we have often behaved as if it were. We gain if, like Freud, we sustain curiosity about the unconscious in a broader world including and beyond the consulting room. We also gain when we lose the sense of superiority that has often been our way of encountering that world and meet it with a more helpful humility. This was rather summed up for me in my 'getting experience under my belt' years when, once a week when our days coincided, I would travel into work at Guy's Hospital with my line manager, Paul van Heeswyk. Paul had heard a very senior analyst at a conference intone the phrase: 'when I have completed an analysis'. We both collapsed in giggles. The first thought was 'Gosh! *Are* there completely analysed people?'; the next that it spoke either to a reductivism of the personality or, more worrying, a hypothesis as to what the human personality ought to be. The task of working with the unconscious remains a *joint* undertaking for therapist and patient together, taking place in that co-created space between them. Development itself is a life-long task. With children, we hope that with more appropriate defences, less driven by anxieties, they are helped to regain the developmental track and urgency that should have been theirs by right.

There is also the task of communication. Freud – like Al Alvarez – wrote simply, clearly and extremely well. That tradition is one that we have tried to continue – the task in this sense is to seek clarity with no need for a jargon that obfuscates, for Klingon as the staff working at the Portman Clinic used to call it. Adam Phillips, following Rycroft, has resurrected and developed the essay form as a splendid vehicle for psychoanalytic reflection. We owe him an enormous debt. We ourselves try, in our book series, to engage good, new, qualified student writers and occasionally we publish stunning ones. Writing should not be undertaken in order to separate us, create 'us' and 'others' – it should seek to engage and involve us.

A question of technique

[this heading could be seen as an advertising ploy . . . Of course, it's not. . .]

The real world

The origins of child psychotherapy lie on the couch in work with adult patients and in Freud's seeking that 'scientific method for studying the unconscious' – indeed, we find analysts whose child analytic work remains boundaried by this model. There is a place for that still. For most of us, however, there has been what might be best expressed as a 'Winnicottian shift', a recognition of the outside world and the environment necessary to engage the developmental impulse in the child. For Winnicott, it included 'placement' which he takes to be the entire environment around the child – it may be the family, for example, as it is in 'The anti-social tendency' (Winnicott 1956), or specialist school. There is also the 'real world' of the clinic rather than the private consulting room – and today's child psychotherapists work in a large range of settings including voluntary agencies and social services where consultation is as important as therapy. Once weekly work, too, has ceased to be a poor relation of analysis and has become a deliberate treatment of choice. On beginning our training at the BAP, as Psychiatric Social Workers in child guidance work, both Verena Crick and I were accustomed to whole family work, yet the ethos of the time was one of anxiety that this might dilute – or split – the transference. Child Psychotherapists did not see whole families. We had many animated debates. In the case of my third training patient, Sally, it was vital that I had begun as co-worker with the male Senior Registrar for six weeks in family work – a parental couple for a widowed father and his six children – and that Sally and I moved together to individual therapy, the family – with her – continuing monthly work with the SR. Her experience of losing and being very lost after her mother's death (Freud 1967) would otherwise have made it impossible for her to have what her siblings could not; and the family work allowed the other children to draw their father's attention to Sally's need (Horne 1989).

I also recall huge concern at the idea of communal toys, that I was really challenged by my teachers about this when it became apparent that these were in my room. Your average Peckham Child Guidance Unit had in the office (more office than therapy room. . .) one dolls' house, a few soft toys, some large and small Lego bricks, two chairs for grown-ups/adolescents, a small table and small chair for toddlers, a filing cabinet and shelf and a desk and swivel chair – to which I added two big home-made floor cushions and one throw. We collected cardboard boxes from the supermarket to contrive individual boxes (oops – getting Pythonesque. . .) – but some things simply had to be common.

It was while working at the Portman Clinic that I realised the true *advantage* of communal toys. For the gender dysphoric child, having a cupboard available with what might be perceived as gender specific toys free to be played with and used as ways of expressing desire and anxiety was enabling. To put e.g. girls' jewellery in a boy's box makes a statement of the therapist's perception – or even wish; the communal cupboard precludes that. Marianne [Parsons] [colleague at the Portman, former Head of the Anna Freud Centre training and good friend] and I had a lot of discussions of what was essential, what permissible, in our shared room. In each of these areas, we adapted.

'A whole ball of string!'

The phrase comes from Pat Radford [senior member of staff at the Anna Freud Centre and Brixton Child Guidance Unit, and original member of the Training Committee]. It has shades of Lady Bracknell, does it not! It comes to mind as I think on the contents of the child's box. I was seeing another 5-year-old at Guy's, the Bloomfield Clinic. Work there, and in the other half of my split post in Greenwich, consisted mainly of keeping my head down and getting a lot of experience – and encountering a large number of traumatised and very active patients. James was another highly anxious little boy for whom separations felt like annihilations. Aged 5 he was a short, solidly round and very appealing lad whose capacity for sudden speed over a short distance was unexpected in relation to his girth. He frequently behaved in a very babyish fashion in inelegant attempts to keep his object close; this made him seem and feel younger. We had worked for some time and to considerably good effect. Like many children whose inappropriate defences lessen as more age-appropriate ones are adopted, he had also physically changed and become more of a boy. The possibility of ending had been raised. . . . He picked up the ball of string and began tying me to my chair. It was an upright ordinary office chair with wooden arms and he wrapped the string around my wrists and the chair arms, then around my body and the back of the chair. I was intrigued and slow thinking. Then he added the two big floor cushions, onto my lap so that I couldn't see over them. Finally, he topped it off by throwing the blanket over my head – and dashing out the door. I waited, aware that, although I had held my arms an inch or so above the chair arms, it would still take more than a few moments to get out of this. There was a muffled giggle.

A voice said, 'I can see you! Through the keyhole!' Who said mothers have to be there to be left?

I had gossiped about this with friends at a conference, overheard by Pat who – utterly unconcerned for my plight – ruthlessly focused on the fact that I allowed a child 'a *whole* ball of string!' It does raise that interesting issue of what one provides – and again how – for each child patient. My whole balls of string were, I confess, simply provided without thought. My experience of bondage led me to review this – and I continued to provide whole (if smaller) balls of string . . . We recall Winnicott writing of the many meanings of string (Winnicott 1960) – it is a simple and useful tool and, as both he and James would have it, 'a technique for communication'.

To be – and how to 'be'

Deportment

I recall Eileen Orford telling us that in her Tavistock training days they were encouraged (even enjoined) to wear the same clothes with a patient – tricky if that involved five times weekly work and a small wardrobe . . . Juliet Hopkins has described work with a girl with a foot and shoe fetish – work that involved her therapist wearing suede boots for a considerably long time (Hopkins 1984). Perhaps the summers were not so hot? This regularity of garb can be understood as not provoking the fetish and allowing the therapy to happen. It is sensible. However, the effacement of the therapist that the injunction to trainees to wear the same clothes indicates is a different matter and questions finding one's own voice, one's own therapeutic person. There *are* limits to what one should wear, of course there are – we are back to Winnicott and his aim as a therapist of 'being myself and behaving myself' (Winnicott 1962: 166). 'Behaving myself' includes our dress and an awareness of what, for a particular child, might be a stimulus to high anxiety or an extreme provocation exciting inappropriate defences and actions. But we *have* changed – there is no automatic dressing down, no humble inconspicuousness of self. As Dorothy Lloyd Owen [a good colleague in the Portman] has said, one could perceive a nun-like approach amongst child psychotherapists going to waiting rooms to collect their patients when there was an assumption that there is a right and constant way to be.

Stanley[2], a 19-year-old referred because of his fetishistic preoccupations, had adopted an omnipotent, barren position of not needing people and of not being separate – of not having to mourn the developmental achievements of individuation and separation. He could not entertain a sense of 'going-on-being' (in himself or his object) but appeared to exist in the moment, denying separation or our week apart between sessions. This precluded development (necessitating the fetish as the only route for sexuality) and reflection (the idea of the 'third' so well outlined by Britton (1989)). I had to think carefully about intimacy and distance. I took care to engage him calmly in the waiting room, greeting him; and in the therapy room, when he instantly reached for his backpack of papers, drawings of his preoccupations that he had done over the months and years, as we sat down, I would ask how he was, catching his gaze. This made him pause, reminding him of our separateness. Sometimes he would brush it aside as if unheard, but increasingly he responded in kind. At times, he could manage not to reach for his drawings. I saw this as progress. He would even spontaneously tell me of aspects of his week – I noted that we *had*, then, been apart – and how he felt.

Leaving the room after one session, still in the basement, he said, 'See you next week'. At the start of therapy, he never said goodbye; he also did not say hello but simply arrived and began, as if to deny any breaks and abandonments. For the six months prior to this new farewell he had said obliquely, 'See you next week' upstairs as he exited the clinic, while facing the main door. He had now found the capacity to be separate and to leave me. Yes – mothers are there to . . . And mothers adapt to their different children. With Stanley, engaging him and being present from the waiting room mattered.

The writing of Anne Alvarez has also been helpful here, although it is notable that when she teaches clinical practice at the BAP she exhorts: 'But this is easy for you Independents! You know this!' Her choice, in 1992, of the title *Live Company* for her first book was not accidental – it makes the case for an at times enlivening therapist, geared to the individual patient's need.

The sound of silence

I was talking, anxious that I should be a decent enough therapist and aware of the literature that said interpretation produces change, one should seek the life-altering inspiring mutative interpretation. Interpreting was what I was doing. Charlie looked at me and said: 'Shut up!' The tone was mild but firm. I narrated this interaction to Rose Edgcumbe in supervision. There was a pause; quietly she said, 'Listen to him!'

It isn't easy to teach quiet waiting but it does matter that we do. It is not new – old trousers again – but so important for supervisors to encourage. When I left Scotland to train as a psychiatric social worker in London, my good colleague and friend Margie gave me a book by Bill Jordan who had trained Probation Officers for many years. In the preface, he mentioned his first senior PO whose axiom had been 'when in doubt do nothing'. Not responding to the compulsion to 'do', holding one's anxiety (and quieting one's superego) – the theory reminds us that activity – 'doing' – can mean not thinking.

Thinking

Charlie was intrigued. He poked his head round my shoulder and gazed at my face. 'Are you thinking?' he asked with some considerable awe.

Thinking is of course not new! But we have to remind trainees that they can reach for time to think – especially when chaos and frantic activity threaten to take over. Sometimes survival is all that one can manage; but often the confidence quietly to take a thinking space – and say one is doing so – can surprise in its calmness and difference and startle the child who is unused to being thought about at all. Thinking takes us to Bion. I struggled with Bion until I came across Edna O'Shaughnessy's 'A commemorative essay on WR Bion's theory of thinking':

> He does not mean some abstract mental process. His concern is with thinking as a human link – the endeavour to understand, comprehend the reality of, get insight into the nature of . . . oneself and another. Thinking is an emotional experience of trying to know one's self and someone else.
>
> (O'Shaughnessy 1981: 181)

For Charlie, the emotional experience of having a separate other keeping him in mind, thinking about him, was revelatory and a profound event in enabling his separation anxiety to abate. He was in turn able to internalise a thinking, remembering object.

Understanding and working with aggression

Charlie was livid with me. He finally gave up scowling and lowered his fists, his body shaking with rage, and turned to gaze out of the large picture window with its views of the busy Peckham Road. The back of his head bristled with upset indignation and impotent fury. Words simply would not do. There was a considerable pause. He leaned his elbows and forearms on the windowsill, maintaining a rigid back towards his therapist. I was silent, wondering how to interpret this rage without humiliation of his 4-year-old self – and not being successful in my thoughts. Suddenly a loud clatter of dropped scaffolding poles came from outside. Charlie jumped. He turned round with a questioning and anxious look. I said that he had heard a very loud noise outside and it had startled him – but perhaps it had been more shocking because he was so angry with me and had such angry noises *inside* him. He stared at me, sniffed – and turned back to gaze outwards. A silence followed. The scaffolding poles fell once more. Charlie turned and this time smiled: 'Outside noise!' he said, then, knocking his fist against his temple, 'Inside noise!' He laughed. We could now talk about his rage.

It is essential that today's trainees can understand the origins of aggression and distinguish what is developmentally an achievement and the advent of potency, what is a primitive defence and that which is affect that overwhelms, where words cannot be found to make sense of it and bind it. So we go down the usual trouser leg of time and teach Anna Freud (1949). But we also need to travel a few decades on and invoke Glasser: the concepts of core complex and self-preservative violence – aggression in the service of defending against a perceived threat to the ego – are essential theoretical tools today (Glasser 1996; 1998). Where we get it wrong, we label children – when we can only think of ourselves, as therapists, being attacked we lose the plot and continue to be blind to the defence that is being summoned as the only position the child can find.

Charlie stood on my desk. (Don't ask – it only embarrasses. . . .) It did not seem the safest place for a 3-year-old. I told him that I thought it wasn't very safe.

At times like this, one feels either panicky or wimpish and always foolish. He stomped across it triumphantly. After a pause – for my own benefit – I said that it really wasn't safe and I would help him down. More delighted stomping. I said I was going to lift him down. I picked him up, my hands round his torso. In mid-air he quickly bent down and bit me, clinging on to my forearm with his teeth. If you're thinking counter-transference, what was going through my mind went: 'Bloody sore arm! I can't let go – I'd drop him. What do I do with this? It hurts! And I've got to tell Miss Edgcumbe in supervision on Friday that Charlie bit me!' Superego? I put him down on the floor at one end of my very small office when blessedly he let go with his teeth. I retreated, trying to regain thought, and said sharply – rather as one would to one's dog – 'Stay!' Charlie stayed, patently avidly curious as to what I might do next. I found the monosyllable as much as I could safely manage. Then, after a few breaths, a comment about being so angry with me that he had to eat me came to mind from somewhere and I tried it. Charlie turned to his box and began to play.

Charlie is not the only child who has bitten me. You may think – like Winnicott who was bitten on the buttocks three times by his delinquent training patient – that I might have learned. The second and last occasion entailed a humiliating trip to Occupational Health at Guy's Hospital for a hepatitis injection. Even more difficult, I find, is being spat at; other desperate aggressive encounters can usually be thought about but spitting leaves me brainless.

Some of you may recall Katiebelle whom I have talked of in the past [*vide* Chapter 6 from which some of this section has been taken] – abused, neglected and beginning to abuse her brother at age 7. Through a long once weekly therapy, Katiebelle began eventually to be able to get in touch with anger, aggression and hate, for her a developmental achievement and necessity. Board games could have her taking great delight in obliterating my pieces, sending them back to the start. At times, this felt a very appropriate rehearsal of the aggression that develops into agency and potency; at others it was simply rage. The counter-transference gave the clue as to which – and that really mattered. Waiting while she manoeuvred the dice until she threw a 6, I could feel real distress for her; but there were many times when I felt furious and excluded. Endings of sessions could be times of high anxiety, delaying, panic and resistance. Despite my always giving her warning when the end of our session time neared, Katiebelle frequently tore around the room, desperately seeking something to take with her, often shouting and swearing at the top of her voice to let any colleagues within earshot know how horrible a therapist I was. For most of the therapy, I dreaded such endings. I did take practical steps like ensuring that there was always a gap of 20 minutes before the next appointment, giving time to focus on the ending, to tidy the room which was often left in chaos, and for my recovery; but I knew that being open to her fury and despair would mean that I would be drained at the end. Surviving this mattered; resilience in the therapist (who does need ways of becoming available to the next patient) depends greatly on listening, thinking colleagues and one (Dorothy Lloyd Owen) was often around after Katiebelle's session, offering coffee and a processing ear.

All therapists have to survive aggression and rage and still think, even when that thought is about the inability to think. As trainees face more overtly acting children, helping them regain the capacity for thought has become an important part of the toolkit that we encourage them to acquire. In this, I think, we move down a different leg of the trousers. . . . I recall sitting in on a clinical meeting at the Hampstead Clinic (later Anna Freud Centre) when a diagnostic of a 9-year-old bed-wetting girl was presented. Miss Freud's comment – 'This is just the sort of nice neurotic child for whom child analysis was invented!' The implication was that, even then in 1980, the patient group was changing. But we work today with young people who would have been deemed 'unworkable' in the past: the 'nice neurotic child' of Miss Freud's recollection has in the main given way to children whom others really struggle to understand and contain. Where thought is terrifying to the child or absent, it becomes important for us to create a space where it might become a possibility. In doing this, we have to reflect constantly on the nature of the anxiety that the child struggles with, that necessitates the only discoverable response of mindless activity.

Bodies

The novelist Hilary Mantel, in *Wolf Hall*, describes the import of silence which can be not empty but filled with words unspoken (Mantel 2009: 644). This resonates with our thinking about the body. The Italian analyst, Gaddini, reminded us over three decades ago (1980) that the mind exists throughout the body and Winnicott saw as a major task the integration of 'psyche in soma' (Winnicott 1972: 7). Indeed, it was Freud who wrote that 'the ego is first and foremost a bodily ego' (Freud 1923: 26). That the body has a memory system seems evident; and in repetition-compulsion it is often physiological as well as psychological sensation that is being reprised. Charlie's come-back session, in a mild way, involved his body – testing out the little chair to see if his body still fitted into it and remembered it, and the physical sensations and excitement of spinning in the big chair.

In my own analysis I have a very clear recollection of my analyst shifting forward in her seat – I could hear it – at two regular points: when I brought a dream and when I spoke of a child whom I was seeing. One day I mentioned that Charlie had climbed up the back of my chair, struggled over my head and slid none too gently down my front and on to my lap. He grinned at me in some triumph before sliding off. A shocked voice said, 'You don't *touch* the children?' 'No – we don't touch them but there are few embargoes on them using you as required.' Not touching is an important issue – again not new but we know more now of how acute this is with a patient group for whom the body may never have become or been only theirs.

For the child or young person who acts, who might be viewed as functioning at a level of body-based defensive manoeuvres, one can address the body as a separate entity that cannot think but which does operate as a source of memories and at times acts on these. Katiebelle had been abused by her half-brother from age 3; he in turn had been abused by their mother. Her compulsive sexual activity started at age 6 with peers and a little brother. She found it impossible to talk of it – words, indeed, were dangerous entities where to speak them might make them concretely real. Finally we managed a brief conversation about her body and the very interesting way it remembered things that had been done to it. When her body found it had to do things to her brother, it was remembering these things that had been done to it. She was overwhelmed – there was a reason for her behaviour; she understood it; and she was not simply 'bad'.

The humanity of working in the displacement and thoughts on shame

It has long been a feature in psychoanalytic work with children to take issues up in the displacement, especially when the child's anxiety is too great to enable a transference interpretation to be made or when words have for the child a concrete reality. Talking of murderous rage can be heard as accusing the child of *actually* killing the objects. Displacement is especially effective with younger children where it allows high emotion to be explored in a safe, removed arena . . . as it did for me with Stanley (see Chapter 8), who could manage to think about relationships initially only in displacement. His choice of Thomas the Tank Engine was perhaps unusual for a 20 year old but enabled Thomas's feelings – and Stanley's – to begin to have a place in our thoughts.

It is a method that has from time to time been scorned as not proper psychoanalysis – as once was taking a developmental as well as relational stance in work with developmental lacunae and affect recognition (Hurry 1998).

> Anna Freud has pointed out that the procedure of giving interpretations about a person or figure onto whom the child has externalised aspects of his own self, thus accepting the externalisation for the time being, is not necessarily collusion but, rather, a way of approaching threatening mental content gradually
>
> (Sandler, Kennedy & Tyson 1980: 165)

Charlie had problems parking his toy cars; they kept smashing together in an excitingly dangerous intimacy. We spent some time in this displacement of oedipal desires and phallic fears! For the *abused* child, however, it is often through such displacements that affects can begin to be recognised and given the symbolism of words for the first time. To use an example from Chapter 10:

> Maria had suffered extreme sexual abuse at the hands of her alcoholic mother's partner, and severe emotional and physical neglect. She tended to deal with her world by dissociation, inhabiting a realm of wild animals, which seemed to her to be more honourable in their interactions with each other than untrustworthy humans. For several months, conversation between trainee child therapist and child concerned these animals – rapacious only when necessary, at the mercy of humans, strong yet vulnerable. Only once extremes of

affect could gradually be recognised and named in the animals could Maria
begin to tolerate their resonance with parts of herself and their relevance to
the transference relationship.

In this way she slowly, in Miss Freud's words, 'came near the defended content'
(*ibid*: 169). We may be more inclined to think of such a technique when we have
the child's shame in mind – e.g. shame about murderous feelings towards siblings –
or narcissistic pain, where too direct an approach may reinforce and strengthen
inappropriate defences as Marianne Parsons reminded me. We also need to be
able to use it, I think, when affect, if reawakened too quickly, may overwhelm and
drive the child to more desperate defences.'

With adolescents in particular, one has to be careful to avoid humiliating them
with one's interpretations. Anne Hurry describes the work of assessing troubled
adolescents at Brent (Hurry 1986) where she used neutral words – 'strange' feelings, for example, rather than 'fearful' or shameful ones. Splitting off the infantile
part from the more adult, thinking part can also help the young person and engage
them with the mature part of the self that can reflect on the activity-based defences
of the infantile part. 'Isn't it interesting what your body gets up to?' Addressing
this with curiosity – joining with the thinking part – follows: with the risk-taking
delinquent one can comment on the little part of them that wished it could run or
escape the past traumatic experiences, and how this part still repeats the feelings
of risk, fear and high adrenalin surge, hoping this time to be in control of them.
One can then be curious about why this still happens – and space for thought is
created amidst mainly body-based defence mechanisms.

I think this is an area where we have returned to earlier theory. Lampl-de Groot
writes of the ego ideal and the sense of shame in relation to delinquency in 1949;
Don Campbell returned to it in 1994. For today's troubled, delinquent youths it is
again essential learning: being 'dissed' (disrespected and shamed) is the corollary
of respect and quickly summons the need Glasser noted to protect the ego from
perceived insult (Glasser 1998).

A note on endings

I began this paper with Charlie's return and final farewell because recently a BAP
trainee chose 'endings' as the subject of her doctoral dissertation and Charlie
came to mind. It is an extremely interesting choice of topic and she helped me
realise that teaching on endings still does not feature enough in training. The
subject used to arise if a therapy came to a planned end – with Charlie, I recall
Rose Edgcumbe, my supervisor, telling me that it is best not to have endings
coincide with the end of term: the import of the one gets lost in the other and
work can be diverted. But otherwise we did not have the time limitations of today
when therapy can be constrained by the end of a trainee post, for example. It was
not unusual in my day to request (and be granted) permission to continue with
a patient, even when one had moved clinic, to allow a good ending, an assessment with child and family of strengths and defences and good-enough on-going

functioning. So we clearly had ending in mind and its importance, but I cannot recall formal teaching and reading on the subject. Another leg of the trousers, then, if we now pay attention to the increasing literature on the matter.

Finding one's voice – the aim of training

There are three brief issues that I find matter. First, Albert Einstein is said to have remarked: 'It's the theory that determines what we observe.' There is real danger that this is so. Perhaps a new research ethos will ensure that it is not.

When we train we gain a certain comfort from theory – when we are not struggling to understand it. But part of the training must be a growing capacity to question, at least to test, theory, to have as an aim the production of curious, grounded critics. I enjoyed my parent-infant observation but struggled with some of the early developmental literature. Eventually I came to a seminar: 'See symbiosis? I just don't see it!' feeling a failure, to have Juliet (Hopkins) respond: 'Perhaps it isn't there to be seen.' We must retain the capacity to distinguish theoretical framework from gospel and to test where we can. Our new trouser leg of research – our trainees are doctoral students – helps.

Second, a quote that I find enormously important:

> Modifications of technique are departures from the 'normal' range of techniques applicable to neurotic children. **There is no absolute psychoanalytic technique for use with children, but rather a set of analytic principles which have to be adapted to specific cases.** Variations in technique represent appropriate specific adaptations of the basic set of analytic principles rather than deviations from standard technique
> (Sandler, Kennedy & Tyson 1980: 199, my emphasis).

Once we are freed from a tyrannical sense of the right way to do or to be, we can appreciate that child psychotherapy is the humane application of psychoanalytic theory to the understanding and psychological treatment of children. What seem rules are often ways of holding the frame of good practice. But others may have become needlessly enshrined in stone. We have 50-minute sessions because Freud's concentration ran out after that; we have a couch because eyeball to eyeball was intolerable at times and it offered a less humiliating and possibly regressive platform – and it was a chaise longue, a day bed, and not the flat single bed of most of today's therapy rooms. Some children – especially very little ones – find 40 or 45 minutes easier; some, like Katiebelle and Charlie until he speedily learned where the big hand moved to, find time and the whole notion of time to be a ruthlessly out-of-tune imposition – which is different. I think we follow Miss Freud in applying a set of analytic principles, adapting them to the setting and to the patient.

And finally – 'I aim at being myself and behaving myself' (Winnicott 1962: 166). Like Winnicott, we aim at being ourselves, finding our *own* voices, not becoming clones – and we also include behaving ourselves, keeping a compassionate ethical sense that does not abuse the analytic method even while we explore extensions of our technique and understanding to a wide range of settings. The framework of the psychoanalytic approach is not rigid: it gives us a sure foundation and encourages us as individuals to find creative pathways in the variety of encounters that now form our working days.

To end with as many mixed metaphors as possible – perhaps the past is only in part another country and is not really such a foreign one. It contains our theoretical gene pool and harbours a good deal of our technical DNA as well. In our evolution, we adapt not simply to survive but to meet present-day challenges with creativity. Over the life of this BAP Child Training we have certainly added to that – in training, technique, supervision, organisation, continuing education and writing. In having the freedom of an Independent mother ship (sorry. . .) we have been able to voyage to the past and back, down several trouser legs, creating on our journey our own rather splendid pattern on the cloth of psychoanalysis.

Notes

1 This paper was given as a talk at the British Association of Psychotherapists in July 2011 as part of the celebration of the BAP's 60 years. The child training had begun 29 years before. I was asked to reflect on changes over time.
2 See Chapter 8 for a fuller description of Stanley and our work together.

References

Alvarez, A (1992) *Live Company: Psychoanalytic Psychotherapy with Autistic, Borderline, Deprived and Abused Children* London: Routledge

Alvarez, Al (1967) *The New Poetry* Harmondsworth: Penguin

Alvarez, Al (2006) *The Writer's Voice* London: Bloomsbury

Britton, R (1989) The missing link: parental sexuality in the Oedipus complex. In R Britton, M Feldman. and E O'Shaughnessy (eds.) *The Oedipus Complex Today: Clinical Implications* London: Karnac

Campbell, D (1994) Breaching the shame shield: thoughts on the assessment of adolescent sexual abusers *Journal of Child Psychotherapy* 20(3): 309–326

Freud, A (1949) Certain types and stages of social maladjustment. In KR Eissler (ed.) *Searchlights on Delinquency* New York: International Universities Press

Freud, A (1967) About losing and being lost *Psychoanalytic Study of the Child* 22: 9–19

Freud, S (1923) The Ego and the Id *SE* 19 London: Hogarth Press

Furman, E (1982) Mothers have to be there to be left *Psychoanalytic Study of the Child* 37: 15–28

Gaddini, E (1980) Notes on the mind-body question. In A. Limentani (ed.) *A Psychoanalytic Theory of Infantile Experience: Conceptual and Clinical Reflections* London & New York: Tavistock Routledge 1992

Glasser, M (1996) Aggression and sadism in the perversions. In I Rosen (ed.) *Sexual Deviation* 3rd edition Oxford: Oxford University Press

Glasser, M (1998) On violence: a preliminary communication *International Journal of Psychoanalysis* 79(5): 887–902

Hopkins, J (1984) The probable role of trauma in a case of foot and shoe fetishism: aspects of the psychotherapy of a six-year-old girl. *International Review of Psycho-Analysis* 11(1): 79–91

Horne, A (1989) Sally: a middle group approach to early trauma in a latency child *Journal of Child Psychotherapy* 15: 79–98

Hurry, A (1986) Walk-in work with adolescents *Journal of Child Psychotherapy* 12(1) 33–45

Hurry, A (1998) *Psychoanalysis and Developmental Therapy* London: Karnac

Jordan, B (1979) *Helping in Social Work* London: Routledge and Kegan Paul

Lampl-de Groot, J (1949) Neurotics, delinquents and ideal formation. In KR Eissler (ed.) *Searchlights on Delinquency* New York: International Universities Press

Mantel, H (2009) *Wolf Hall* London: Fourth Estate

O'Shaughnessy, E (1981) A commemorative essay on WR Bion's theory of thinking *Journal of Child Psychotherapy* 7

Sandler, J, Kennedy, H & Tyson, R (1980) *The Technique of Child Psychoanalysis: Discussions with Anna Freud* London: Hogarth Press & Institute of Psycho-Analysis

Stone, S & Wesley, J (1866) The Church's One Foundation *Hymns Ancient and Modern*

Strachey, J (1940) letter to Glover, 23rd April. Quoted in E Rayner *The Independent Mind in British Psychoanalysis* London: Free Association Books 1991

Winnicott, DW (1945) Primitive emotional development. In *Collected Papers: Through Paediatrics to Psychoanalysis* London: Hogarth Press 1975

Winnicott, DW (1956) The anti-social tendency. In *Collected Papers: Through Paediatrics to Psychoanalysis* London: Hogarth Press 1975

Winnicott, DW (1960) String: a technique of communication. In Winnicott *The Maturational Processes and the Facilitating Environment: Studies in the Theory of Emotional Development* London: Hogarth Press 1965

Winnicott, DW (1962) The aims of psychoanalytical treatment. In DW Winnicott *The Maturational Processes and the Facilitating Environment: Studies in the Theory of Emotional Development* London: Hogarth Press 1965

Winnicott, DW (1972) Basis for self in body *International Journal of Child Psychotherapy* 1(1): 7–16

Publications

Horne, A (1989) Sally: a middle group approach to early trauma in a latency child *Journal of Child Psychotherapy* 15: 79–98

Horne, A (1999) Sexual abuse and sexual abusing in childhood and adolescence. In M Lanyado & A Horne (eds.) *The Handbook of Child & Adolescent Psychotherapy: Psychoanalytic Approaches* London: Routledge

Horne, A (1999) Normal emotional development. In M Lanyado & A Horne (eds.) *The Handbook of Child & Adolescent Psychotherapy: Psychoanalytic Approaches* London: Routledge

Horne, A (1999) Thinking about gender in theory and practice with children and adolescents *Journal of the British Association of Psychotherapists* 37(July)

Horne, A (2000) Keeping the child in mind: thoughts on work with parents of children in therapy. In J Tsiantis (ed.) *Work with Parents* EFPP Clinical Monograph Series London: Karnac Also published in Russian in 2006

Horne, A (2000) Jak myslet na dítě – úvaha o práci s rodiči děti v terapii *Revue Psychoanalytické Psychoterapie* 2(1): 28–34

Horne, A (2000) Sexuální zneužití a senzuální zneuživání v dětství a adolescenci *Revue Psychoanalytické Psychoterapie* 2(1): 35–46

Horne, A (2000) Krátké zprávy z rizikového kraje: psychoterapei s náročnými adolescenty *Revue Psychoanalytické Psychoterapie* 2(1): 55–62

Horne, A (2000) Úvahy o pohlaví v teorii a praxi s dětmi a adolescenty *Revue Psychoanalytické Psychoterapie* 2(1): 63–71

Horne, A (2000) O těle a dětech: sexualita a sexuální teorie v dětství a adolescenci *Revue Psychoanalytické Psychoterapie* 2(1): 72–75

Horne, A (2001) Of bodies and babies: sexuality and theories about sex in childhood and adolescence. In C Harding (ed.) *Sexuality: Psychoanalytic Perspectives* London: Routledge

Horne, A (2001) Brief communications from the edge: psychotherapy with challenging adolescents *Journal of Child Psychotherapy* 27(1)

Also published in M Lanyado & A Horne (eds.) *A Question of Technique* London: Routledge 2006

And in Timo Niemi (toim.) *Teit Puhuvat Sanoja Kovemmin – Nuorisopsykoterapian Erityiskysymyksiä 8* Helsinki: Nuorisopsykoterapia-säätiö 2006

And in D Morgan & S Ruszczynski (eds.) *Lectures on Violence, Perversion and Delinquency* London: Karnac 2007

Horne, A (2003) Oedipal aspirations and phallic fears: on fetishism in childhood and young adulthood *Journal of Child Psychotherapy* 29(1): 37–52

Also published in Timo Niemi (toim.) (2007) *Itseään Viiltelevä Nuori – Nuorisopsykoterapian Erityiskysymyksiä 9* Helsinki: Nuorisopsykoterapia-säätiö

Horne, A (2003) L'abuso sessuale subito e perpetrato durante l'infanzia e l'adolescenza. In M Lanyado & A Horne (a cura di) *Manuale di Psicoterapia dell'infanzia e dell'adolescenza* Milano: FrancoAngeli

Horne, A (2004) Gonnae no' dae that! The internal and external worlds of the delinquent adolescent *Journal of Child Psychotherapy* 30(3): 330–346

Horne, A (2004) Jaké zajímavé věci říkat dětem – a proč *Revue Psychoanalytická Psychoterapie* 6(1): 4–14

Horne, A (2005) Clinical commentary by a child and adolescent psychotherapist trained at the British Association of Psychotherapists *Journal of Child Psychotherapy* 31(1): 116–120

Horne, A (2006) Clinical commentary: Sam *Journal of the British Association of Psychotherapists* 44(1): 64–67

Horne, A (2006) Interesting things to say – and why. In M Lanyado & A Horne (eds.) *A Question of Technique* London: Routledge

Also published in Timo Niemi (toim.) (2007) *Itseään Viiltelevä Nuori Nuorisopsykoterapian Erityiskysymyksiä 9* Helsinki: Nuorisopsykoterapia-säätiö

Horne, A (2006) The Independent position in psychoanalytic psychotherapy with children and adolescents: roots and implications. In M Lanyado & A Horne (eds.) *A Question of Technique* London: Routledge

Horne, A (2009) From intimacy to acting-out: assessment and consultation about dangerousness. In A Horne & M Lanyado (eds.) *Through Assessment to Consultation: Independent Psychoanalytic Approaches with Children and Adolescents* London: Routledge

Also published in 'Psykodynamik – vad är det?' *Mellanrummet* Nr. 22 (2010) Stockholm

Horne, A (2010) Rhythm, blues, affirmation and enactment: it's tough soloing without a rhythm section *British Journal of Psychotherapy* 26(1): 1–21

Hornova, A (2011) Děti, které používají tělo k vypořádání se s traumatem *Revue Psychoanalyticá Psychoterapie* XIII(1): 16–27

Horne, A (2012) Winnicott's delinquent. In C Reeves (ed.) *Broken Bounds: Contemporary Reflections on the Anti-social Tendency* Winnicott Studies Monograph Series London: Karnac

Horne, A (2012) Entertaining the body in mind: thoughts on incest, the body, sexuality and the self. In P Williams, J Keene & S Dermen (eds.) *Independent Psychoanalysis Today* London: Karnac

Horne, A (2012) On delinquency. In A Horne & M Lanyado *Winnicott's Children: Independent Psychoanalytic Approaches with Children and Adolescents* London: Routledge

Horne, A (2012) Body and soul: developmental urgency and impasse. In A Horne & M Lanyado *Winnicott's Children: Independent Psychoanalytic Approaches with Children and Adolescents* London: Routledge

Horne, A (2015) Introduction. In A Horne & M Lanyado (eds.) *An Independent Mind. Collected Papers of Juliet Hopkins* Hove & New York: Routledge

Horne, A (2016) Play, culture and the use of objective reality. Introduction to Volume 8: 1967–68 *The Collected Writings of Donald Woods Winnicott* eds. L Caldwell & H Taylor Robinson London & New York: Oxford University Press

Horne, A (2016) Clinical Commentary *Journal of Child Psychotherapy* 41(3): 345–348

Horne, A (2018) *On Children Who Privilege the Body: Reflections of an Independent Psychotherapist. Selected Papers* Hove & New York: Routledge

Horne, A (in press) O dětech, které dávají přednost tělu – s důrazem na ideální self *Revue Psychoanalyticá Psychotherapie*

Horne, A (in press) Reflections on the ego ideal in childhood. In C. Harding (ed.) *Dissecting the Super-Ego: Moralities under the Psychoanalytic Microscope* Hove & New York: Routledge

Horne, A & Lanyado, M (eds.) (2009) *Through Assessment to Consultation: Independent Psychoanalytic Approaches with Children and Adolescents* London: Routledge

Horne, A & Lanyado, M (eds.) (2012) *Winnicott's Children: Independent Psychoanalytic Approaches with Children and Adolescents* Hove & New York: Routledge

Also published as A Horne & M Lanyado (Hrsg.) (2016) *Übergangsobjekt und Möglichkeitsraum: Die Kreativität Winnicott'schen Denkens für die klinische Praxis* Frankfurt: Brandes & Apsel

Horne, A & Lanyado, M (eds.) (2015) *An Independent Mind: Collected Papers of Juliet Hopkins* Hove & New York: Routledge

Berelowitz, M & Horne, A (1990) Child mental health and the legacy of Child Guidance: lessons for the 1990s *Newsletter of the ACPP*

Lanyado, M & Horne, A (eds.) (1999) *The Handbook of Child & Adolescent Psychotherapy: Psychoanalytic Approaches* London: Routledge

Also published as Lanyado, M & Horne, A (a cura di) (2003) *Manuale di psicoterapia dell'infanzia e dell'adolescenza: approcci psicoanalitica* Milan: FrancoAngeli

And as Lanyadoová, M & Hornová, A (eds.) (2005) *Psychoterapie děti a dospívajících – psychoanalytický přístup* Prague: Triton

Lanyado, M & Horne, A (eds.) (2006) *A Question of Technique: Independent Psychoanalytic Approaches with Children and Adolescents* London: Routledge

Lanyado, M & Horne, A (eds.) (2009) *The Handbook of Child and Adolescent Psychotherapy: Psychoanalytic Approaches* 2nd edition London: Routledge

Published in Japanese in 2013.

Parsons, M & Horne, A (2009) Anxiety, projection and the quest for magical fixes: when one is asked to assess risk. In Horne & Lanyado (eds.) (2009) *Through Assessment to Consultation: Independent Psychoanalytic Approaches with Children and Adolescents* London: Routledge

Smith, S & Horne, A (1988) Working together: a singular case of school non-attendance *Maladjustment and Therapeutic Education* 6(2): 107–119

Tsiantis, J, Boalt Boethius, S, Hallerfors, B, Horne, A & Tischler, L (eds.) (2000) *Work with Parents: Psychoanalytic Psychotherapy with Children and Adolescents* London: Karnac EFPP Monographs

Also published as *Работа с родителями* Russia: Когито-Центр 2006.

Horne, A & Lanyado, M Series Editors – Independent Psychoanalytic Approaches with Children and Adolescents London & New York: Routledge

Index

For Product Safety Concerns and Information please contact our EU
representative GPSR@taylorandfrancis.com
Taylor & Francis Verlag GmbH, Kaufingerstraße 24, 80331 München, Germany

9 780815 399827